BEYOND BORDERS

NEW CONTEXTS OF MISSION IN LATIN AMERICA

BEYOND BORDERS
NEW CONTEXTS OF MISSION IN LATIN AMERICA

MIGUEL ÁLVAREZ

CPT

CPT Press
Cleveland, Tennessee

Beyond Borders
New Contexts of Mission in Latin America

Published by CPT Press
900 Walker ST NE
Cleveland, TN 37311
USA
email: cptpress@Pentecostaltheology.org
website: www.cptpress.com

Library of Congress Control Number: 2017953704

ISBN-10: 1935931652
ISBN-13: 9781935931652

To
Roland Vaughan
Proverbs 13:20a

CONTENTS

FOREWORD

Everyone who has an interest in Latin American mission and theology will welcome this work of Miguel Álvarez's *Beyond Borders: Emerging Contexts of Mission in Latin America*. This well written and expertly documented work surveys the history of both the Pentecostal and Evangelical churches with their various theologies of missions that have characterized these movements from the beginning. Álvarez extends his study back in time to examine the mission theologies of both the Roman Catholic Church and the protestant missionary churches that preceded the arrival of Evangelicals and Pentecostals to Latin America in the early 20th Century.

In his work, the author explores in particular some significant issues facing Pentecostalism as the movement has grown exponentially all over Latin America in recent decades. He details the pressures of social and political policy that the movement faces as it matures into a strong force in Latin American life and culture. Along the way he discusses the differences between North American and South American Pentecostal theologies of mission as well as the dynamics of neo-Pentecostal mega-churches with their growing popularity and the challenges of other contemporary charismatic movements.

Álvarez is well qualified to write this book. He has experience as a pastor, missionary, and educator. He holds a Master of Divinity from the Pentecostal Theological Seminary of Cleveland, Tennessee, a Doctor of Ministry from Ashland Theological Seminary in Ohio, and a PhD from the Oxford Centre for Mission Studies in the UK. He has also been a successful pastor in Honduras, seminary president in the Philippines and administrative leader in the United States. For several years he has been engaged in denominational and non-denominational leadership in Latin America, Asia, and the United States. Miguel has been able to integrate scholarship and ministry into his life as an educator, pastor, and missionary. This book is a product of a thorough academic research and observation on the topics studied. That is one significant reason I recommend the careful reading this work.

Of course, this book interacts with anthropological, sociological, historical, and cultural studies. Here, the reader will find that mission is seen as God's active work of integral transformation for humanity in various fields. The redemptive work of God extends beyond denominational borders and is always available to all of those who take hold of his gracious favor.

Being a Latin American, Álvarez writes about his love and commitment to God's mission on behalf of the people of that latitude. In his own life experience Miguel is also part of the early history of Pentecostalism in Central America and his country of origin in particular.

After several years of ministry in the city of Tegucigalpa, in 1992 he was commissioned to serve as president of the Asian Seminary of Christian Ministries (ASCM) in Manila, Philippines. During this time in Asia/Pacific, Álvarez was also co-founding vice-president of the Asian Center for Missions (ACM) and associate pastor at Word Community Church in Metro Manila.

Upon his return to the United States in 2001, he was later commissioned by the Church of God to serve as the bishop of the Northeast Hispanic Region, with offices in Allentown, Pennsylvania. When his term expired, he accepted to serve as president of the South American Seminary and senior pastor of Capilla del Valle in Quito, Ecuador.

In more recent years he has worked closely with Gordon Robertson as associate representative of Superbook at the Christian Broadcasting Network as a liaison to Hispanic ministries. Álvarez is also Director of Hispanic Ministries for the Church of God in Virginia. During these years, he has also been able to train pastors and Christian leaders in church planting and leadership development. He lectures internationally and serves as academic advisor of mission and renewal studies. Álvarez networks with a variety of organizations and Christian leaders. He connects pastors, educators and church ministers with resources available in different locations. Since 2002 he has served as an adjunct professor of Theology and Mission at Regent University in Virginia Beach, Virginia where he lives with his wife Mireya. They have four children: Daniel, Michelle, Miguel, and Mariadela.

Vinson Synan, PhD
Dean Emeritus
Regent University School of Divinity, Virginia Beach, VA

PREFACE

I grew up as a preacher's kid to Church of God parents in South Honduras; I am the eldest of eight children. My parents became Christians when I was at elementary school and it was in those days that I joined the Pentecostal tradition.

In those days, the Pentecostal movement had just arrived in our area, so there were few believers of the same tradition near us. Incidentally, I understood there were only two churches in the world: The Catholic Church, where most people attended, and the Church of God. Sometime later, I heard that there were other Christians who called themselves Baptists, or *Centroamericanos*. To me, that was something new and I did not hesitate to ask my parents why there were other churches with different names. In my mind, I had it clear: there should only be two churches; one that had control over most people in our community and the Church of God. My Father, Miguel Antonio, graciously explained to me that there were also other churches in the world, but I did not have to worry about that, for we were in the 'right' one.

I dedicated my life to the Lord at nearly the young age of seven; that event happened during my grandfather's preaching. Abraham was an outstanding evangelist and church planter in South Honduras and East El Salvador. The night of my conversion, we had been at an open-air service, and several families came to listen to his preaching. When he asked if there was anybody in the crowd who wanted to receive Jesus as Savior and Lord, I felt convicted. I knew I needed Jesus in my heart, so I moved forward to surrender my life to Him.

During those days, my mentors were my grandfather and my father, and in that order. They were solid preachers, and I believed everything they spoke was truthful. They knew the Bible and taught the congregation to practice true holiness. They taught us that once we committed our lives to the Lord, we had to become holy inside and out. So we had to dress, speak, and conduct ourselves as true Christians: we were not allowed to listen to non-Christian music; we could not attend any parties, sport activities or go to movie theaters. Those places and activities were considered sinful. Faithful Christians were taught to avoid them in order to please the Lord and to persevere in holiness.

Right after I started middle school, things became complicated for me. The school required that all students become involved in sports, artistic, and musical activities. All of a sudden I found myself between two worlds. Soon the school requirements became a problem with my Christian lifestyle. I knew my parents knew the situation, but they could not do a thing to help me in my bewilderment. I wanted to please the Lord and the church, yet I had to go to school and did not want to fail. Moreover, I was growing physically, and new needs arose that also affected my social activities. I found myself trapped between two contradicting worlds. However, there were two things I wanted for my life: I wanted to serve the Lord, and I also wanted to study. So I prayed that the Lord would help me out to understand my world, do the necessary adjustments and excel in the two things I loved to most – Christian service and education. The Lord did answer my prayer by granting me those desires.

When I was eleven I knew within me that I was going to be a minister. Deep in my heart I had the testimony of the Holy Spirit that I was on my way to becoming a minister of the gospel. Nonetheless, I also knew I was going to become a theologian too. Yet to accomplish both goals I had to stay in school and learn as much as I could for the benefit of God's work and for myself as well.

On November 1973, I was baptized in the Holy Spirit. I remember speaking in tongues for several hours. A young seventeen-year old received a charismatic blessing that launched him into a new stage in his life. Everything was different; I was still in high school, but deep in my heart all I wanted was to speak about Jesus to everyone I knew and everywhere I could. Doors opened for me, so I began to serve in ministry on a regular basis. By God's grace I stayed at school and was able to preach and plant churches with great passion.

In 1974 I met Roland Vaughan, an American missionary who had recently arrived in Honduras. For some reason we connected well, and right after those days he helped me to enter into ministry. I believed the Lord ordained it that way, so Roland could become a paternal figure to me during those days of my ministerial formation. He was able to read my expectations, understand my background and quickly make plans to get me into ministry while attending school at the same time. I remember one time after I had finished Bible school; he called me to his office and spoke very clear to me: 'You must register at the local university and continue your education. If you do not do it, you will have serious issues with me.' Of course, this was like ordering a frog 'to jump into a pond'. Since those days I have done those two things intentionally: full-time ministry and full-time school. My life has been like that ever since, and I am thankful that I was able to thrive in ministry and education.

In 1977 I was appointed Pastor in Tegucigalpa, Honduras where I met my wife Mireya. This mission gave us the opportunity to lead a congregation that made an impact to the city in those days. We worked with vibrant youth that eventually set new standards for church life and ministry in the country.

In 1992 I was commissioned by the Church of God to serve as President of the Asian Seminary of Christian Ministries in Manila, Philippines. My wife and I and our four children moved halfway around the world. This development exposed us to another world. The cross-cultural experience trained us to serve internationally and to see firsthand the fulfillment of the Great Commission through leaders with excellent cross-cultural mentality.

Mine is a Pentecostal story. If we examine the story of most Pentecostals in Latin America, we will find similar patterns. Most of us come from simple lifestyles and were formed through the hardships of poor neighborhoods and many limitations. Every born again person in these community-churches is providentially guided by the Holy Spirit to access and enjoy the blessings of God's kingdom. If an individual is willing to follow the Spirit's guidance, he or she may experience holistic redemption, and in the course of time they become passionate agents of transformation.

In this volume, I open the story of most Pentecostals in Latin America. I admit that there are differences at some places and scenarios. Nevertheless, as I said earlier, a significant number of Pentecostals would share similar patterns in the socio-economic contexts.

Currently, the size of the congregation or the increased number of believers seems to have introduced significant changes within some Pentecostal constituencies. We have become important, which is good, but are we aware of the perils that our congregations face under the present situation?

In this volume we study about mission and public theology in Latin America; and, as my introduction indicates, I will be speaking from a Pentecostal point of view. However, I will present not only the strengths of Pentecostal missiology but also the weaknesses. As a scholar, my purpose is to initiate a healthy dialogue about *Missio Dei* in Latin America, which I believe is needed in our context of ministry.

In this work I dialogue with both the Evangelical and Pentecostal streams. I also review some of the Catholic teachings of social responsibility in order to find common grounds of understanding in the development of a Latin American missiology that is integral in its nature and practice.

I envision the day when Christian leaders will sit down around the table to dialogue on common concerns, whether these have to do with social issues, economics, public service, or environmental concern. It is about time to recognize one another and to open up to fellow believers in Christ Jesus who share similar goals in the practice of the Great Commission. This book is written in good faith, and I pray that the Holy Spirit will enable the reader to understand its missiological message.

With much appreciation,
Miguel Álvarez

ABBREVIATIONS

AB	Anchor Bible
CBL	The Complete Biblical Library
HNTC	Harper's NT Commentaries
ICC	International Critical Commentary
JPT	*Journal of Pentecostal Theology*
JPTSup	*Journal of Pentecostal Theology*, Supplement Series
JSNT	*Journal for the Study of the New Testament*
JSNTSup	*Journal for the Study of the New Testament*, Supplement Series
LSJ	H.G. Liddell, R. Scott and H.S. Jones, *Greek–English Lexicon* (Oxford: Clarendon Press, 9th edn, 1968)

INTRODUCTION

This work overviews recent developments on *Missio Dei* in Latin America and explores current trends about public theology in the region. It analyzes the impact of the Pentecostal movement in the community and includes a discussion of weaknesses and challenges confronting Pentecostals in Latin America today. The study reviews current mission trends in academic scholarship and pays attention to emerging contemporary ministries, such as church expansion and other tendencies. It explores mission among the poor and marginalized in Latin America.

We will examine works that have contributed significantly to the understanding of mission in the area[1] and consider issues in contemporary Pentecostalism, such as the emphasis on numerical growth and the expansion of the church within the cultures of Latin America. At the end, we anticipate new opportunities for public service that have emerged in the Latin America. Some of these components have to do with theological developments and social concerns that are associated with Pentecostalism.

---

[1] The following have written classic works about Pentecostalism in Latin America: Emilio Willems, *Followers of the New Faith: Culture Change and the Rise of Protestantism in Brazil and Chile* (Nashville, TN: Vanderbilt University Press, 1967); Francisco C. Rolim, *Religião e Classes Populares* (Petrópolis: Vozes, 1985); *idem*, *Pentecostais no Brasil, Uma Interpretação Socio-Religiosa* (Petrópolis, Brasil: Vozes, 1985); Jean Pierre Bastian, 'Disidencia Religiosa en el Campo Mexicano', in Martin de la Rosa and Charles A. Reilly, (eds.) *Religión y Política en México* (México, DF: Siglo XXI, 1985), pp. 117-92 and Pierre Bastian, 'Religión Popular Protestante y Comportamiento Político en América Central, Clientela Religiosa y Estado Patrón en Guatemala y Nicaragua', in Karl Kohut, (ed.), *Religiosidad Popular en América Latina* (Frankfurt, Germany: Vervuert Verlag, 1998), pp. 81-103.

Most Pentecostal and evangelical networks have reached nearly one hundred years of history in Latin America. The first known Pentecostal 'outpouring' occurred in Chile in 1909. This spiritual awakening that began in the early twentieth century can now be seen in every nation. In this study we take a general look at evangelical and Pentecostal churches of Latin America, drawing information from general observations and the scholarship of the movement specialized in mission.

This study observes that Pentecostals and Evangelicals have had a successful numerical growth in recent years and that the presence of evangelical and Pentecostal churches is evident in most cities of Latin America. Logically such substantial growth generates collateral circumstances that have to be addressed with healthy levels of maturity. For that reason, church leaders are now looking for ways to operate peacefully in environments of multiple congregations of different denominations. Thus, they have created pastoral and inter-denominational fellowships that gather them under common causes and lead them to mutual recognition and support.

This work studies the missional influence of Evangelicals and Pentecostals over social action within some contexts of Latin America. It also reviews their participation in public service. It explores the transformation that occurs or does not occur in the communities where Pentecostal and evangelical churches operate.

We will also look into the general spectrum of Christianity in Latin America. In the study there is a valid suggestion that a dialogue is necessary between the different denominational streams, including the Catholic Church. Such dialogue may lead to mutual understanding and friendly co-existence among Christians in the region.

The study focuses on new contexts of mission in the area and leans heavily on mission literature that has been produced in recent years. In the case of Pentecostals, they seem to be growing numerically, but they are learning quickly that Christian mission extends beyond the spiritual nature, so they are now reaching out to the entire person, including his or her habitat and the social, economic, and political environment. They are learning that those conditions are integral to the lives of people and the communities. So they are committed to share the whole gospel to the whole person and his or her society.

I must also add that during the time of this research I was not aware of the book of Amos Yong, *In the Days of Caesar: Pentecostalism and Political Theology*, which would have added valuable insights to this work. Yet, I found it interesting that my research did coincide with some topics that are thoroughly discussed in Yong's book.[2]

This study is presented in good faith. Most specific observations are done in the context of the churches in Honduras, where the author is from. However, there are similarities with other contexts of Central and South America that should be considered carefully. Also, this contribution is presented with great respect and appreciation of those who faithfully serve the Lord in the congregations of Latin America.

---

[2] See Amos Yong, *In the Days of Caesar: Pentecostalism and Political Theology* (Grand Rapids, MI: Eerdmans, 2010).

1

RECENT MISSION STUDIES IN LATIN AMERICA

Recent scholarship, especially among missiologists has observed the changing role of public theology in Latin America.[1] While these works have spurred Western interest in the development of mission thinking in the region, Latin Americans themselves have been researching *Missio Dei* since the 1960s.[2] One significant research forum in the region was initiated by the *Red Latinoamericana de Estudios Pentecostales* (RELEP) (Latin American Network of Pentecostal Studies) to study several mission fields. They have convened in countries such as Chile, Mexico, Brazil, and Ecuador to discuss Pentecostal history, theology, and ministry. RELEP has published a number of articles in a series of volumes known as *Voces del Pentecostalismo Latinoamericano*[3] (Voices of Latin American Pentecostalism).

---

[1] See for instance, David Martin, *Tongues of Fire: The Explosion of Protestantism in Latin America* (Cambridge: Basil Blackwell, 1990); David Stoll, *Is Latin America Turning Protestant? The Politics of Evangelical Growth* (Berkeley, CA: University of California Press, 1990); Harvey G. Cox, *Fire from Heaven: The Rise of Pentecostal Spirituality and the Reshaping of Religion in the Twenty-first Century* (Reading, MA: Addison-Wesley, 1995); Edward L. Cleary and Hannah W. Stewart-Gambino (eds.) *Power, Politics, and Pentecostals in Latin America* (Boulder, CO: Westview Press, 1997); and Allan H. Anderson, *An Introduction to Pentecostalism: Global Charismatic Christianity* (Cambridge: Cambridge Academic Press, 2004) among other works.

[2] See Jorge Soneira, 'Estudios Sociológicos sobre el Pentecostalismo en América Latina', *Sociedad y Religión* 8.1 (1991), pp. 29-47.

[3] One example is the article by Luis Orellana, 'El Futuro del Pentecostalismo en América Latina', in Daniel Chiquete and Luis Orellana (eds.), *Voces del Pentecostalismo Latinoamericano* (vol. 4; Concepción, Chile: RELEP, 2011), pp. 141-56.

Furthermore, several Latin American scholars like Darío López, Juan Sepúlveda, Norberto Saracco, and Bernardo Campos have made significant contributions to mission theology in the region.[4] Some other evangelical writers have also done important research on mission theology, such as Manuel Gaxiola, Luis Segreda, Samuel Escobar, and C. René Padilla.[5] In these cases, it is common for researchers of *Missio Dei* to cite the classic works of Emilio Willems, Christian Lalive d'Espinay, Francisco Rolim, and Jean Pierre Bastian.[6]

From his evangelical point of view, Samuel Escobar studied *Missio Dei*, and through his contributions to mission theology he gained credibility among Latin American scholars.[7] Escobar engaged sociological and anthropological issues in his various books and articles. In reference to evangelism Escobar and other scholars also recognize that the new era for the evangelization of Latin America and other sites of the world is closely related to the advancement of Pentecostalism.[8] Along with Escobar, other scholars such as Ed-

---

[4] Juan Sepúlveda, 'Reflections on the Pentecostal Contribution to the Mission of the Church in America', *JPTSup 4;* 1.1 (1992), pp. 93-108; Norberto Saracco, 'Mission and Missiology from Latin America', in William D. Taylor (ed.), *Global Missiology for the Twenty-First Century* (Grand Rapids, MI: Baker Academic, 2000), pp. 357-66; Darío López, *El Nuevo Rostro del Pentecostalismo Latinoamericano* (Lima, Perú: Ediciones Puma, 2002), pp. 65-68; Bernardo Campos, 'Pentecostalism: A Latin American View', in Hubert van Beeck (ed.), *Consultation with Pentecostals in the Americas* (San José, Costa Rica: WCC, 1996), pp. 4-8; Miguel Álvarez, 'The South and the Latin American Paradigm of the Pentecostal Movement', *Asian Journal of Pentecostal Studies* 5.1 (2002), pp. 135-53.

[5] Among other scholars see Manuel J. Gaxiola, 'Latin American Pentecostalism: A Mosaic within a Mosaic', *Pneuma* 13.2 (1991), pp. 107-29; Luis D. Segreda, 'Informe de Viaje', in Harold D. Hunter and Peter C. Hocken (eds.), *All Together in One Place* (JPTSup 4; Sheffield, UK: Sheffield Academic Press, 1998), pp. 134-48; and C. René Padilla, *Bases Bíblicas de la Misión: Perspectivas Latinoamericanas* (Grand Rapids, MI: Nueva Creación, 1998).

[6] See Willems, *Followers of the New Faith*, p. 68; and Lalive d'Espinay, *El Refugio de las Masas*, pp. 110-14. See also Francisco C. Rolim, *O Que é Pentecostalismo* (São Paulo, Brasil: Primeiros Pasos, 1978).

[7] See for instance Samuel Escobar, 'The Promise and Precariousness of Latin American Protestantism', in Daniel R. Miller (ed.), *Coming of Age: Protestantism in Contemporary Latin America* (Lanham, MD: University Press of America, 1994), pp. 26-38.

[8] See Samuel Escobar, *Changing Tides: Latin America and World Mission Today* (New York, NY: Orbis Books, 2002).

ward Cleary and Doug Petersen have added significant data to recent challenges and opportunities faced by mission theology in the region.[9]

In the Pentecostal circles of Latin America Darío López has urged Christians to assume *Missio Dei* by making the message and practice of gospel relevant to the poor and marginalized. López maintains that Christians ought to pay attention to the arduous challenges that poverty and marginalization demand from the churches of Latin America. He also argues that the fact that most Pentecostal congregations are located in marginal areas should motivate Pentecostal scholars to defend the dignity of all human beings.[10] From his pulpit in a marginalized zone in Lima, López encouraged a change of attitude in the church that seeks and labors for the spiritual and social transformation of the poor, the weak, and the marginalized.[11]

Another scholar with significant works on Pentecostal topics is Bernardo Campos. He introduced the concept of *Pentecostalidad* (Pentecostality) to the church, which he defines as 'the universal experience that expresses the occurrence of Pentecost'[12] in the body of Christ. Campos maintains that the Pentecostality of the church must be understood as 'a pluralist and diverse action of the Spirit'.[13] Christologically, Pentecostality is the 'the strength of the Spirit'[14] that enables the church as the body of Christ to engage *Missio Dei* as modeled by Christ.[15] In principle, Pentecostality surpasses any

---

[9] Edward L. Cleary, 'Latin American Pentecostalism', in Murray W. Dempster, Byron D. Klaus, and Douglas Peterson (eds.), *The Globalization of Pentecostalism: A Religion Made to Travel* (Oxford: Regnum Books, 1999), pp. 127-45.

[10] Darío López, *Pentecostalimo y Transformación Social* (Buenos Aires, Argentina: Ediciones Kairós, 2000), p. 29.

[11] See Darío López, *Los Evangélicos y Los Derechos Humanos* (Lima, Perú: Centro Evangélico de Misiología Andino-Amazónica, 1998), pp. 65-75.

[12] See Bernardo Campos, *De la Reforma Protestante a la Pentecostalidad de la Iglesia: Debate Sobre el Pentecostalismo en América Latina* (Quito, Ecuador: Ediciones CLAI, 1997), pp. 90-106.

[13] Bernardo Campos, 'El Influjo de las Huacas: La Espiritualidad Pentecostal en el Perú', in Tomás Gutiérrez (ed.), *Protestantismo y Cultura en América Latina: Aportes y Proyecciones* (Quito, Ecuador: Ediciones CLAI, 1994), p. 18.

[14] Campos, 'El Influjo de la Huacas', p. 26.

[15] See also Bernardo Campos, 'In the Power of the Spirit: Pentecostalism, Theology and Social Ethics', in Benjamin F. Gutiérrez and Dennis A. Smith (eds.), in *In The Power of the Spirit: The Pentecostal Challenge to Historic Churches in Latin America* (Guatemala City, Guatemala: CELEP, 1996), pp. 41-50.

historical Pentecostal event that would claim to be the only model of Pentecost, denying others the uniqueness of their own Pentecostal experience.[16] According to Campos, the Pentecostality of the church refers to the mission of all believers who after being filled with the Holy Spirit operate in the world showing the marks of the incarnate Christ who redeems human beings and their world holistically.

The work of Campos is significant, for it makes Pentecostality the common experience of all believers throughout history. Every person that follows Christ Jesus and obeys his commands can show the marks of Pentecost in his or her life and public service. Thus Pentecostality is the mark of the church and can be seen in its nature and mission.

Since the Holy Spirit is the initiator of Pentecost then all who are led to Christ by the Spirit are Pentecostals. Campos' notion of Pentecostality deconstructs the classic Pentecostal exclusivity of the reception and implementation of the gifts of the Spirit. He has introduced a significant dialogue by suggesting that potentially all Christians are Pentecostals for all are brought by and follow the same Spirit who is the initiator of the Pentecostal experience. This insight should foster cooperation and stimulate fellowship among Christians as they engage *Missio Dei*.

Expected Stereotypes

It is well known that Evangelicals and Pentecostals are a large community with different cultural backgrounds.[17] These movements have been enriched by a colorful blend of race, language, and geography including history and politics. In the book, *Crisis and Hope in Latin America*,[18] William D. Taylor described the generational transformation that has taken place in Latin America after the revolutionary days. There were significant political and socio-economic

---

[16] Campos, *De la Reforma Protestante a la Pentecostalidad de la Iglesia*, pp. 90-91.

[17] Among those works we can mention, Virginia Garrard-Burnett and David Stoll (eds.), *Rethinking Protestantism in Latin America* (Philadelphia, PA: Temple University Press, 1993); Cecil M. Robeck, 'Selected Bibliography on Latin American Pentecostalism', *Pneuma* 13.1 (1991), pp. 193-97.

[18] See Emilio Antonio A. Núñez and William D. Taylor, *Crisis and Hope in Latin America* (Pasadena, CA: William Carey Library, 1996), p. 3.

changes that forced Christians from all denominations to make accelerated adjustments to their lives. Taylor pictures this change by recalling stereotyped images such as

> a man sleeping under his *sombrero* [broad brimmed hat]; or with the son of a former *guerillero* [guerrilla], who in recent years held on tensely to a machine gun, but now, his grandson or granddaughter holds on to a smart phone to keep in contact with his or her own business.[19]

Drastic changes took place in the cities, and entire nations have been affected by contemporary socioeconomic shifts. They have also changed the church and changed Pentecostalism.

Moreover, Houtart and Pin remind us that sometime ago, Latin American Christians operated in a region where liberation theology emerged. This was particularly the case of the decades of the 1960s and 70s. For Houtart and Pin liberation theology proposed an approach that combined Marxist ideology with Christian theology in a path that both fascinated and repulsed, but it soon faced its own crisis due to the collapse of European Marxism at the end of the 'Cold War'.[20]

In recent years Latin American Evangelicals and Pentecostals have grown numerically in a region of crisis. Political corruption and a poor economy have created an unstable environment. However, these movements emerged strong and confident with a message of hope in such chaotic scenario. Evangelicals and Pentecostals made their impact through evangelism and church planting, particularly in the most remote and marginalized areas of the cities.[21] In spite of those challenging scenarios these movements practiced their faith in an attitude of obedience to the great commission of Christ.

---

[19] Núñez and Taylor, *Crisis and Hope in Latin America*, p. 3.

[20] See Francois Houtart and Emile Pin, *The Church and the Latin American Revolution* (New York, NY: Sheed and Ward, 1965), pp. 65-74.

[21] See for instance John J. Considine, *The Religious Dimension in the New Latin America* (Notre Dame, IN: Fides Publishers, 1966).

Mission and the Expansion of the Church

To understand the role of Evangelicals and Pentecostals in Latin America, we need to examine some factors that may correlate with their significant numerical growth. For instance Berg and Pretiz have identified some of the values of Pentecostalism in Latin America.[22] These features can be observed in most Latin American contexts, although some similarities can be found in other regions of the world where Pentecostalism is also expanding.

Historical Connection

In Latin America, Classic Pentecostals generally identified the Catholic Church as a fallen religious system. The Catholic Church had the doctrine, the Scripture, and theology, but the religious system obscured these from the people. Hence, Pentecostals resented the fact that for centuries the Catholic Church alienated them from the experience of communion with the Holy Spirit that they have now re-discovered. For that reason they saw the Catholic religious system as an agent of alienation, oppression, and complicity with evil powers that ruled the world.[23] So for Pentecostals, the Spirit of Pentecost represents the new 'wine' that must be preserved in 'new wineskins'.

For Pentecostals in Latin America then, the action of witnessing was directed to those who have remained ensconced within the obsolete religious system.[24] Pentecostal conversion occurs when the individual understands the gospel as revealed by Scripture or by the Holy Spirit. By faith, the person receives Christ Jesus into his or her heart and joins the Pentecostal family. This is followed by a new paradigm for life and ministry, which is offered by the community of believers.

Yet as much as Pentecostals continued to perpetuate this anti-Catholic rhetoric, there is also no denial that Pentecostal converts from nominal Roman Catholicism bring their previous tradition

---

[22] Mike Berg and Paul Pretiz, *The Gospel People of Latin America* (Monrovia, CA: MARC/LAM, 1992), pp. 118-20; and Guillermo Cook, *Let My People Live: Faith and Struggle in Central America* (Grand Rapids, MI: Eerdmans, 1988), pp. 65-70.

[23] David M. Howard, 'Great Things to Come', *Christianity Today* 36.4 (April 1992), p. 39; and Andrés Tapia, 'Why is Latin America Turning Protestant?', *Christianity Today* 36.4 (April 1992), pp. 28-29.

[24] Tapia, 'Why is Latin America Turning Protestant?', p. 29.

with them, including their Catholic theological background. Their basic knowledge of Christianity is informed by Catholic faith, tradition, and practice.[25] As such, there may be more continuity between Catholicism and Pentecostalism than the either are willing to admit. Perhaps this is why Pentecostals, Charismatics, and Neo-Pentecostals are successful in evangelizing nominal Roman Catholics. The Holy Spirit refreshes their common Catholic background to become solid witnesses of Christ. Eventually Latin America may produce a new breed of Christianity, which combines Roman Catholic theology and culture with Pentecostal zeal and empowerment.[26]

Response to Poverty and Marginalization

With the exception of some classical denominations of North American origin, most Evangelical and Pentecostal movements in Latin America are indigenous in leadership.[27] They mobilize their congregations in the poorest and most marginalized communities. That is why most of these churches have taken root among the poor masses, contrary to what has happened with the majority of historical protestant churches that have developed their congregations predominantly among the middle class.

The poverty amidst which many Evangelicals and Pentecostals live provides occasion for the poor to voice and articulate their understanding of the revelation of Christ. For these Christians there can be no dichotomization between theory and praxis.[28] Here, theo-

---

[25] Enrique Dussel, *A History of the Church in Latin America: Colonialism to Liberation* (Grand Rapids, MI: Eerdmans, 1981), pp. 123-32.

[26] See Eduard L. Cleary, *The Rise of Charismatic Catholicism in Latin America* (Gainesville, FL: University of Florida Press, 2011), pp. 46-50.

[27] Among the most influential North American denominations in Latin America we can mention the Assemblies of God and Church of God. Their involvement in social concerns seems to have been limited. Hence, their leaders and administrators have become dependent on the mother church in the United States. Few members are committed to social and cultural transformation. Both denominations seem to have been permeated by fundamentalism, which teaches a dualist point of view between the world and the church. See for instance Carmelo E. Álvarez, 'Historic Panorama of Pentecostalism in Latin America and the Caribbean', in Benjamin F. Gutiérrez and Dennis A. Smith (eds.), *The Power of the Spirit: The Pentecostal Challenge to Historic Churches in Latin America* (Guatemala City, Guatemala: CELEP, 1996), pp. 29-40.

[28] See for instance Cheryl Bridges Johns, 'Pentecostals and the Praxis of Liberation: A Proposal for Subversive Theological Education', *Transformation* 11.1 (1994), pp. 11-15.

ry derives from praxis and leads back to ecclesial and social transformation. Evangelicals and Pentecostals in Latin America are now
serving the poor and marginalized. They are becoming aware that
their service is decisive in the transformation of the poor.

Importance of the Supernatural

In the case of Latin American Pentecostals, they accept the baptism
with the Holy Spirit as an initiation into a new reality. The believer
is radically reoriented to experience a new relationship with God
and is enabled to serve his or her community effectively. Naturally,
it is expected that different gifts of the Holy Spirit will operate in
the lives and ministry of believers who will either sacrifice themselves for the cause of Christ or will simply experience the power
of the Holy Spirit in their Christian service.[29]

In Latin America most Pentecostals anticipate the return of
Christ and arrival of a new world order where there will be peace
and justice. However, this will not occur until the completion of the
work of Christ at his return. In the meantime, the use and impartation of the supernatural, of which manifestations demonstrate the
presence, testimony and power of God is needed. Miraculous healings and supernatural events in families and the community convict
sinners and strengthen faith in Christians. As a result, conversions
ensue, church attendance increases, and believers are mobilized.

When supernatural phenomena are experienced, Pentecostals are
certain that they are moving in the power of the Holy Spirit. Signs
and wonders confirm the presence and ministry of the Holy Spirit
in their service.[30] Their hearts overflow with love, joy, and expecta-
tion. They believe this leads to experiencing the promises of God.
The gifts of the Holy Spirit are sought and exercised for the benefit
of the community of faith and taken as a sign to unbelievers. Pentecostals lay hands on the sick and expect healing to follow. They
attempt to remain in close connection with the Holy Spirit and anticipate that supernatural events may occur.

---

[29] López, *Pentecostalimo y Transformación Social*, p. 29
[30] L. Grant McClung, "'Try to Get Them Saved": Revisiting the Paradigm of
an Urgent Pentecostal Missiology', in Murray W. Dempster, Byron D. Klaus, and
Douglas Petersen (eds.), *The Globalization of Pentecostalism: A Religion Made to Travel*
(Oxford, UK: Regnum Books International, 1999), pp. 30-51.

Mobilization for Cross-Cultural Ministry

Pentecostals in Latin America emphasize participation of the laity in the ministry of the church. This feature differentiates Pentecostal congregations from denominations of North American origin and from the Catholic Church. It also differs from those American-based Pentecostal denominations in which hierarchical power has relegated the laity to limited participation in ministry.[31] Contrary to that, most Pentecostal churches in Latin America have adopted a different attitude towards laity. However, there are some North American Pentecostal scholars who have embraced lay leaders as active participants in church ministry. One of them is Cheryl Bridges Johns. She said that, 'the active presence of the Holy Spirit in the Pentecostal congregation calls for a radical balance in ministry between men and women, blacks and white, rich and poor'.[32] Obviously Johns' argument has a prophetic purpose for a North American context; however, the message fits what is happening among Latin American Pentecostal ministries today.

The priesthood of all believers has become one of the most effective tools in their practice of mission.[33] In fact, most prominent Pentecostal leaders in Latin America are lay ministers. Some of them are professionals who have left aside their professional fields to devote themselves completely to ministry. Most of them are practitioners in ministry and do not have adequate theological training; however, the success of these pastors is evident. They have been able to plant new and strong congregations and some are pastors of mega churches. Others are head leaders of social and development organizations.[34]

Pentecostals thus understand the 'Great Commission' as an inescapable mandate in which all believers participate diligently. The task of evangelization knows no racial, political, or cultural barriers;

---

[31] Campos, *De la Reforma Protestante a la Pentecostalidad de la Iglesia*, pp. 47-50.

[32] Johns, 'Pentecostals and the Praxis of Liberation', p. 11.

[33] See Chris Armstrong, 'Embrace your Inner Pentecostal', *Christianity Today* 50.9 (September 2006), p. 86.

[34] One example is the testimony of Misael Argeñal, *Crónicas de una Gran Cosecha: Cómo Pasar de la Visión a la Acción* (Miami, FL: Editorial Vida, 2012), pp. 36-42. Argeñal explains how he transferred from a small classic Pentecostal church to a mega-pastor in San Pedro Sula, Honduras. Argeñal's story is also an example of the many variations that Neo-Pentecostalism has caused even among classic Pentecostals.

it is an undertaking of all the saints and not just of a few specialized in missions.[35] This is a key element of the cross-cultural vocation of the Pentecostal church.

The difference between the cross-cultural evangelization practiced by the Pentecostal movement and the one practiced by the evangelical movement lies in their stance on the Great Commission. For Pentecostals, evangelization is a corporate responsibility, and the main objective is to plant churches that can be reproduced in every cultural context where all believers live. For traditional evangelicals, cross-cultural mission is the responsibility of a few missionaries, who in the majority of cases, leave everything behind and go to a chosen place to carry out their mission. Generally, such efforts are costly and demand a great sacrifice for the 'career missionary'.[36] Most Pentecostal churches do not have career missionaries. They approach cross-cultural missions corporately. They enable great-commission-committed believers who are sent to evangelize and plant churches in all places and contexts where the Holy Spirit leads.

This approach to mission is exhibited by the impressive and rapid growth of Pentecostal congregations in the world. Some have mistakenly criticized Pentecostals for not having a vision for cross-cultural ministries. On the contrary, the goal of Pentecostals is to fulfill the Great Commission of which all are a part.[37] It is true that they do not have many 'career missionaries' because in their mindset all believers are career missionaries. This assessment may stand in conflict with the traditional Evangelical conception that it is necessary to recruit, train, and send cross-cultural missionaries to the unreached people groups. Such conception could be justified in spiritual settings where the community of faith has not experienced a true Pentecostal experience. That is not the case of Pentecostal

---

[35] With regards to specialized agencies of mission, see C. René Padilla, 'Toward the Globalization and Integrity of Mission', in Gerald H. Anderson, James B. Phillips, and Robert T. Coote, (eds.), *Mission in the Nineteen Nineties* (Grand Rapids, MI: Eerdmans, 1991), pp. 30-32.

[36] See William D. Taylor (ed.), *Too Valuable to Lose: Exploring the Causes and Cures of Missionary Attrition* (Pasadena, CA: William Cary Library, 1997), pp. 3-14.

[37] On the matter of mission mobilization among Pentecostals, see Miguel Álvarez, *La Palabra, El Espíritu y la Comunidad de Fe* (Cleveland, TN: Editorial Evangélica, 2007), pp. 73-76.

congregations; for them the formation and training of missionaries refers to equipping of all believers to carry the great commission to all people groups.

One way to reconcile these opposing views would be for traditional denominations to incorporate those Pentecostal dynamics and passion for ministry into their career missionary endeavors, while Pentecostals should incorporate the well-designed mission strategies of traditional Evangelical churches to their passion for ministry. This attempt to integrate a cross-cultural missionary outreach will prove to be more effective than those carried out today.

Practices of Mission

Latin American Pentecostals also have some limitations. They are confronted by problems such as: lack of training, limited resources, the temptations of prosperity theology and other factors. They also face social alienation and marginalization in their communities.[38]

Theological and Leadership Training

Most Pentecostal churches are led by pastors without formal and theological education. In most cases, they were chosen from the laity for their testimony of commitment to the church and for their natural ability to lead other believers. Such lack of theological training leads many to embrace doubtful teachings. Church growth generates wealth, which is attractive to the people who profess having the latest revelations of God but in the end causes division and suspicion.

Conversely, neo-Pentecostal pastors are prone to embrace contemporary teachings related to financial prosperity, spiritual authority and extreme supernatural experience.[39] Every new Christian fad finds fertile grounds in neo-Pentecostal congregations for they do not have ways to regulate any approach to these teachings. These

---

[38] See for instance Everett Wilson, 'Guatemala Pentecostals. Something of their Own', in Edward L. Cleary and Hannah W. Stewart-Gambino (eds.), *Power, Politics and Pentecostals in Latin America* (Boulder, CO: Westview Press, 1997), pp. 139-62.

[39] On the matter of the prosperity gospel, see David Jones and Russell S. Woodbridge, *Health, Wealth and Happiness?* (Grand Rapids, MI: Kregel Publications, 2011), p. 93.

issues are a matter of concern, particularly with those who have a prophetic perspective on the new developments of ministry.

Nevertheless, after the era of violent revolutions and the surge of the Internet information, Pentecostals are learning to interconnect as individuals and as institutions. They have engaged the ranks of higher education to seek viable solutions to their common concerns and to excel in Christian service. Furthermore, it is known that some Pentecostals in Latin America are now developing comprehensive educational programs. Most of these programs are in the stage of formation but may become stronger as time goes by and more students join.

However, Pentecostals still lack biblically and theologically grounded leaders, but this scenario may change due to more Pentecostal participation in several international forums. Those platforms offer constructive ideas for the advancement of leadership and administrative skills. In addition, they provide in-depth views of formal studies, pastoral training, and psychological formation suitable for the community of faith.

Limited Resources

Contrary to Neo-Pentecostalism, Pentecostals have limited resources and labor under financial constraints. There are, however, some pastors who are from the middle class and have the capability to fund their ministry. They are able to mobilize and attract other Christians into their church programs. However, most pastors have limited resources, and because of that they struggle to maintain their ministries.

As a result, members of classic Pentecostal churches migrate over time to the most attractive mega-church in town. In Latin America today it is customary to see former members of small congregations as new leaders of faster growing mega-churches. This situation raises issues with regards to evangelism, church growth, and ethics in ministry.

Even in the first quarter of the twenty-first century, Pentecostals continue to move their resources toward evangelization and planting of new churches. They are also developing strategic ideas to address social concern. Some Pentecostal leaders are becoming involved in the political arena with mixed results. Others are involved in theological reflection. Some are exploring ways to participate in cross-cultural service.[40] This may be an optimistic stance on what the Holy Spirit has been doing among Pentecostals in general. However, the limitations are still tremendous compared to the current statistics of numerical growth.

The Challenge of Prosperity in the Presentation of the Gospel

It is very significant that church growth is occurring in multiple fronts with many congregations of different denominations and growing rapidly, especially in the urban areas. Nevertheless, this phenomenon also has its critics. Some are concerned about their theology, that is, the validity of supernatural manifestations and other practical issues among Pentecostals.

In response to some of those concerns, Samuel Escobar has highlighted the topic of spiritual life in Latin America.[41] Escobar calls for the solid education of leaders. He advocates for honest evangelical-evangelical, Pentecostal-Pentecostal, and evangelical-Pentecostal dialogues.[42] Those dialogues may provide wisdom and understanding for spirituality, strategic evangelism, church planting, and social concern among evangelicals and Pentecostals.[43]

Between Tradition and Change

Guillermo Cook also referred to the dynamic tensions caused by social, political, and religious changes that are now taking place in Latin America. A few years ago he published a book called *The New Face of the Church in Latin America: Between Tradition and Change*. In a significant statement Cook affirmed, 'The new face of the church in Latin America is also largely a history of Pentecostalism'.[44] Cook

---

[40] Núñez and Taylor, *Crisis and Hope in Latin America*, p. 4; see also Daniel E. Grey, 'Revive, Argentina!' *Eternity* (July-August 1987), pp. 22-26; and Stephen Sywulka, 'A Latin American Evangelical View of Base Communities', *Transformation* 3.3 (1986), pp. 20-32.

[41] See for instance Guillermo Cook, 'Growing Pains', *Christianity Today* 36.4 (April 1992), pp. 36-37.

[42] See Samuel Escobar, 'A New Reformation', *Christianity Today* 36.4 (April 1992), pp. 30-34.

[43] Samuel Escobar, 'Mission in Latin America: An Evangelical Perspective', *Missiology: An International Review* 20.2 (1992), pp. 241-53.

[44] This issue was addressed by Guillermo Cook (ed.), *New Face of the Church in Latin America: Between Tradition and Change* (Maryknoll, NY: Orbis, 1994), p. xiii.

also acknowledged that there is not a single face that identifies the church in Latin America. By saying so he recognized the multiplicity of expressions of the Christian faith that coexist in the continent.

In countries like Guatemala, El Salvador, and Honduras, Pentecostals have grown considerably; however, they are yet to experience a significant socio-economic and political impact. Up to this point, Pentecostals seem to have been more focused on numerical growth and new sensational spiritual teachings rather that facing the severe human reality of their communities. Extreme poverty remains untouched. Violence and drug trafficking continue to harm those Central American countries. It is clear that Pentecostals have a share in their society, so their participation in the solution of these social ills is vital.

Strategic Training

For now, the priority of the Pentecostal movement in Latin America seems to be strategic training and equipping the leadership. Solid theological formation will secure the foundations of ministry for the emerging generations.

Samuel Escobar has suggested a few indicators to watch for those interested in the numerical growth of Latin American Pentecostalism: (1) Spiritual factors: the free action and sovereign work of the Holy Spirit; (2) anthropological motives: hunger for God; (3) sociological elements: these provide believers with a sense of personal and communal identity and a sense of refuge and security in a hostile world; (4) pastoral methodology: how the priesthood of all believers is promoted; (5) psychological and cultural reasons: freedom of worship and the expression of emotions; and (6) creative worship: the use of contemporary music allowed in the service.[45] These elements are already observed in growing Pentecostal congregations. Even Protestant and evangelical churches as well as the Roman Catholic Church have adopted them in their liturgy, particularly in praise and worship.[46] Pentecostals have extensively influenced the life and ministry of Christianity in Latin America.[47]

---

[45] These indicators are observable in Latin American Pentecostalism. See the reports of Escobar, 'Latin America: An Evangelical Perspective', pp. 241-48; and John Maust, 'Revival in Zacatecas', *World Pulse* 29.2 (1994), pp. 1-5.

[46] Escobar, 'Latin America', p. 247.

[47] Escobar, 'Latin America', p. 248.

Facing Social Needs

Much has been said and written about the isolation that characterized Latin American Pentecostalism in recent years. For example, in
his 1965 analysis of Chilean Pentecostalism, Christian Lalive
d'Espinay discovered among other things that most evangelical pastors, including Pentecostals, believed that the proclamation and
practice of the gospel should not mix with politics.[48] They also affirmed that the church should not get involved in the sociopolitical
problems to the point of not even mentioning them from the pulpit.[49] A lot has changed since 1965. A new generation of Pentecostals is now getting involved in politics, addressing socioeconomic
problems, and proposing solutions to the community at large. Although this thrust is still limited, there is hope that further participation will contribute to the transformation of Latin America.

In addition, evangelical and Pentecostal thought was labeled as
one that polarized the spiritual versus material and the church versus the world. Both Evangelicals and Pentecostals were identified
with those who rejected the present world in anticipation of the
future. In Latin America, this dichotomy emerged as a consequence
of the alliance of the Catholic Church with the wealthy class.[50]
These circumstances sparked the longing for liberation among
those who yearned for a better world where justice and equality
would be practiced. Naturally during those days Pentecostals were
incapable of denouncing injustice they observed in the socio-
political structures of power. They found comfort in the spiritual
teachings of the Scriptures. Others were required by North American missionaries to submit to the government without questioning
whether these forces were politically just or unjust.[51]

Due to their extreme apolitical inclination, most Latin American
Pentecostals have not questioned the establishment, especially in

---

[48] See Pablo Alberto Deiros (ed.), *Los Evangélicos y El Poder Político en América
Latina* (Grand Rapids: Eerdmans, 1987), pp. 8-12.

[49] On this issue, see Lalive d'Espinay, *El Refugio de las Masas*, p. 157.

[50] See Joaquín Piña, 'Juntos, para Defender los Derechos Humanos', *Iglesias,
Pueblos y Culturas: Evangélicos en América Latina* 37-38.1 (1995), p. 175.

[51] See for instance, Darío López, *La Misión Liberadora de Jesús: Una Lectura Mi-
siológica del Evangelio de Lucas* (Lima, Perú: Ediciones Puma, 1997), pp. 101-109;
and Eldin Villafañe, *The Liberating Spirit: Towards an Hispanic American Pentecostal
Social Ethic* (Grand Rapids: Eerdmans, 1992), pp. 143-62.

cases of injustice or immorality. North American missionaries had taught them that being apolitical was a Christian virtue.[52] However, some leaders had begun to question the role that Pentecostals could assume to promote socio-political changes in the region. In the twenty-first century, a new generation of Pentecostal thinkers is emerging with new hermeneutics concerned about the holistic needs of the community.[53] There are also Pentecostal voices that call out for social justice and are opting to serve and defend the poor, the weak and the marginalized.[54] However this awareness of social justice issues and opting in favor of the poor and marginalized are incipient among Pentecostals. Nonetheless, more people are uniting efforts to elevate social concern in the church. Hence, theological education, pastoral formation, and Christian service are being challenged to adjust to the fullness of the gospel in the context of church and society.

New Possibilities

At the end of the twentieth century Latin American Pentecostals were confronted by the tendencies of a postmodern society. Relativism, liberalism, materialism, secularism, and individualism were the common denominator in a world of rapid changes. In contrast, the world was experiencing an unprecedented spiritual revival with the coming of the new millennium. The great majority of members of the Christian church were undergoing unusual levels of concern due to the eschatological implications of the end of a millennium and the start of a new one.

It is clear that Latin American Pentecostals in the twenty-first century are at a crossroads. On one side there is a segment of the

---

[52] See Paul E. Sigmund, 'The Transformation of Christian Democratic Ideology: Transcending Left and Right, or Whatever Happened to the Third Way', in Scott Mainwaring and Timothy R. Scully (eds.), *Christian Democracy in Latin America: Electoral Competition and Regime Conflicts* (Stanford, CA: Stanford University Press, 2003), pp. 30-55; also, Vicente C. Peloso (ed.), *Work, Protest and Identity Twentieth-Century Latin America* (Wilmington, DE: Jaguar Books, 2003), pp. 129-32.

[53] López, *La Misión Liberadora de Jesús*, pp. 11-14.

[54] For more information on the subject, see World Evangelical Fellowship, *The Grand Rapids Report on Evangelism and Social Responsibility: An Evangelical Commitment* (Exeter, UK: Paternoster, 1982), pp. 43-44.

church that has become satisfied, established, and wealthy. This is the case of most neo-Pentecostal churches, which will continue to emphasize the condition of prosperity as a result of true faith. This stance is more visible in areas influenced by Western cultures and mainly affects the wealthy class of Latin America. Some Neo-Pentecostals and Charismatics embrace this tendency, which may culminate in a post-Christian society. Consequently, this neo-Pentecostal movement may experience a spiritual decay in the up-coming years. Eventually people get tired of the fallacies of the same rhetoric day after day. The spiritual level of such congregations could reach a low level, where secularism supported by technological and information advances could endanger the health of the church.

But on the other side, there will remain a solid and radical congregation composed of Pentecostals that will remain committed to the practice and teachings of the Word. They will obey the leading of the Holy Spirit. These have interpreted the arrival of the twenty-first century as the best opportunity ever granted to the church. However, this level of commitment could be an enormous cost to those who are devoted to the Great Commission. Nonetheless, historically Pentecostals have operated well under socio-political and religious distress. Latin American Pentecostals will need to operate wisely and in the mind of the Holy Spirit in this time of opportunities and new developments.

2

CONTEXTS OF MISSION IN LATIN AMERICA

Pentecostals in Latin America share similar characteristics in their approach to mission thinking and practice. Pentecostal churches are now engaging with poverty and marginalization for missiological purposes. They are implementing the principles of the gospel to the most critical issues. Thus, Pentecostals seem to have started offering solutions to the socio-economic, political and spiritual problems of their countries.

In this section we explore mission thinking among Pentecostals in recent history. The first part examines the sequels of the conflict between North and South and the differences between East and West during the 'Cold War' in the development of mission theology in Latin America. The second part studies a Pentecostal praxis of social responsibility. It looks at the formation of social responsibility among Pentecostals and their response to the challenges of social service, community development, and their attitude toward violence and social injustice.

Emerging Contexts

In Latin America, the term integral mission is also known as transformational development, Christian development, or holistic mission.[1] The proponents of integral mission argue that the concept of

---

[1] The term 'integral mission' was used in Spanish as *misión integral* (integral mission) in the 1970s by members of the Latin American Theological Fraternity (FTL) (Fraternidad Teológica Latinoamericana) to describe that understanding of

integral mission is rooted in Scripture and exemplified in Jesus' own ministry. Hence, Charles Van Engen suggests that integral mission defines a distinct term for a holistic understanding of mission that has become noteworthy in the past forty years.[2] This vocabulary distinguishes it from widely held approaches that emphasize either evangelism or social responsibility.

A commitment to integral mission is often reflected in a particular concern for those living in poverty and a commitment to pursuing justice. In Latin America, some Pentecostals have begun to grasp the concept of integral mission as advocated by other evangelical thinkers.[3]

During the last quarter of the twentieth century, several scholars have written about the attitude of isolation that characterized the Pentecostal movement in those days vis-à-vis the tendency to ignore the deep socio-economic situations that affected Latin America at that time. In his Chilean study from 1965 to 1966, Christian Lalive d'Espinay reported, 'among other things, the majority of pastors, both Evangelical and Pentecostals, believed that the gospel should not be involved in politics'.[4] He also found that 'Christians should

---

Christian mission, which embraces both the proclamation, and the demonstration of the Gospel. The word integral is used in Spanish to describe wholeness. Theologians use it to refer to Christian mission as that which affirms the importance of expressing the love of God through every means possible. Its proponents (e.g., René Padilla, Samuel Escobar) wanted to emphasize the integration of the good news with Christian mission, and used the word integral to signal their discomfort with conceptions of Christian mission based on a dichotomy between evangelism and social involvement. See C. René Padilla, 'Integral Mission and its Historical Development', in Tim Chester (ed.), *Justice, Mercy & Humility: Integral Mission and the Poor* (London, UK: Paternoster Press, 2002), pp. 86-94; Samuel Escobar, 'Christian Reflections from the Latino South', *Journal of Latin American Theology* 1.2 (2006), pp. 12-16; and Vinay Samuel and Chris Sugden, *The Church in Response to Human Need* (Oxford, UK: Regnum Books, 1987), pp. 62-71.

[2]   Charles Van Engen, *Footprints of God: A Narrative Theology of Mission* (Monrovia, CA: World Vision Publications, 2000), p. 116.

[3]   Recent activity shows that Pentecostals are paying attention to ministry focused on relief and development. For more information, see G.A. Haugen, 'Micah Declaration on Integral Mission', in *Micah Network* (2001). http://www.micahnetwork.org/en/integral-mission. Viewed 12 January 2010.

[4]   Christian Lalive d'Espinay, *El Refugio de las Masas* (Santiago de Chile: Editorial del Pacifico, 1968), p. 157.

not concern themselves with the socio-political problems of the country, to the point of not even talking about them'.[5] This line of thought seems to be very similar to the fundamentalist ideas that focused on maintaining the purity of the gospel against the threats of worldly influences.[6] The early Pentecostal church in Latin America had to deal with these ideas. They had to incorporate definitions for what was considered sinful, carnal, or unethical in the practice of faith.

Engaging Mission

Historically, Pentecostals had the tendency to stress a dichotomy between the church and the world, Christ and society, and the spiritual and material.[7] Due to their theological approach to mission, Pentecostals have rejected the present order of things on account of the anticipation of the new world that is going to be established by Christ upon his return.[8]

Latin American Pentecostals inherited this dichotomy from the North American denominations and the historical influence of the Roman Catholic tradition, which tended to ally itself closely with the upper class of society. This has been a pattern since the Colonial Era in order to subdue the masses of the region.[9] Some historians have interpreted the alliance between the RCC and the upper class as the spark that ignited liberation theology among those who longed for greater justice and equality in the region. Such opinions

---

[5] d'Espinay, *El Refugio de las Masas*, p. 145.

[6] See for instance Heinrich Fries, *Fundamental Theology* (Washington, DC: Catholic University of America Press, 1996), pp. 11-22 and George M. Marsden, *Fundamentalism and American Culture* (Oxford, UK: Oxford University Press, 2006), pp. 43-47.

[7] See Valentín Menéndez Martínez, *La Misión de la Iglesia: Un Estudio Sobre el Debate Teológico y Eclesial en América Latina* (Roma, Italia: Universidad Pontifica Gregoriana, 2001), pp. 276-79.

[8] See for instance Wolfgang Vondey and Martin William Mittelstadt, *Theology of Amos Yong and the New Face of Pentecostal Scholarship. Passion of the Spirit* (Leiden, The Netherlands: Brill, 2013), p. 11.

[9] John A. Mackay, *The Other Spanish Christ: A Study in the Spiritual History of Spain and South America* (Eugene, OR: Wipf and Stock Publishers, 2001), pp. 43-51. See also Alberto Rembao, *El Orden de Dios y el Desorden del Hombre* (México, DF: Casa Unida de Publicaciones, 1964), pp. 24-26.

were not exclusively religious, however; some were influenced by Marxist ideology, for example, which supported the revolutionary movements in the second half of the twentieth century.[10]

Conversely, the Pentecostal movement did not issue any prophetic response to the injustices present in the social, political, and economic structures of Latin America in the same way as liberation theology.[11] Instead, they tended to submit meekly to the powers that controlled the area politically and socio-economically. Though the RCC hierarchy served the interests of the upper class, Pentecostals were immersed amongst the poor but lacked a clear understanding of their role in the mission of the church. It was not until they grew so rapidly, in terms of adherents, that Pentecostals learned new ways and opportunities to express their opinions and positions in the areas that affected their communities.

This was the time when democratic regimes returned throughout Latin America in the 1980s and 1990s after a string of military dictatorships. This meant that participation in political life was again open to the general population. However, research, reflection, commitment, and participation in social concerns did not begin immediately. During that time, they learned that some RCC scholars had been involved in the movement labeled as liberation theology, which was initially based upon the Vatican II's 'option for the poor'.[12]

---

[10] Juan A. Oddone, 'Pautas de Indignación: Contenidos y Ambigüedades', in Leopoldo Zea (ed.), *América Latina en sus Ideas* (Madrid, España: Siglo Veintiuno Editores, 2006), pp. 201-209.

[11] Peruvian Dominican priest-theologian, Gustavo Gutiérrez coined the term 'Liberation Theology', and gave the movement its most famous and enduring presentation in his book. See Gustavo Gutierrez, *Teología de la Liberación: Perspectivas* (Salamanca, España: Ediciones Sígueme, 1971, 1990), p. 71. Liberation theology is a Christian theology in which the teachings of Jesus Christ are understood in terms of liberation from unjust political, economic, or social conditions. Its theologians consider 'structural sin' to be a root cause of poverty and oppression, and consider the primary responsibility of the Church to be its 'option for the poor'.

[12] See López, *La Misión Liberadora de Jesús*, pp. 101-109; See also Benedicta Da Silva, *Benedicta Da Silva: An Afro-Brazilian Woman's Story of Politics and Love* (Oakland, CA: A Food First Book, 1997), pp. 193-201; Villafañe, *The Liberating Spirit*, pp. 143-62.

In their early history, Pentecostals in Latin America thought of themselves as being apolitical,[13] and for that reason they did not question or challenge the establishment. For a time, there was no Pentecostal response to the problems of society. It took a new generation with a contemporary approach to hermeneutics to express concerns for the needs of humanity in the region.[14] There were other voices, together with Pentecostals, that asked for social justice, opting for the poor and defending the weak.[15]

At this point in time, awareness and analysis on issues related to social justice and options for the poor are still incipient but continue to emerge among grass-roots leaders. By the same token, theological education, pastoral formation, and Christian service are now being challenged and will continue to be challenged to adjust to the fullness of the gospel in the context of the church and society.

Clash Between North and South

Here, let us turn the discussion to examine the historical conflict between the Northern and Southern Hemispheres.[16] This study is important in order to explain some of the socio-economic and po-

---

[13] However, there are those who argue that there is no such thing as being apolitical for even those who spiritualize the issue, still follow certain political alignment toward the fundamentalist belief that all the things of this world are under judgment. See for instance Núñez and Taylor, *Crisis and Hope in Latin America*, pp. 245-99.

[14] López, *La Misión Liberadora de Jesús*, pp. 11-40; and Norberto Saracco, 'Mission and Missiology from Latin America', in William D. Taylor (ed.), *Global Missiology for the 21st Century* (Grand Rapids, MI: Baker Academic, 2000), pp. 357-66.

[15] C. Rene Padilla, 'Evangelism and Social Responsibility from Wheaton '66 to Wheaton '83', *Transformation* 2.2 (1985), pp. 27-33; see also Peter Kuzmic, 'History and Eschatology: Evangelical Views', in Bruce J. Nicholls (ed.), *In Word and Deed* (Grand Rapids, MI: Eerdmans, 1986), pp. 152-57.

[16] The discussion does not have anything to do with geography, but rather with that division of North and South as proposed by political, economic, social, and theological thinkers. In some instances, this division is seen as West versus East. However, for its social and economic implications, I had chosen to use the terms North versus South. See for instance Jürgen Moltmann, *God for a Secular Society* (Minneapolis, MN: Augsburg Fortress, 1999), pp. 46-55.

litical issues that affected Latin American missiology,[17] particularly during the Cold War, and how they affect the understanding and practice of mission among Pentecostals today. At some point, Pentecostal missionaries from North America were referred to as instruments of domination to buttress those social forces, which they saw as containing the advance of communism in the region.

The Cuban revolution was a particularly salient point in this; a revolution that Washington was determined to contain and (if possible) subvert. Policy towards Latin America in the 1960s and 1970s was imbued by the need to win the region for free-market capitalism, and there were frequent interventions by the US to this end, of which possibly the most egregious example was the role of the US in the 1973 coup in Chile. This was a conflict that affected the Pentecostal churches. Furthermore, there were some branches of the RCC that associated them with revolutionary change, and these were active at the grass roots in a number of countries. Nevertheless, there were other sectors in the RCC, which were notably more conservative in socio-economic, political and spiritual issues, particularly in the hierarchy. Christian democrats sought to forge a midway course, but when the social problems became difficult they tended to side with the conservatives as in Chile.[18]

Pentecostal churches were not immune to this ideological conflict, especially in Central America where they tended to lend support to conservative causes. In that region, the revolution in Nicaragua in 1979 and the civil war in El Salvador from the 1980s onward had a highly polarizing effect from which Pentecostal churches were far from immune.

During the second half of the twentieth-century, the socio-economic and political differences between North and South became very obvious. Some of those differences continue to be unresolved even today. Geographically the rich were in the North and the poor in the South. Likewise, in the 1960s and 70s these two poles were reflected in the church. Prosperous North America had its gospel of faith and prosperity, and poor and oppressed South

---

[17] See C. Rene Padilla, *Mission Between the Times* (Grand Rapids, MI: Eerdmans, 1985), p. 120.

[18] See for instance Anderson, *An Introduction to Pentecostalism*, pp. 78-86.

America had its liberation theology. Those were two irreconcilable doctrines that even today remain unresolved.

The financial superiority of the North remained under control of the free market,[19] while the fluctuation of the free market determined the economic capability of people, entities, and institutions. Capitalism had bought people's values and services and had used them to build a capitalist consumers' society.

The debt crisis of the early 1980s led to an abrupt change in Latin America with interventionist states giving way to more liberal regimes, mainly in the economic sense, in which markets ruled supreme. It was in this context that poverty levels increased and social divides widened. In recent years, a number of countries have seen a political reaction against neo-liberal governments, notably in Venezuela, Bolivia, Ecuador, Argentina, and Brazil. In Central America too, left-of-center governments have been in office in El Salvador and Honduras but with different outcomes. The leftist government of Honduras collapsed in 2009 under the pressure action of nationalistic forces that battled against a totalitarian government backed by Venezuelan President Hugo Chavez.

Pentecostalism could not escape the model of Christianity that was born in North America. Pentecostal missionaries from the North travelled South to reach the 'unreached' people groups.[20] In the case of Pentecostals, most missionaries brought with them their culture, economic, and spiritual models.[21] This culture was highly

---

[19] The theological difference between North and South is discussed by Miguel Álvarez, *El Rostro Hispano de Jesús* (Barcelona, España: Editorial CLIE, 2014), pp. 114-17.

[20] The term 'Unreached People Groups' was created by Ralph Dana Winter and used for the first time in his 1974 presentation at the Congress for World Evangelization in Lausanne, Switzerland. This was an event organized by evangelist Billy Graham, which became the watershed moment for global mission. Winter was an America missiologist and Presbyterian missionary who became well known as the advocate for pioneer outreach among 'unreached' people groups. He was the founder of the U.S. Centre for World Mission (USCWM), William Carey International University, and the International Society for Frontier Missiology. More information on this subject is available at Ralph D. Winter, *I Will Do a New Thing: The U.S. Centre for World Mission and Beyond* (Pasadena, CA: William Carey Library, 2003), pp. 29-36.

[21] For a legal definition of colonialism and neo-colonialism, see Jean Salmon (ed.), *Dictionnaire de Droit International* (Bruxelles, Belgique: Bruylant, 2001), pp.

conservative in every sense or at least that is a widely accepted perception. Local people were converted to this Pentecostalism, and they were taught to represent the faith that they had now received. A new breed of Pentecostalism was being born in a context of very poor and political oppressed societies,[22] especially in a very Catholic Latin American region.

The South also experienced a different scenario, whereby some Christians seemed to have openly challenged the context of poverty and oppression that took place in most countries. Most of these were RCC adherents, although some did not subscribe to any specific religious faith. They were deeply involved in the struggle for liberation of the poor, persecuted, and oppressed.[23] In some cases, revolutionary movements arose, which turned against despotic governments and, in some cases, these proved strong enough to remove such regimes from power. This was the case of the revolution in Nicaragua in 1979.[24]

In other cases, people were able to give an impetus to governmental reforms through popular pressure in the implementation of justice and socio-economic development for the people. In the South, people were motivated to develop a social consciousness to speak and act against unjust rulers who served as agents of repression for the benefit of the dominant class. Consequently, the context demanded a theology that would motivate Christians to oppose

---

193-94. For a broader definition, see Le Roy Étienne, 'Colonies', in S. Rials and D. Alland (eds.), *Dictionnaire de la Culture Juridique* (Paris, France: PUF, 2003), p. 231.

[22] On this matter, see the report of John Simpson, *In the Forest of the Night: Encounters in Peru with Terrorism, Drug Running and Military Oppression* (New Haven, CT: Arrow Books, 1993), pp. 23-29.

[23] See for instance Gustavo Gutierrez, *The Truth Shall Make You Free: Confrontations* (Maryknoll, NY: Orbis Books, 1990), pp. 19-22.

[24] The Sandinista National Liberation Front (FSLN) is a socialist political party in Nicaragua. Its members are called Sandinistas. The party is named after Augusto César Sandino who led the Nicaraguan resistance against the United States occupation of Nicaragua in the 1930s. The FSLN overthrew Anastasio Somoza in 1979, ending the Somoza dynasty, and established a revolutionary government in its place. See the account of the Sandinista revolution in Nicaragua as reported by Thomas W. Walker, *Nicaragua: The Land of Sandino* (Boulder, CO: Westview Press, 1981), pp. 32-46.

those oppressive systems and to work in favor of social justice, economic and political freedom for the poor.[25]

In recent years, Latin America has become an open field for confrontations, not only political, social, and economic, but also theological. With the demise of communism, liberation theology lost strength, so the cause for social justice and freedom from oppression migrated to the teaching podium and the pulpit. Workers unions were forced to abdicate, and the poor did not have a voice against social injustice.

In the meantime, some theologians from North America showed their capitalistic allegiance in their doctrine, teaching, and preaching. Hence, their fundamentalist views on politics and economics were clear in their theological stance. They were very antagonistic towards the ideas generated by liberation theologians. North American preachers arrived in Latin America teaching their gospel of faith and prosperity to the middle and upper classes. Eventually, these actions gave birth to the mega-church phenomenon. In the marriage of the prosperity gospel and the mega-church system, a new model of leadership was born that was called the Apostolic and Prophetic Movement. Incidentally, that Apostolic and Prophetic movement is now evolving into what is now known as the 'gospel of the Kingdom here and now'. For obvious reasons this evolution will have to be left for further studies.

Recent Latin American history has witnessed an increase in poverty and oppression in many countries. Some theologians acted responsibly when they reflected upon their reality and made significant proposals, which guided people in the local churches to think according to their Christian values and principles in response to poverty, oppression and persecution.

A number of theologians from the RCC were prompted to offer an immediate response to the context of injustice through a new way of thinking and doing theology that sought social justice and liberation of the oppressed. This new proposal became an academic

---

[25] See Phillip Berryman, *Liberation Theology: Essential Facts About the Revolutionary Movement in Latin America and Beyond* (New York, NY: Harper&Row, 1987), pp. 43-47.

manual in the work of a then fairly young Catholic priest from Peru, Gustavo Gutiérrez.[26]

There are some significant things to be considered in regards to the theological debates taking place in Latin America: (1) Theologians from the Northern hemisphere may have been inaccurate when they accused those from the South as heretics for involving themselves overtly in the field of politics and in social concerns. Northern theologians may have ignored or overlooked the poverty and political oppression in which Southern hemisphere theologians developed their mission thinking and practice. (2) Such a context forced theologians from the South to assume prophetic positions to denounce injustice and to act in favor of the common good of their fellow citizens.

As far as Pentecostals in Latin America are concerned, some may have become involved in the social and political debate. There is no clear evidence of this, except for some isolated cases. Nevertheless, Pentecostals have experienced complications in their approach to social theology due to the following premises: (1) Some Pentecostal churches are direct descendants of classical North American Pentecostal denominations.[27] These Northern missionaries, although most of them were poor in their own context, brought with them a capitalistic understanding of the gospel. Every denomination is free to join the cause that they deem as compatible. The free market could also be applied to churches as the model to be observed by local converts in the mission field. (2) Consequently, Latin American theologians had been identified as heretics and in some cases instruments of demonic activity.[28]

---

[26] Gutiérrez, *Teología de la Liberación*, pp. 12-34. Gutiérrez's position was that social injustice is a form of violence arising from sin. He urged the poor – and those acting in solidarity with them – to reflect on Scripture from the perspective of the poor.

[27] Pentecostals in North America seem to be nationalistic and very tied to their economic and political system, which they reflect in their teachings and practice of ministry. See for instance, Braden P. Anderson, *Chosen Nation: Scripture, Theopolitics and the Project of National Identity* (Eugene, OR: Cascade Books, 2012), pp. 36-43.

[28] See for instance Tim Rutten, 'Glenn Beck's Liberation Theology Obsession', *Los Angeles Times* (1 September 2010).

Therefore, it can be concluded that these missionaries could neither conceive nor understand another way of thinking about or practicing church mission. Local Pentecostals have thus had to learn to live and serve in a continuous contradiction. On one hand, they wanted to be loyal to their North American denominational leaders, but on the other hand, they had become aware of the responsibility to take a stand against corrupt systems that oppress the people whom they serve in their communities.

In these circumstances, Pentecostals have been officially forced out of political involvement, or they were not allowed to participate in politics due to their denominational adherence. Nevertheless, they still found a way to carry out their mission and transform local congregations into places for the advancement of humanity. They grew out of poverty and from that reality were able to assist and meet the needs of people.

Moreover, the contexts of their ministry have begun to experience transformation. The recent development of Pentecostal communities is evidence of a significant social involvement at the grass roots level. Nevertheless, Pentecostals are politically challenged, for they have not holistically engaged in politics.

Conflicting Theological Views

As we have seen, from the context of prosperity in the newly successful Charismatic movement of North America originated a theology of faith and prosperity, commonly known as the 'prosperity gospel'. In the South of the continent, the context of poverty and oppression in most Latin American societies gave way to the idea of a theology of liberation. Incidentally, these theological approaches to the gospel emerged as opposing axes at the same time, one widely spread in the North and the other seriously engaged in socio-political concerns in the South.

Both streams had their foundations in their socio-economic, political, and religious realities that prevailed in their respective contexts. In the North, there were theologians and pastors who preached prosperity as a sign of freedom and spiritual blessing.[29]

---

[29] Theology of prosperity or prosperity gospel is a belief found among Christians from wealthy countries who are centered on the notion that God

Mostly neo-Pentecostal or charismatic, they insisted that economic prosperity was the evidence of a life blessed by God, and that lack of financial prosperity was the evidence of a life in disobedience to the gospel.[30]

At the same time, in the context of oppression, persecution and poverty of the South, there emerged theologians who proclaimed a theology of liberation as a means to experience the entire gospel amongst all people. The objective of this theology was to create awareness among Christians about the reality of poverty and oppression created by unjust government systems and powers structures tilted against the poor. They taught that Christians should not ignore the spiritual and material needs of the oppressed and the poor. Structural sin was to be denounced not only from a moral and personal perspective but also from a socio-economic and political dimension. There were structures of power that served as instruments of evil[31] that had to be opposed and overturned if necessary in order to bring peace and freedom to all people.

In Central America, liberation theologians were active in the socio-political affairs of Guatemala, El Salvador, and Nicaragua. Honduras was no different. What happened in these neighboring countries had a significant effect on Honduras. However, to this day in spite of decades of struggle, the polarization between the privileged and the poor still remains unresolved.

These two theological positions have struggled across the American continents for at least a half a century; one denouncing the other with the difference that the theologians from the North had enough financial resources to discredit the theologians of the South and their thrust for freedom. Ironically, with the demise of the So-

---

provides material prosperity for those he favors. The doctrine has been defined by the belief that 'Jesus blesses believers with riches' or more specifically as the teaching that 'believers have a right to the blessings of health and wealth and that they can obtain these blessings through positive confessions of faith and the "sowing of seeds" through the faithful payments of tithes and offerings'. See for instance Gordon Fee, *The Disease of the Health and Wealth Gospels* (Vancouver, Canada: Regent College Publishing, 2006), p. 56; see also Obed Minchakpu, 'Materialism, Heresy Plague Churches', *Christianity Today* 43.6 (1999), p. 12.

[30] Gregorio Venables, *et al*, *Fe y Prosperidad: Reflexiones Sobre la Teología de la Prosperidad* (La Paz, Bolivia: Editorial Lámpara, 2008), pp. 28-33.

[31] Alberto M. Piedra, 'Some Observations on Liberation Theology', *World Affairs* 148.3 (1985), pp. 151-58.

viet Union in 1989, there was no other political system or government that would take the poor as its cause, although there have been some 'populist' governments who have taken up the cause of the poor in Latin America[32] in recent years.

Thus, the space was wide open in the upper classes of Latin America for the gospel of prosperity to continue to expand. Incidentally, at the turn of the century, most mega-churches in Latin America were teaching the gospel of prosperity.[33] These mega-churches have become influential throughout Latin America but mainly in Brazil and Guatemala. They are immensely wealthy and most of their ministry is performed after North American models of faith and prosperity.

The mega-church movement controls the Christian media and is actively involved in the political arena. Mega-church pastors and leaders have relinquished any denominational ties with Pentecostals and preferred to create a new apostolic and prophetic movement, which aims to restore all of the gifts to the church. These apostles and prophets teach that the historical church became ineffective; therefore, their movement represents the new reformation for the church worldwide.[34] Church observers are waiting to see the result of this new movement's proposal.

New Emphasis on Mission

Some scholars have thought of Pentecostalism as a by-product of the North American evangelical movements that grew and acquired

---

[32] This would be the case of countries like Cuba, and more recently, Venezuela, Bolivia and Ecuador. This is not to be taken as a judgment for or against these particular governments; however, in the rhetoric at least they propose much concern about the poor and the negative effects of globalized capitalism. In recent history, the only political system that had the cause of the poor as part of its ideology was the communist system. That system is no longer in place as it was for most of the 20th century, so the poor do not have an advocate on their side. On this particular subject, see Bryant L. Myers, *The New Context of World Mission* (Monrovia, CA: MARC, 1996), pp. 94-96.

[33] Venables, *Fe y Prosperidad*, p. 56.

[34] This is the opinion of C. Peter Wagner, a widely known propulsor of this movement. For more details, see his book, C. Peter Wagner, *Churchquake!* (Pasadena, CA: Regal Books, 2000), pp. 280-86.

its own characteristics in the beginning of the 20th century.[35] According to Grant McClung, 'the real event that preceded Azusa Street by five years and actually precipitated the Pentecostal revival in Los Angeles began at the outset of the century in a students' environment in Topeka, Kansas'.[36] Since they did not have a theological framework besides the evangelical one of the time, they were prompted to adjust their experience to the common doctrines of their day.

Incidentally, recent studies reveal that most evangelicals in Latin America are now Pentecostals.[37] This may be due to the fact that Pentecostals have been the most visible evangelistic force in the area although they have been widely known for their tendency to retreat from the 'world'. However, Latin American Pentecostalism has been considered to be 'the haven of the masses'.[38] Perhaps this is mostly due to significant rates of church growth. There has been a tendency to think that Pentecostals find some kind of compensation in their new faith for their social alienation. As a result, they have been perceived to harbor a degree of indifference toward social issues and socio-political involvement.

While Pentecostalism appears evasive in regards to social issues, as in any religious movement, there are some exceptions to the general attitude of its members. In the twenty-first century, there are significant signs of change in the new generation of leaders. For instance, some have concluded that the crucial element for understanding the 'great Pentecostal reversal'[39] was the fundamentalist reaction to the 'liberal social gospel' after the 1900s.[40] Fundamentalists understood social concerns as non-related to the mission of the

---

[35] Bernard Martin, 'From Pre to Postmodernity in Latin America: The Case of Pentecostalism', in Paul Heelas (ed.), *Religion, Modernity and Postmodernity* (Oxford, UK: Blackwell, 1998), pp. 34-46. See also Pablo A. Deiros and Everett A. Wilson, 'Hispanic Pentecostalism in the Americas', in Vinson Synan (ed.) *The Century of the Holy Spirit: One Hundred Years of Pentecostal and Charismatic Renewal* (Nashville, TN: Thomas Nelson, 2001), p. 293-323.

[36] Grant L. McClung, (ed.) *Azusa Street and Beyond* (South Plainfield, NJ: Logos, 1986), p. 5.

[37] Núñez, *Crisis and Hope in Latin America*, p. 404.

[38] d'Espinay, *El Refugio de las Masas*, p. 112.

[39] See Núñez and Taylor, *Crisis and Hope in Latin America*, pp. 401-406.

[40] Marsden, *Fundamentalism and American Culture*, p. 86.

church, which was simply to share the gospel of salvation of the souls. This could be the main theological and historical explanation that most Pentecostals used to justify their lack of social concern.

It is important to notice that during the era of consolidation of the Pentecostal mission in Latin America, the struggle between liberalism and fundamentalism also took place in North America. In those days, the fundamentalists considered social gospel to be the fruit of liberal theology. It was also considered as a symbol of humanistic and anthropocentric Protestantism.

In Central America, most Pentecostal missionaries were afraid of falling into the trap of liberation theology. At that time, Pentecostals as well as evangelicals thought of liberation theology as socio-political involvement, which they did not favor, for it was not considered part of their mission.[41] Those Pentecostals who did not want to betray the gospel message preached the improvement of the individual through enhanced spirituality instead. Their hope was not in human progress but in the Lord's return.[42] They preferred not to invest time, money, and human resources in establishing large institutions.

Some historical protestant denominations that dedicated their efforts in the mission field mainly to institutional work had little success in spiritual growth, and this was a warning to the pioneers working under the leadership of North American and European Pentecostal missions.

Those devoted pioneers assumed the outlook of some missionaries in other fields: 'We are in the mission field to evangelize, not to educate'.[43] A misunderstanding of the Protestant emphasis on the New Testament teaching that humanity is not saved 'by works' was also the cause of social alienation in Latin America.

The doctrine of justification by 'faith alone' produced a profound change in many religious circles.[44] They understood that the

---

[41] See for instance Daniel Salinas, *Latin American Evangelical Theology in the 1970's: The Golden Decade* (Leiden, The Netherlands: Brill, 2009), p. 10.

[42] Salinas, *Latin American Evangelical Theology in the 1970's*, p. 47.

[43] Marsden, *Fundamentalism and American Culture*, p. 92.

[44] David Martin, *Tongues of Fire: The Explosion of Protestantism in Latin America* (Oxford, UK: Blackwell, 1990), pp. 254-55; and David Stoll, *Is Latin America Turning Protestant? The Politics of Evangelical Growth* (Berkeley, CA: University of California Press, 1990), pp. 180-217.

RCC had encouraged people to work hard for their salvation, so they had to accumulate more merits in preparation for the day-of-judgment.[45] Thus, Pentecostals taught the opposite that they were not supposed to do anything but receive the gift of God by faith alone, so good works receded from the picture. The emphasis was not on works. They just had to believe. It was not a matter of doing. This seems to be one of the reasons that Pentecostals were not concerned about social action.[46] Therefore, they were not properly made aware of the social implications of the gospel and their responsibility to transform their surrounding culture.

For most Pentecostals in Latin America, there was a 'world' beyond the walls of the church where they had to go to rescue souls for Christ. Their responsibility to society was to preach the gospel of spiritual and eternal salvation, hoping that those who responded in faith to their gospel message would become a blessing to society by telling others about the gospel of Jesus Christ. Their goal was to expand the congregation numerically, so the more converts, the greater the changes that would take place in their communities.

Incidentally, due to their significant numerical growth, Pentecostals have been instrumental in the hands of God in bringing change to the homes and personal attitudes of individuals who then eventually affect the communities where they live, dwell, and interact. All of these changes were brought about by a genuine conversion to Christ and the work of the Holy Spirit in the lives of the individuals and the community of believers. Nonetheless, in the twenty-first century, more Pentecostals have become aware of and have become intentionally involved in socio-economics and human transformation.

---

[45] These conclusions could be seen in the remarks of Edward L. Cleary, *The Catholic Church in Latin America* (New York, NY: Orbis Books, 1985), p. 24.

[46] See Mariano Arteaga Avila, *Toward a Latina American Contextual Hermeneutics: A Critical Examination of the Contextual Hermeneutics of the Fraternidad Teológica Latinoamericana* (PhD Dissertation, Westminster Theological Seminary, 1996). Also, Jean Pierre Bastian, *Historia del Protestantismo en América Latina* (México, DF: Casa Bautista de Publicaciones, 1990), pp. 13-16. Although these were evangelical accounts of recent history in Latin America, Pentecostals were inclined to observe the same position. This is also sustained by Núñez, *Crisis and Hope in Latin America*, pp. 405-406.

This new attitude began to emerge when some Pentecostal scholars introduced a new concept of mission.[47] Some leaders began to ask whether the mission of the church should prioritize good works on behalf of the needy and the poor inside or outside the congregation. However, the question still remains whether or not believers should become involved in transforming the basic structures of society, since a significant number of leaders in the Pentecostal community are not yet actively involved in social concerns.[48] They do not seem to look for the validity of social transformation as part the mission of the church even though the greatest challenge for Christians in Latin America seems to be social responsibility and political action to produce positive change.

Social Service

The changes experienced at the end of the twentieth-century and the beginning of the new millennium accelerated the awakening of social awareness among Pentecostals. Examples of emerging trends included the concern for the demographic explosion, the ecological problem, the awakening of the masses to the sub-human conditions in which they live and their cry for social justice.

Vital areas of attention are the advancement of science and technology, the rise of globalization and its different implications, the creation of the Internet and the increase of interaction between people of different geographical locations as a result of the widespread availability of numerous forms of communication.[49] Other concerns are related to the massive migration of peoples to urban centers. There is also the ever-present danger of losing one's indi-

---

[47] One of those scholars is Darío López. He has served among the poor of Lima, Perú for several years. His goal is to bring about transformation to the communities that have been deprived by poverty and social disadvantage. See López *Pentecostalimo y Transformación Social*, p. 29; also López, *Los Evangélicos y los Derechos Humanos*, pp. 65-75; and Campos, *De la Reforma Protestante a la Pentecostalidad de la Iglesia*, pp. 90-106.

[48] Enrique Dussel, *The Church in Latin America, 1492–1992* (Tunbridge Wells: Burns and Oates, 1992), p. 65.

[49] A broader discussion over the new paradigms facing church mission today can be found at Christopher J. H. Wright, *The Mission of God* (Urbana, IN: Intervarsity Press, 2006), pp. 78-86.

vidual freedom in a society that is becoming controlled by a new class of technocrats and the new wave of socialism emerging in several countries of Latin America.[50]

On the ecclesiastical scene, social conscience is being accelerated by the influence of such ecumenical organizations as the World Council of Churches.[51] There is also a new generation of Pentecostal leaders and scholars who are committed to the task of doing theology on the basis of Scripture in response to the social, economic and political challenges of the twenty-first century.[52]

Recent Contribution to Social Action

The social, economic, political and spiritual needs of most Latin American communities have increased in recent years. These conditions have worsened drastically as the population increases with more people living in poor conditions. There are, of course, many other factors that have had a significant impact on the context of many countries. This study, however, focuses on the current situation, especially in the light of recent developments in social, economic, and political spheres. Nonetheless, historical development and cultural traits are elements that contribute heavily to the disposition of people to advance socially, economically and politically.[53] To these, one must add physical factors of climate and natural disasters, which have a great influence over the way some people relate to one another over periods of time.[54]

---

[50] Wright, *The Mission of God*, p. 86.

[51] Current information on the Development of social responsibility in Latin America can be found in an article written by Cecilia Castillo-Nanjari, 'Pastoral de la Mujer y Justicia de Género', *Consejo Latinoamericano de Iglesias* (2009). http://www.claiweb.org/mujeres/mujeres_genero/mujeres_1.htm. Accessed 12 March 2009.

[52] Campos, *De la Reforma Protestante a la Pentecostalidad de la Iglesia*, p. 96.

[53] Peter. L. Berger, *The Desecularization of the World: Resurgent Religion and World Politics* (Grand Rapids, MI: Eerdmans, 1999), pp. 120-25.

[54] In 1998, Honduras was literally devastated by Hurricane Mitch. The impact of such catastrophe was not fully evaluated, but 90% of the public infrastructure was severely damaged or destroyed by the storm. Due to its geographical location every year the country faces these kinds of weather attacks.

Pentecostals in Social Action

The recent growth of Pentecostalism provides a broad base with which to work and a plurality of expressions and practices open to academic investigation. However, a definition of Pentecostal mission is foundational in order to understand Christian service and the particular role that the church must play within that mission.[55] Pentecostal evangelism has given priority to witnessing and church planting, while Christian education and social concern have by and large only been addressed when the church sees the need for special intervention.

Pentecostals have not shown intentionality in this particular area of Christian service.[56] Their theology seems to emphasize the immediate and personal aspects of personal salvation and the life hereafter.[57] However, some Latin American voices have boldly confronted the lack of involvement in social concerns. They are calling for the church to advocate on behalf of the poor and to stand for justice.[58] This has resulted in a new awareness and a spur to action in several sectors of the movement.[59]

---

[55] Mario E. Fumero, *La Iglesia: Enfrentando el Nuevo Milenio* (Miami, FL: Spanish House, 2004), pp. 16-21.

[56] See Gabriel O. Vaccaro, *Indentidad Pentecostal* (Quito, Ecuador, CLAI, 1990), p. 106. Also from an evangelical angle, see Orlando Costas, *Missional Incarnation. Christ Outside the Gate: Mission Beyond Christendom* (Maryknoll, NY: Orbis Books, 1982), pp. 47-48; and Costas, 'Dimensiones del Crecimiento Integral de la Iglesia', *Misión* 21.8 (1982), pp. 14-17.

[57] Modern Pentecostalism gave prominent emphasis to biblical eschatology. Gerald Sheppard made this point in his observation: 'Pentecostals commonly thought of the 20th century outpouring of the Spirit as evidence of the latter rain or at least as a sign of a last days' restoration of the apostolic church prior to the return of Christ'. He also observed that 'the influence of Dispensationalism caused Pentecostals to focus on preparing the church for the imminent return of Christ, thus neglecting the social and economic and political situation of their society'. See Gerald T. Sheppard, 'Pentecostals and the Hermeneutics of Dispensationalism', *Pneuma: The Journal of the Society for Pentecostal Studies* 3.1 (1984), pp. 5-31.

[58] Recent Pentecostal scholarship has addressed these issues of poverty, peace, and justice with a missional perspective. See for instance Benjamín F. Gutiérrez, *En la Fuerza del Espíritu; Los Pentecostales de América Latina: Un Desafío de las Iglesias Históricas* (Ciudad Guatemala, Guatemala: CELEP, 1995), pp. 22-38; also L. Gill, 'Like a Veil to Cover Them: Women and the Pentecostal Movement in La Paz', *American Ethnologist* 17.4 (1990), 708-21; and Maria das Dores Campos Machado,

Part of the failure to accept social responsibility could be attributed to the fundamentalist milieu of the early pioneers of the movement.[60] However, many of the North American missionaries who followed the first pioneers seemed to be even more negligent in their social concern than those who initiated the movement in Latin America.

The ferment and division caused by the fundamentalist controversy in North America helped create the dichotomy between evangelism and social transformation in the early part of the twentieth century[61] that continues to have a great influence on most Pentecostals in Latin America.[62] Historically, this has been considered a significant challenge that Pentecostals will have to overcome. Nevertheless, Pentecostals have made progress toward a more integrated understanding of their responsibility to the social, economic, and political needs of the world.

Community Development

At this point we examine some of the current trends of Pentecostal churches on social service and community development. One example is *Brigadas de Amor Cristiano* (Brigades of Christian Love) where the *Victoria Project* was founded.[63] The *Victoria Project* is a ministry that has served as a model in Honduras to rehabilitate alcoholics and drug addicts. Through the efforts of *Brigadas de Amor Cris-*

Carismáticos e Pentecostais: Adesão Religiosa na Esfera Familiar (São Paulo, Brasil: Editora Autores Asociados, 1996), pp. 68-82.

[59] One example the creation of Pentecostals and Charismatics for Peace and Justice, an organization committed to reflection and social action. See, PCPJ, 'Charismatics peacemakers and peacemaking', *Pentecostals for Peace and Justice* (2009). http://www.pcpj.org/index.php/resources-topmenu-45/86-charismatic-peacemaking-and-peacemakers. Accessed 10 November 2009.

[60] McClung, *Azusa Street and Beyond*, pp. 8-9.

[61] Donald W. Dayton, *Discovering an Evangelical Heritage* (New York: Harper and Row, 1976), pp. 121-41.

[62] In Brazil, for instance, Cecilia Mariz, reports of the difficulties found by the Agencies of relief and development with the theology and practice of ministry among Pentecostals. Intentionality is yet to be found among Pentecostal denominations with regards to assisting the poor strategically. See Cecilia L. Mariz, *Coping with Poverty: Pentecostals and Christian Base Communities in Brazil* (Philadelphia, PA: Temple University Press, 1994), pp. 12-31.

[63] The Victoria Project (Proyecto Victoria) was established in 1976 by Cuban missionary, Mario Fumero. It aimed to rehabilitate alcoholics and drug addicts.

tiano, a rehabilitation center has been established, and many lives have been transformed and restored to their communities. *Victoria Project* has developed from a once isolated social project into a model program, impacting people's lives in different parts of the country. Every year, more churches join this effort and positive results are being obtained.[64]

With this kind project among others, Pentecostals began to show intentionality in their approach to community service and solidarity with the needy. Previously remote and inaccessible, the *Victoria Project* was opened nationwide to serve many people in need of assistance. As a result of this, a positive awareness of the project increased. In recent years, there has been more participation of church members in the area of social justice and political violence.

Social Injustice and Violence

The emergence of guerrilla movements in Central America during the 1970s and 1980s forced the church to re-think its position regarding the new social and political circumstances. During those years, guerrilla movements renewed their long-standing fight against the military-oriented governments while voices of protest were raised from the religious sector as well.[65] As politics became increasingly polarized, Pentecostals were forced to re-define their relationship to both the government and the dissenting groups.[66]

In Latin America, most Pentecostals are respectful and supportive of governmental authority. However, such ready docility has sometimes placed them on the side of oppressive and unjust forces. At other times, according to André Corten, the church has attempted to be supportive of the government in a general way without

---

[64] Proyecto Victoria has rehabilitated alcoholics and drug-addicts in Honduras since the 1970s. Victoria was among the first rehabilitation centers established in Honduras. Now there are several others serving the needs of the country. Some are run and operated by leaders and members of Pentecostal congregations.

[65] Carmelo Álvarez, *People of Hope: The Protestant Movement in Central America* (New York, NY: Friendship Press, 1990), p. 65; and Gordon J. Spykman, *et al.*, *Let My People Live: Faith and Struggle in Central America* (Grand Rapids, MI: William Eerdmans, 1988), pp. 70-75.

[66] Edward T. Brett and Donna W. Brett, 'Facing the Challenge: The Catholic Church and Social Change in Honduras', in Ralph Lee Woodward, (ed.), *Central America: Historical Perspectives on the Contemporary Crises* (New York, NY: Greenwood, 1988), pp. 41-54.

endorsing the terrorist and inhuman tactics employed by the armed forces.[67] However, there was a time when questions about the validity of the government were asked by some sectors of the church mainly among the younger members who were either high school or university students and by some of the local organizations in the countryside. Some of these people had already given tactical support to the protest movements in areas of conflict in the country, and some decided to join the ranks of those actually fighting to overthrow the corrupted government.[68] Nevertheless, entire congregations disappeared, and some pastors were even killed under army repression in most Central American countries.[69] Others were forcefully expelled from their homes.[70] The guerrillas, of course, played the role of the liberators and were careful to present themselves in heroic light usually avoiding any direct or violent confrontation with the humble peasants and the poor.

Another case was reported in Honduras. Carlos Reyes was a member of an independent Pentecostal church in Lepaguare, Olancho. He worked for Caritas de Honduras, a relief and development agency. On July 18, 2003, Reyes was assassinated because he was a leading member of a campaign to protest against the deforestation of the Olancho region by national and international logging companies.[71] That made him a target for assassination by groups believed-to-be allied to the logging companies in the area.

---

[67] André Corten and Ruth Marshall-Fratini, *Between Babel and Pentecost: Transnational Pentecostalism in Africa and Latin America* (Bloomington, IN: Indiana University Press, 2001), pp. 112-18.

[68] Coten, *Between Babel and Pentecost*, pp. 112-18.

[69] One example is the account of Pastors and churches disappeared in Guatemala during the 1970s and 1980s by Virginia Garrard-Burnett, *Protestantism in Guatemala: Living in the New Jerusalem* (Austin, TX: University of Texas Press, 1998), pp. 15-16.

[70] Although Honduras approached the guerrilla war in Central America with a different attitude from that of El Salvador, Guatemala, or Nicaragua, still Christians split between right and left, politically. However, one could find Pentecostals in all groups in conflict. This happened because Pentecostals had already permeated most social groups. This matter is discussed by Mandy Macdonald and Mike Gatehouse, *In the Mountains of Morazán: Portrait of a Returned Refugee to His Community* (London: Monthly Review, 1995), pp. 12-21.

[71] Caritas, 'Honduras: Anti-Logging Campaigner Murdered', *Independent Catholic News* (July 2003), pp. 2-3.

The 21-year-old Carlos Reyes and other church activists had been on a hit list for many months. Reyes had been forced to flee his house as a result of intimidation and threats. His death came after the march for the Defense of Life[72] in June 2003 where 30,000 people walked 200 km to the capital, Tegucigalpa, to protest against excessive logging.[73] Other protesters said the government also needed to address the environmental problems. Reyes lost his life fighting to change the unjust logging policies of his province.

Historically, the unwritten political stance of Pentecostals is that its members should stay out of politics and concentrate on the preaching of the gospel. However, this has begun to change, and the Pentecostal church has accepted the fact that its members are free to participate in the political processes of the country, including that of belonging to a certain party or holding a given political ideology when it does not usurp one's loyalty to the church and the gospel.[74]

In their approach to social struggles, Pentecostals tend to be non-violent and observe a peaceful stance against participation in civil strife echoing the earlier Pentecostal counter-cultural and pacifist traditions.[75] In the twenty-first century, new voices are being heard in the Pentecostal world, and their voices call for the integration of spirituality, evangelism, education, and social transfor-

---

[72] The march for the defense of life was held on June 12, 2003, at the initiative of Catholic organizations for the protection of the environment in Honduras.

[73] National and international timber companies log at least 150,000 hectares of forest a year for export to North America and Europe. At least two thirds of the original forest in Olancho has been lost over the last decade with as many as 10,000 loggers currently working in the area. Caritas Honduras says the environmental damage caused by the logging has been massive, especially to local farmers. There has been a 60 percent loss in the water supply and the soil has been badly damaged. Over half of the population has migrated out of the area. See Caritas, 'Honduras: Anti-Logging Campaigner Murdered', pp. 2-3.

[74] Honduran scholar, Raúl Zaldívar, has written about the political participation of Evangelicals in the country. The study also includes Pentecostals. See Raúl Zaldívar, 'Relación Estado-Iglesia y su Apertura al Protestantismo en Honduras', *Vida y Pensamiento* 25.2 (1996), pp. 90-114.

[75] Jay Beaman, *Pentecostal Pacifism: The Origins, Development and Rejection of Pacific Belief Among the Pentecostals* (Hillsboro, KS: Center for Mennonite Brethren Studies, 1989), p. 87.

mation.[76] The future may well see a more holistic emphasis given to the life and mission of the church.

---

[76] On the need for integration of spirituality, evangelism, education, and social transformation, see Miguel Álvarez, 'The South and the Latin American Paradigm of the Pentecostal Movement', *Asian Journal of Pentecostal Theology* 5.1 (2002), pp. 135-53.

3

NEW APPROACH TO SOCIAL CONCERN

Pentecostalism has been studied from different angles and in different contexts. Therefore, in order to study the mission of Christ incarnated in the context of poverty, we will confront issues of poverty versus riches against the background of the Scriptures as it deals with the reality of human life.[1]

This section ends with a theological approach to the redemptive action of God in favor of the poor and marginalized. It sets the foundation for understanding theology of mission as practiced by the Pentecostal community which in this case makes reference to the general context of Pentecostal mission.[2]

---

[1] Ample information on this subject was documented on occasion of the VIII Encounter of the Study Commission of the History of the Church in Latin America in Lima, Peru. Several scholars presided by Enrique Dussel provided a broad approach to mission among the poor in the region. See Enrique D. Dussel, 'Resistencia y Esperanza: Historia del Pueblo Cristiano en América Latina y el Caribe', in Pablo Richard (ed.), *Materiales para Una Historia de la Teología en América Latina* (San José, Costa Rica: Dei-Cehila, 1981), pp. 641-50.

[2] The most recent scholar who began to organize the history of mission in the context of Honduras was Medardo Mejía, *Historia de Honduras* (Tegucigalpa, Honduras: Editorial Universitaria, 1983). His work sets anthropological, cultural, and religious bases to understand the history of Honduras since the days of the Colonia Española. This Roman Catholic scholar argues that Christianity could be examined from a non-religious point of view.

New Perspectives of Mission

Es que lo llevamos en la sangre (It is that which we carry in our blood). This seems to be a negative attitude used by Latin Americans to justify misfortunes and tragedies that happen to them. Thus, understanding the people of this region requires knowledge of this cultural epithet and other traditions that have long stood with the culture. Transforming the negative into a positive mentality requires an injection of hope.[3] God's people, with the transformational message of the gospel, are now bringing such hope.

In the particular context of Central America, the area suffers different degrees of chronic features of underdevelopment that manifest through endemic political corruption and unbearable administrative bureaucracies.[4] Admittedly there are different terms which can be used to classify the Latin American countries according to their national wealth. Whether it is Honduras at the bottom or Chile at the top, they all are part of a continent that struggles to reach higher levels of progress. Nevertheless, the entire region is rich with natural resources.

Moreover, Christianity has been present in the region for more than five centuries. What makes this background so difficult? In this section we take a look at the history of the region through the insightful lenses of anthropological, sociological, cultural, and spiritual factors.

In Honduras, for example, recent years have witnessed severe conditions of political corruption aligned with natural disasters that have forced people to create their own survival devises. For example, youth turned to gangs at the arrival of the twenty-first century.[5]

---

[3] Núñez and Taylor, *Crisis and Hope in Latin America*, pp. 102-103. The authors discussed the theme of racial inheritance and its influence over mentality and traditional thinking among Latin Americans.

[4] Sebastian Edwards, *Crisis and Reform in Latin America. From Despair to Hope* (Oxford, UK: Oxford University Press, 1995), p. 29. The author discusses how external economic pressures and domestic policies have affected political behavior of Latin Americans in recent years.

[5] Jon Wolseth, *Jesus and the Gang: Youth Violence and Christianity in Urban Honduras* (Phoenix, AZ: The University of Arizona Press, 2011), pp. 68-71. Wolseth takes individual case studies in Honduras to discover the motivation behind gang members in the inner city.

Months later the drug-lords bought the gangs. The gang-drug[6] combination made Honduras one the most violent countries of the world.[7] Current reports show, as of now, that the drug industry has permeated elite government and military officials. Consequently, this evil has reached some of the most significant leaders and influential people of the country.[8]

Mission in the Margins

History shows that conditions in Honduras have alarmingly increased the number of people living in poverty. Corrupt political leaders have perpetuated and nurtured this social problem.[9] The Honduran economy shows severe imbalances in the distribution of wealth. The rich are becoming richer, and the poor are getting poorer. In the legal system, officials continue to struggle in the application and realization of justice. As a result, the number of poor and marginalized continues to increase. The failure of the judicial system creates unbearable conditions for the promotion of humanity.[10] The first decade of the twenty-first century saw Honduras emerge as one of the poorest and most violent countries of the world.

---

[6] Margot Webb, *Drugs and Gangs* (New York, NY: The Rosen Publishing Group, 1998), pp. 39-49. The author discusses the relationship between drugs and gangs. It also explains how this relationship has generated a powerful illegal industry worldwide.

[7] Rita James Simon, *A Comparative Perspective on Major Social Problems* (Oxford, UK: Lexington Books, 2001), p. 36. She found updated information with reference to violence in Central America. Unfortunately, at that time Honduras was one of the deadliest countries of the world.

[8] Thomas P. Anderson, *Politics in Central America: Guatemala, El Salvador, Honduras and Nicaragua* (Westport, CT: Greenwood Publishing Group, 2003), pp. 13-15.

[9] On the matter of political corruption in Honduras, see the article of Michael Radu, 'The Other Side of Democratic Transition', *Democracy at Large* 2.3 (2006), pp. 28-30.

[10] For extensive information on work among the poor and marginalized in Honduras, see Vilma Elisa Fuentes, 'Reconstruction: An Opportunity for Political Change', in Marisa O. Ensor (ed.), *The Legacy of Hurricane Mitch: Lessons from Post-Disaster Reconstruction in Honduras* (Phoenix, AZ: The University of Arizona Press, 2009), pp. 100-28.

In search for better conditions of life, a significant number of young people migrated to the United States. Recent migration data reports that most rural communities of Honduras were left with grandparents taking care of grandchildren. As a natural consequence of migration, marriages are destroyed, families split, and children grow up without parents. The new generation is growing at an unnerving rate without parental figures and moving forward into an uncertain future.

As a result of severe measures taken by new immigration laws in the United States, thousands of undocumented immigrants have been deported to their homelands.[11] Upon returning to their country, migrants are faced with a new decision. They either return to the United States, or they join a gang. Gangs are already associated with the drug-trafficking industry in the country. Tragically, the government agencies that assist the deportees have nothing to offer to them in the re-entry process.[12] The government does not have the political strength, financial capability, or honorable stance to overcome this need.

Under the present conditions, Honduras seems to be very vulnerable and with little hope for the future. Foreign assistance and financial aid are needed. However, people will have to be re-educated through a new system of values that will save the country from self-destruction. Therefore, it is under these circumstances that Pentecostals are expected to play a major role in the solution to the problems of society.

Pentecostals on the Scene

Pentecostalism in Honduras has grown significantly in recent years. This growth can be observed mainly thorough high numbers in church attendance which is currently seen in a significant number

---

[11] Vladimir López Recinos, 'Desarrollo Migración y Seguridad: El caso de la Migración Hondureña Hacia los Estados Unidos', *Migración y Desarrollo* 11.21 (2013), pp. 65-105.

[12] Daniel Álvarez, 'No More Violence: Renewal Theology Reflections on Violence in the Context of Honduras and Its Immigrants to the United States', in Sammy Alfaro and Néstor Medina (eds.), *Pentecostals and Charismatics in Latin America and Latino Communities* (New York, NY: Palgrave Macmillan, 2015), pp. 81-95.

of recently established congregations. In addition, these new churches and ministries have impacted local communities in a number of fields that benefit humanity.

Why is this happening? There may be many reasons that explain it, but I focus this discussion on the Pentecostal service to the community.[13] Much has been said about the response of Pentecostalism towards disaster, poverty, and social unrest in the country. Historically, Hondurans have responded positively to the Pentecostal message of hope in times of crisis.[14] However, such a message has had a positive impact due to the significant service provided by Pentecostals in the communities. Pentecostal believers are committed to a devoted life that serves the community in obedience to the Great Commission.[15]

Pentecostals have learned to depend on prayer and fasting for most of their actions.[16] They believe these disciplines are necessary in order to sharpen their focus on ministry. At the local congregations they are taught that holiness is the standard of life for God's people. They also realize how important it is to experience sanctification and the baptism of the Holy Spirit. Such experience enables them to serve effectively and prepares them well to serve people in their communities.

Pentecostals believe that if every believer uses his or her priestly call from God, then each one is capable of serving people effectively. This notion leads them into a prayerful life as the main source of spiritual enrichment. This discipline is highly esteemed and remains active at all levels of Christian service.[17] Pastors and local church leaders emphasize the importance of prayer and fasting. The pur-

---

[13] See for instance Daniel Chiquete, *Haciendo Camino al Andar. Siete Ensayos de Teología Pentecostal* (San José, Costa Rica: DEI 2007), p. 32. The author offers fresh ideas over the approach of Pentecostals to service to the community. See also Cox, *Fire from Heaven*, p. 82.

[14] Andrés Tapia, 'Growing Pains', *Christianity Today* 40.2 (February 1995), pp. 38-41.

[15] The Great Commission as mandated by the Lord Jesus Christ in the gospel of Matthew (28.19).

[16] See my article, Álvarez, 'The South and the Latin American Paradigm', pp. 135-53.

[17] López, *Pentecostalimo y Transformación Social*, p. 29; also López, *Los Evangélicos y los Derechos Humanos*, pp. 65-75. López is one of the first scholars to address the issue of transformation from the margins of society.

pose is to strengthen believers in their personal spirituality and to enable them to serve people effectively.

Recognition of the Community at Large

As we have seen, Pentecostals teach that personal conversion, commitment to Christ, sanctification, and the baptism of the Holy Spirit enable believers to be effective in ministry. They are capable of reaching out to the needy, the poor, and the marginalized.[18] Once people respond to the preaching of the gospel, those who accept Christ are consolidated into the congregation through a program that leads new believers into solid discipleship.

These actions create a culture of evangelism and discipleship, which is intentionally planned and executed through community service. Most believers are part of a small group where they experience most of their Christian life. As a result, local communities are transformed. Local leaders grow in faith and are now capable of influencing local authorities for the good of people. Thus, civil authorities are now paying attention to the voices of Pentecostal congregations.[19] Pentecostals are now taking part in the decisions and plans of local authorities.

Facing Destructive Forces of Evil

It is clear that this kind of spiritual influence causes positive effects in society. For instance, Honduras is facing one of the most dramatic situations in its social and spiritual realms. There are two extremes that can be clearly identified: on one side there is the transforming power of the gospel, and on the other there is the destructive source of evil that still remains strong in the country.[20] The

---

[18] A discussion of the personal transformation of Pentecostal lives in Latin America can be found at Álvarez, *La Palabra, El Espíritu y la Comunidad de Fe*, p. 56.

[19] Wilma Wells-Davies, 'La Naturaleza de la Conversión Pentecostal en la Argentina: Implicaciones Missionológicas', in Daniel Chiquete and Luis Orellana (eds.), *Voces del Pentecostalismo Latinoamericano* (Concepción, Chile: Red Latinoamericana de Estudios Pentecostales, 2009), pp. 157-78.

[20] Bühne Wolfgang, *Explosión Carismática* (Terrassa, España: Editorial CLIE, 1994), p. 141. The author does a critical analysis of the doctrines and practices of

church seems to be growing strong, and it continues to transform people's lives and communities. However, it seems that evil also continues to manifest its destructive power over those who remain apart from the gospel.

There is a spiritual conflict battling for the control of the country. Evil increases through violence, death, destruction, and immorality in economic, social, and political structures. However, the church intensifies prayer and Christian action for the sake of those who are the direct victims of such evil schemes.[21] Because of this spiritual conflict, Honduras is now going through a historical spiritual battle.[22] Pentecostals understand this well, so they are intentionally increasing and intensifying their prayer. They have no doubt that the Holy Spirit is at work in the transformation of the country.

Identifying Evil Agents in Political Structures

Political authorities that democratically enter into power are capable of manipulating the country's constitutional order once they are into position. They do this so that they can remain in control of the government without term limits. The situation becomes worse with the support of the international community.[23] The international community practices double standards toward governments and countries depending on the interests of those who control politics. Thus, corruption is found at all levels and seems to have permeated most political structures.

---

so-called 'Three Waves' of the Holy Spirit. He studied the most current trends of Charismatic and neo-Pentecostal leaders and churches.

[21] About the fervent prayers of Pentecostals in favor of peace and against the forces of evil in Honduras, see Joseph F. Manning, *Cristianismo Milenario* (México, DF: Editorial Pax México, 2001), p. 94.

[22] María Ramírez Nieves, *Ángeles en Guerra Espiritual* (Bloomington, IN: Palibrio, 2012), p. 56. The author presents evidence of spiritual warfare, such demonic deliverance, healings, and miracles that take place in the context of Pentecostal congregations of Honduras.

[23] By 'international community', Hondurans understand the associations or groups of nations that gather together for common purposes. The United Nations represents the largest body of nations worldwide. In Latin America there is the American Organization of States. Cf. the behavior of the international community as observed by Gary Goertz and Paul F. Diehl, 'International Norms and Power Politics', in Frank W. Wayman, and Paul F. Diehl (eds.), *Reconstructing Politics* (Detroit, MI: University of Michigan Press, 2001), pp. 101-22.

This phenomenon is clearly observed in several Latin American governments. Such political structures and personalities deform the culture of economics, social relationships, and people's moral behavior. This reality has given birth to new forms of evil such as drug trafficking, gangs, and diverse forms of violence. Civility has been severely affected by the negative power of corruption at all levels. Honduras is undergoing one of its darkest times in history under the attack of these evils. As previously mentioned, the country has been recently labeled as one of the most violent ones in the world. Similar situations are also taking place in other Central American nations and Mexico that are also known as drug-dealing states.

Spiritual Response of the Church

Pentecostals have understood the serious responsibility that they have assumed under the circumstances of this time. For them there is no turning back in their commitment to the truth of the gospel.[24] In the midst of corruption, poverty, and violence they are aware of their role in the redemption of their nation – the opportunity is now. Daniel Chiquete argues that Pentecostals who are aware of this situation are now mobilized to evangelize the poor, the weak, and the marginalized.[25] They focus their efforts to spread hope for new life conditions. This hope becomes the main source of strength to counterattack the destructive forces of evil. They realize victory is possible if they observe and practice their faith. They can do this by showing solidarity with those who are hurting.

Pentecostals are also practicing an intelligent reading and interpretation of the Scriptures. Such reading strengthens their commitment to the Great Commission even if this means sacrifice or suffering. Their personal relationship with the Holy Spirit keeps them focused on their mission. The Holy Spirit makes them strong in the battle against evil. In the church the altar is still occupied by the poor, the weak, the sick, and the marginalized. That is one reason why Pentecostal congregations continue to witness effectively and win people for Christ.

---

[24] Cleary, 'Latin American Pentecostalism', pp. 127-45.
[25] Chiquete, 'Haciendo Camino al Andar', p. 124.

The Challenge of Social Evils

Pentecostals have been criticized for claiming large numbers of adherents, yet the country remains one of the most violent and corrupt of the region. Such criticism does not seem to be accurate. It does not report what actually happens with the two extremes that struggle for control. Pentecostals are using every way possible to counterattack the forces of evil.[26] As stated earlier, prayer has intensified, and social work has increased dramatically and intentionally in most communities.[27] Assistance to the poor and marginalized has also been intensified. Believers are making every effort possible to advance the transformational power of the gospel in politics and socio-economic terrains.

Poverty, marginalization, and insecurity about the future lead people to a search for ultimate answers. Pentecostals come from the most marginalized segments of society. The movement was born in the midst of the poor masses. It represents the voice that articulates the revelation and hope that the Holy Spirit has given to those who had no other voice. In some circles, Pentecostalism has been referred to as a revolution of the poor.[28] For them there cannot be a dichotomizing between theory and praxis in a world of poverty and insecurity. Here theory arises from praxis to further praxis that eventually leads to change and to the building of a different society. It is the community of faith that determines the destiny and ultimate answers that edify believers. The community sends a prophetic message to the world to find answers in the incarnated Jesus.[29]

Pentecostals have made a significant impact in the process of the evangelization of Latin America. Pentecostals understand evangelization as the action of proclaiming the gospel of Jesus Christ as

---

[26] See for instance Juan Driver, *La Fe en la Periferia de la Historia* (Ciudad Guatemala, Guatemala: Semilla, 1997), pp. 76-81.

[27] Bernardo Campos, 'In the Power of the Spirit: Pentecostalism, Theology and Social Ethics', in Dennis A. Smith and Benjamin F. Gutiérrez (eds.), *In the Power of the Spirit: The Pentecostal Challenge to Historic Churches in Latin America* (Ciudad Guatemala, Guatemala: CELEP, 1996), pp. 41-50. Campos' main interest is to examine the role of Pentecostalism in the context of marginalization, which is the typical social and economic condition of Pentecostals in Latin America.

[28] See for instance R. Andrew Chestnut, *Born Again in Brazil: The Pentecostal Boom and the Pathogens of Poverty* (New Brunswick, NJ: Rutgers University Press, 1997), pp. 5-9.

[29] Driver, *La Fe en la Periferia de la Historia*, p. 78.

the fulfillment of the Great Commission. Such proclamation reaches out to every man and woman who is in need of spiritual salvation. Once the message is accepted, it adds transformation to the individual and his or her world.[30] For Pentecostals the first responsibility of a believer is to look for the salvation of others, especially those who are close such as relatives and friends. This thrust generates new conversions that continue to grow in numbers.[31]

Once a community is impacted by the gospel, in most cases transformation starts at home and at the *barrio*. Believers no longer participate in worldly activities and other scenarios of evil. These events are multiplied from one community to another. Congregations continue to grow, and spiritual revival is seen mostly through a devoted prayer life. A subsequent outpouring of the Holy Spirit takes place later with the manifestation of spiritual gifts in the life and ministry of those who believe.

Such growth also brings about social transformation. New converts leave behind old paradigms of life and now look for new options and possibilities.[32] This Pentecostal growth has reached higher levels of influence. Entire communities have changed by the influence of Pentecostal life and spirituality.[33] The results are obvious and can be seen in the family, schools, and social relationships. Once the inner circle of relationships is won for Christ, the next step is to reach out to other families and communities, so the cycle continues to multiply.[34]

---

[30] On the matter of Pentecostalism and evangelism in Latin America, see, Yara Monteiro, 'Congregación Cristiana en Brasil, de la Fundación Centenario: La Trayectoria de una Iglesia Brasileña', in Daniel Chiquete and Luis Orellana (eds), *Voces del Pentecostalismo Latinoamericano* (Concepción, Chile: RELEP, 2011), IV, pp. 77-140 (90).

[31] Rodolfo Girón, 'The Latin-American Missionary Movement: A New Paradigm in Missions', *Celebrate Messiah* (2000). http://www.ad2000.org/celebrate/giron.htm. Accessed 19 November 2010.

[32] Evidence of that kind of transformation could be found in the work of López, *Pentecostalismo y Transformación Social*, pp. 78-83. Also Luis Orellana, 'El Futuro del Pentecostalismo en América Latina', in Daniel Chiquete and Luis Orellana (eds.), *Voces del Pentecostalismo Latinoamericano* (Concepción, Chile: RELEP, 2011), IV, pp. 141-56.

[33] See Lillian Kwon, 'Pentecostal Impact Growing in Latin America', *The Christian Post* (2006). http://www.christianpost.com/article/20061109/ pentecostal-impact-growing-in-latin-america/ Accessed 14 November 2009.

[34] López, *Pentecostalismo y Transformación Social*, p. 82.

4

SPIRITUAL PATTERNS IN LATIN AMERICA

What is our understanding of Pentecostal spirituality in the Latin American context? In the case of Latin America, Pentecostal spirituality can be thought of as that experience lived by believers whose spiritual framework includes beliefs, practices, and sensibilities. The said experience puts the believer in an ongoing relationship with the Holy Spirit, making such awareness useful to the community of faith. In his work on Pentecostal spirituality, Steven Land argues that in order to understand the major qualities of Pentecostal spirituality, one has to proceed in two ways. First is the unique combination of *rituals* and *symbols* used in a Christian congregation as primary factors that affect spirituality in the local context. Steven Land explains that those factors could be observed and practiced in the community, and they symbolize a cluster of sensibilities, qualities, beliefs, and practices connected to spiritual life. Second is a general outline of descriptive symbols that Pentecostals use to explain their *experience with God.*[1]

In light of the above, the verification of those factors occurs in the lifestyle, behavior, and commitment of believers to the principles learned in a process of discipleship. In Latin America, Pentecostals also express their spirituality through the manifestations of miracles, healings, signs, wonders, and other gifts of the Spirit in actual church life.

---

[1] Steven J. Land, *Pentecostal Spirituality: A Passion for the Kingdom* (JPTSup 1; Sheffield, UK: Sheffield Academic Press, 1998), p. 72.

Latin American Pentecostals describe their spirituality using human emotions and feelings attributed to the action of the Holy Spirit in their lives, particularly during the time of praise and worship. They implement diverse forms of human activity in order to affirm their experience with the Holy Spirit.[2] At some point the levels of education of the believer could also measure the nature and quality of the emotions that are linked to spiritual activity. Moreover, the action of the Holy Spirit in the individual affects behavior, attitudes, and emotions that seem to be ways to connect humanity with divine activity. In the same line of thought, Esdras Betancourt furthers the notion that there are sociological, psychological, and spiritual benefits in the exercise of the charismata.[3] He contends that the Holy Spirit does a holistic tune up in the individual thus making every believer a solid witness of the gospel.[4] Therefore, Pentecostal spirituality is more than just a simple spiritual manifestation; it involves the whole person and affects his or her world holistically. Hence, the Holy Spirit enables believers to transform their community using every resource available to develop healthy and faithful lives committed to Christian principles. In order to describe how Pentecostal spirituality works; I suggest the following indicators that could be considered as the most visible spiritual trends observed in Pentecostal churches in Latin America.

Historical Background

The Roman Catholic Church (RCC) arrived in Latin America in 1492 with the first colonizers. It was the kind of Catholicism that had not been affected by the Reformation yet. Henceforth, for more than 500 years after that arrival, the RCC became the main religious tradition that shaped the culture, society, economics, politics, and spiritual life of Latin America. This is the historical heritage of a society that now models family principles and values, cul-

---

[2] Chiquete, *Haciendo Camino al Andar,* p. 125. The author writes from his Mexican context and offers fresh ideas over the approach of Pentecostals to worship and the practice of the spiritual gifts in the Community.

[3] Esdras Betancourt, 'Los Beneficios del Bautismo con el Espíritu Santo', *El Evangelio* (April 1976), pp. 8-9.

[4] Betancourt, 'Los Beneficios psicológicos del Bautismo con el Espíritu Santo', p. 8.

tural traditions, and the religious behavior of an entire continent. It is clear that most Latin American Pentecostals have their theological and spiritual background founded after RCC religious model. Most Pentecostals in Latin America are former Catholics who were born and raised as Catholics. Their culture, education, and spirituality were shaped after the teachings of Catholicism. Based upon this fact, it is fair to affirm that most Latin American Pentecostals are Catholics who have converted to Pentecostalism.

The Catholic Church was instrumental in bringing Christianity for the first time to Latin America, although there are clear evidences that the Church was used by the conquerors to exercise power and control over the natives.[5] For some this was an unfortunate event that affected negatively the work and ministry of the Church. However, at that point in history the Catholic Church was the only source of evangelization for Latin America.[6] As we have seen earlier, the first protestant missionaries did not arrive until the 19th century. In fairness to the Catholic Church, it is important to acknowledge the fact that for about three hundred years this was the only Christian movement known in Latin America.

It was not until the 19th century that the Catholic Church had the first encounters with the protestant movements, thus generating a new approach to evangelization, which brought drastic changes to the mission in ministry practices of the Catholic Church during the colonial times.[7] It is generally accepted that most protestant movements were inspired by the new winds of freedom proposed by the French and the American revolutions.[8] There were liberal ideals that furthered science, philosophy, as well as human growth and transformation in the new societies. Unfortunately, the struggle between conservatives, who wanted to preserve the status quo, and the liber-

---

[5] Magnus Mörner, 'Economic Factors and Stratification in Colonial Spanish America with Special Regard to Elites', *The Hispanic American Historical Review* 63.2 (May 1983), pp. 335-69.

[6] See Ondina E. González and Justo L. González, *Christianity in Latin America: A History* (New York, NY: Cambridge University Press, 2008), pp. 41-57.

[7] Hans-Jürgen, *Christianity in Latin America*, pp. 374-87.

[8] Paul A. Gilge and Howard B. Rock, *Keepers of the Revolution: New Yorkers at Work in the Early Revolution* (Ithaca, NY: Cornell University Press, 1992), pp. 70-72.

als, who proposed a new model of society, continues even to this day.

Traditional Catholic Stand

As we have seen, the Catholic Church brought a Christianity of the Middle Ages that had not been confronted by the Reformation movement yet. This observation is particularly important because of the religious practices that took place during the time of the colonies.[9] The conquerors practiced domination over the natives after the conquests that took place during the Medieval times. The natives were enslaved in their own land, and the conquerors took possession of everything that belongs to them.[10] They used inhuman methods of domination and control so severely that soon the friars intervened on behalf of the natives.

Some Dominican friars, such as Antonio Montesinos, Pedro de Cordova, and Bartolome de las Casas took a stand against slavery and oppression.[11] They advocated for the rights and dignity of the natives. Those friars were concerned for the well-being of the local people.[12] Therefore, for the purpose of this paper, these actions should be regarded as acts of divine grace on behalf of the people of Latin America.

Pentecostalism has about a century of history in the continent. In general, the first Pentecostals of Latin America have their origin in two streams that are largely accepted by most Pentecostal historians. The first was brought by Pentecostal missionaries from North America. They came with a strong evangelical background. A second stream of Pentecostalism was initiated among local free evangelical congregations. One example is the 1909 Pentecostal movement that began in Chile when Methodist believers received the

---

[9] See Patrick W. Carey, *Catholics in America: A History* (Westport, CT: Praeger, 2004), pp. 1-6.

[10] Mackay, *The Other Spanish Christ*, pp. 42-44.

[11] Mauricio Beuchot, 'Bartolomé de Las Casas, el Humanismo Indígena y los Derechos Humanos', *Anuario Mexicano de la Historia del Derecho* 6.1 (1994), pp. 37-39.

[12] Lewis Hanke, 'Free Speech in Sixteenth-Century Spanish America', *The Hispanic American Historical Review* 26.2 (1946), pp. 135-49.

baptism of the Holy Spirit.[13] Another movement took place later in Brazil in 1914, when a group of evangelical believers had their own Pentecostal experience.[14] Those free Pentecostal movements took place after the teachings and practices of holiness by some Methodist congregations that settled in Latin America before the Pentecostal awakening took place in the region. In either case, nevertheless, all of those Pentecostal movements were established and grew strong among Catholic societies and cultures. My contention here is that Pentecostal churches are significantly influenced by Catholic spirituality in their experience of worship, liturgy, and community life.

Pentecostal and Catholic Mission

The dialectic relationship between the historical RCC and the newly arrived Pentecostal streams initiated a third stream of charismatic spirituality. On one hand, there was the Pentecostal faith influenced by the evangelical traditions of North America. Their missionaries planted churches among Catholic masses of poor and marginalized people. The new Pentecostals departed from their commitment to the RCC to embrace a new way of Christianity, which offered them a new and strong spiritual commitment to the gospel. They became passionate at witnessing to other Catholics who eventually joined the new Pentecostal way. As a result, those former Catholics by becoming Pentecostals generated a third stream which is typically observed in the catholic societies of Latin America.

The other was the Pentecostal outpouring that was experienced among middle class Catholics. This stream of those who remained loyal to the RCC was later known as the Catholic Charismatic Renewal movement. Those Catholics had their Pentecostal experience but decided to stay in the Catholic Church, contrary to what happened with the lower class where Catholics left their church and became denominational Pentecostals. This stream of Pentecostals

---

[13] Cf. C.E. Jones, 'Willis Collins Hoover', in Stanley M. Burgess and Gary B. McGeen (eds.), *Dictionary of Pentecostal and Charismatic Movements* (Grand Rapids, MI: Zondervan, 1988), p. 445.

[14] Laura Premack, 'The Holy Rollers are Invading Our Territory: Southern Baptist Missionaries and the Early Years of Pentecostalism in Brazil, 1910–1935' (Master of Arts Thesis, University of North Carolina, 2007).

joined either the historical Pentecostal denominations of the 20th Century or the free Pentecostal organizations available in their communities.

There was another Pentecostal stream initiated among historical and evangelical churches. They also decided to remain loyal to their denominations and called themselves Charismatics. In Latin America, there are two streams of Charismatics: one that is Catholic and another one that was established among the historical and evangelical churches. They have used the name Charismatic in order to separate themselves from the Pentecostal denominations.

The clash between Pentecostals and the historical RCC also initiated new and creative ways of Pentecostal and charismatic expressions. At some point, Latin America has become a melting pot where all of these traditions mingle. In the course of history, Catholics as well as historical and evangelical traditions have been Pentecostalized, and Pentecostals have also been Catholicized. This mingling of Christian streams has generated a new spirituality, which reflects parts of each discipline xin the practice of ministry and the implementation liturgy.[15]

Latin American Pentecostalism is different from North American Classic Pentecostalism. The two regions show different historical backgrounds that cannot be ignored. In North America many Pentecostals come mostly from evangelical traditions, whereas in Latin America Pentecostals carry a strong RCC background.

---

[15] Although from another geographical area, one example of this phenomenon is the El Shaddai movement in the Philippines. Pastor Mike Velarde is a Catholic Pastor (not a priest) who ministers with Pentecostal and charismatic style. Catholics are not suspicious of his affiliation, for his association is with the Catholic Church, yet they receive the benefits of a Pentecostal and Charismatic practice of ministry. This phenomenon is particularly useful in a RCC society like the Philippines. El Shaddai has grown extensively, especially among the Filipino people who refuse to leave their Catholic tradition. See for instance Michael Bailey and Guy Redden, *Mediating Faiths: Religion and Socio-cultural Change in the Twenty-first Century* (Farnham, UK: Ashgate Publishing Limited, 2011) p. 228. Also Katharine L. Wiegele, *Investing in Miracles: El Shaddai and the Transformation of Popular Catholicism in the Philippines* (Honolulu, HI: University of Hawaii Press, 2005), p. 3; also Peter Hocken, *The Challenges of the Pentecostal, Charismatic, and Messianic Jewish Movements* (Farnham, UK: Ashgate Publishing Limited, 2009), p. 3.

The Stand of Liberation Theology

Through liberation theology in the 1970s some Catholic priests took a stand against poverty and oppression in the region.[16] This seed of liberation may have been planted as early as the 16th century by Dominican friars, such as Montesinos, Cordova, and de las Casas, who protected the natives from the atrocities of the conquerors in the Caribbean, Mexico and Central America.

More than a spiritual movement, liberation theology was a social and political movement that was born from the commitment of catholic priests and lay leaders who took a prophetic stand against social and political injustice across the continent. From the pulpit of their parishes, they were able to raise consciousness against financial exploitation, human oppression, social injustice, and political domination.[17] Gustavo Gutierrez continues to insist that the poor are human beings with a dignity that must be recognized. In a recent interview he said:

> We referred to the poor as non-persons, but not in a philosophical sense, because it is obvious that each human being is a person, rather in a sociological sense; the poor, that is, are not accepted as persons in our society. They are invisible and have no rights, their dignity is not recognized.[18]

The North American Stream

North American Classic Pentecostals seem to be continually challenged by numerous social issues plaguing their society. Yet the insufficient solutions they often posit are based on less than adequate understandings of the complexity of the spiritual issues that affect their current cultural context. Their responses often degenerate into one of two inappropriate approaches.

---

[16] Gustavo Gutierrez, *A Theology of Liberation* (Maryknoll, NY: Orbis Books, 1973), pp. 49-51.

[17] Jonathan Fox, Lynn Stephen, and Gaspar Rivera, 'Indigenous Rights and Self-Determination in México', *Cultural Survival Quarterly* 23.1 (1999), pp. 23-64.

[18] Gustavo Gutierrez, 'The Poor are the Starting Point of Liberation Theology', Interview with Andrea Galiarducci, *Catholic News Agency* http://www.catholic newsagency.com/news/fr-gustavo-gutierrez-the-poor-are-the-starting-point-of-liberation-theology-90963/ Accessed 29 January 2016.

The first produces literal propositions that fail to engage the contemporary context seriously. Their approach to mission seems to narrow their action to merely spiritual assistance to people. That position limits the Holy Spirit's ongoing work in equipping the church for contemporary ministry.

The second reduces the authority of Scripture to a minimal role in determining the basis for fundamental Christian actions and attitudes. Hence, brokenness, economic disparity, poverty, health care, undocumented immigration, family, and social concerns continue to challenge authentic Christian witness of the church and its leaders. Moreover, many of these leaders hold a lingering distrust for theological education, and they are unprepared for the academic challenges that an educated society requires.

This is only to mention some issues related to North American Pentecostalism, which reflect a different reality compared to Latin American Pentecostalism. However, a much deeper examination will have to be made in order to explain these affirmations.

The Spirit of a New Movement

In the case of Latin America, the growing disenchantment with the RCC and the search for other spiritual alternatives has moved Pentecostals to identify new ways to experience their spiritual life, while Catholicism is also seen as a fallen religious system. Most of them resent the fact that the Catholic Church kept them alienated for centuries from the new experience they have now discovered. To them, the Catholic Church also represents an agent of alienation, oppression, and compromise with the demonic powers of the world.[19] The Spirit of Pentecost is the 'new wine' that must be preserved in 'new wineskins' in order to keep it sound and effective.[20] Thus, for some Pentecostals in Latin America witnessing about Christ is to unveil the truth to those who have remained deceived or neglected by an obsolete religious system.[21] Conversion then occurs when the individual understands the gospel as stated in the Scriptures and revealed by the Holy Spirit. The new convert joins the

---

[19] See for instance the discussion on this matter of Catholicism as a fallen religious system in Howard, 'Great Things to Come', pp. 38-39.

[20] Cf. Mt. 9.17.

[21] Tapia, 'Why is Latin America Turning Protestant?', pp. 28-29.

Pentecostal family followed by a new paradigm of life in the Spirit experienced by believers in the community of faith.

Here it is also important to highlight the dialectical relationship that occurs between Pentecostals from the North American background and those from the RCC background. Although they may enjoy the same Pentecostal experience, their traditions push them into different wings of reality. This clash also generates a new Pentecostal way of expressing faith, theology, and spirituality. In some cases, this encounter may generate frustration, but intentional understanding may lead believers into exercising comprehension of the historical differences observed on both sides. Thus, a new Pentecostality emerges in the new community of the Spirit in Latin America.

In light of this it seems fair to conclude that there are significant differences between Latin and North American Pentecostalisms. Therefore, it is also fair to present the case for a unique Latin American Pentecostal spirituality.

Pentecostalism appeared in Latin America is a providential act of the grace of God in favor of the poor and marginalized people of Latin America. This is so because Pentecostalism became a movement of the poor. In the Pentecostal congregations the poor found hope and support, which led them to overcome not only their spiritual struggles but also their social and economic limitations. In its approach to the poor and marginalized the Pentecostal message found fertile ground in the region. At some point Pentecostals were able to capitalize on what was earlier initiated by the evangelical movements in the area.[22] According to Calixto Salvatierra Moreno,

> The 20th Century witnessed the rise and development of Pentecostalism. This movement generated the formation of new expressions of religion across the Americas, which had sociological, anthropological and spiritual influence on contemporary societies. Pentecostalism innovated and created various ways to ex-

---

[22] Miguel Álvarez, 'Latin American Mission, Then and Now', in Miguel Álvarez (ed.), *The Reshaping of Mission in Latin America* (Oxford, UK: Regnum Books International, 2015), pp. 1-5.

press the religious beliefs that affected significantly the culture and spiritual ethos of humanity in Latin America.[23]

The Pentecostal lifestyle brought explosive numerical growth in most depressed and marginalized areas of large cities. Pentecostalism made the message of the gospel relevant to the poor, the sick, the depressed, and the weak. The message was simple yet powerful enough to convince people about the relevance of the gospel. The activity of the supernatural was observed in most congregations. At some point, Pentecostalism became instrumental in finding a solution to civil war, natural disasters, disease, and the need for spiritual deliverance.

Henceforth, Pentecostals in Latin America speak of grace as the intervention of God on behalf of the poor. In the power of the Holy Spirit the persecuted may obtain deliverance from their enemies and find a solution to any source of affliction or adversity.[24] For Pentecostals, living in the Spirit denotes spiritual enablement, daily guidance, forgiveness, and protection in the midst of trouble.

Pentecostals also emphasize the importance of simplicity. For them living in community and sharing their lives with other people is the testimony of the grace of God actively operating in the congregation.

This kind of Christianity shook the religious establishment that already existed in the area. Churches and Christian leaders had never seen this church model before. Naturally, the first reaction was to oppose it. The Pentecostal worship style made them nervous. The impartation of spiritual gifts among the congregants was completely different to the order in the church that they had experienced before. Eventually, Pentecostal worship and ministration permeated most evangelical, Protestant, and the Catholic churches. Thus, this influence could also be interpreted as an act of the grace of God to revitalize the church in Latin America. Through the imprints of

---

[23] Calixto Salvatierra Moreno, 'Catholic and Pentecostal Convergence on Practical Theology and Mission', in Miguel Álvarez (ed.), *The Reshaping of Mission in Latin America* (Oxford, UK: Regnum Books International, 2015), pp. 65-83 (65).

[24] A good book on this topic is Yong, *In the Days of Caesar*, pp. 238-51. Yong offers a thorough discussion on the role of Pentecostal empowerment in the incarnational and redemptive mission of God over civilian freedom.

Pentecostalism, churches have become more dynamic in evangelism, social action, and the development of the laity in ministry.

In the 1960s, a new wave of spiritual revival reached Latin America. Lutheran minister Harald Bredesen[25] called this new awakening a charismatic movement. The charismatic movement may also be identified as an act of grace that reached out to the Catholic middle class of Latin America that otherwise would have remained alienated from the gospel.

Charismatics rallied businessmen and professional women to meet the gospel of Jesus Christ. Incidentally, most political leaders of future generations were led to Christ through charismatic gatherings.[26] There were also young professionals affected by the charismatic message of that time.

This message also made Pentecostals nervous. The difference between these two movements was that while Pentecostals ministered to the poor, the charismatics ministered to the middle class and to the political leaders of the countries. It was not until recent years that both movements have been able to dialogue and to accept each other in the evangelization of Latin America.

It seems that during the course of time spiritual revivals tend to reach a plateau. They become comfortable, self-gratifying, and satisfied with their ministry. As a result, their passion for evangelism weakens and the thrust for expansion loses momentum.[27] That is the time when the Holy Spirit begins to work new revivals among his people. This awakening is also portrayed in this book as an act of divine grace.

The emerging Neo Pentecostal movements could also be considered as an act of grace that God is using to revitalize Christianity in the area. Evidently the Lord foresaw the difficulties of the com-

---

[25] Timothy Sims, *In Defence of the Word of Faith: An Apologetic Response to Encourage Charismatic Believers* (Bloomington, IN: AuthorHouse, 2008), pp. 10-13.

[26] Jeff Brumley, 'New Study Documents shifts in Latin American Religious Affiliation', *Baptist News Global* (Monday, January 25, 2016). https://baptistnews. com/culture/item/30862-catholic-decline-in-latin-america-a-lure-for-joyful-churc hes-baptists-say. Accessed 1 February 2016.

[27] Bernardo Campos, 'Neo-Pentecostal Paradigms in Latin American Mission: Megatrends in the Theologies of Mission and Missionary Practices among Neo-Pentecostals in Peru', in Miguel Álvarez (ed.), *The Reshaping of Mission in Latin America* (Oxford, UK: Regnum Books International, 2015), pp. 193-205.

ing days among the different societies of Latin America. The second half of the 20th century witnessed times of war, political unrest, extreme poverty, corruption, and different sources of violence. Thus, it seemed that the Holy Spirit was preparing the church to face all of these adversities with the proper attitude and the efficiency of God's people.

According to Bernardo Campos, Pentecostals and Charismatics had become comfortable and institutionalized, so a new wave of spiritual revival was ignited by the Holy Spirit in order to revitalize the church and start new movements in the area.[28] The time that was coming was critical for the church and the Lord wanted to prepare her for such a time.

In Latin America today, most Christian movements are getting involved in the promotion of human growth and transformation. This effort has not been easy due to the diversity of the body of Christ and because of the multiple efforts that are taking place.

Liberation theology, from its Catholic point of view[29] and Integral Mission, from its evangelical perspective,[30] helped Christians across Latin America to confront social evils and injustice with theological, biblical, and spiritual authority.[31] There were many mistakes and unfortunate circumstances during the process of evangelization, but Christians were able to preach the good news and to reach out to the poor.

Civil wars took place in Cuba, Central America, and South America. Many people suffered violence, expatriation, extreme poverty, and even death.[32] There were also natural disasters that hurt many Latin American nations. Some may argue that the church failed to meet these disasters properly. This could be the case of isolated situations, but in general, Christians were prepared for adversity and were able to respond according to the principles of the

---

[28] Campos, 'Neo-Pentecostal Paradigms in Latin American Mission', pp. 197-99.

[29] Juan Luis Segundo, *Liberation of Theology* (Maryknoll, NY: Orbis Books, 1976), pp. 69-75.

[30] Padilla, 'An Ecclesiology of Integral Mission', pp. 68-70.

[31] R. Andrew Chesnut, *Competitive Spirits: Latin America New Religious Economy* (Oxford, UK: Oxford University Press, 2003), pp. 132-35.

[32] Todd Hartch, *The Rebirth of Latin American Christianity* (Oxford, UK: Oxford University Press, 2014), pp. 59-62.

gospel. Therefore, the credibility of the churches drew people in need into the congregations. Typically, after a natural disaster, large crowds gathered in the churches, so these had to enlarge their facilities to all kinds of people.

Grace, Peace, and Justice

Although there are still challenging levels of injustice, Christians in Latin America are making every possible effort to influence transformation in their communities. They know that this can be possible through the implementation of the principles of the gospel.

In recent years, violence has claimed thousands of lives. Mostly young people have died or have being mistreated at the hands of the gangs and drug trafficking.[33] Insecurity causes people to migrate to safer places. Weak economies cause the search for better options at other sites of the world. Political instability forced people to flee for safety purposes. Administrative corruption has driven people against political authority. All of these social evils hurt society and raise a legitimate demand for social justice and peace that can only happen when civil authority is held accountable under civil law.

As Christianity grows in Latin America a new generation of leaders has begun to lead the church. They are aware of the challenges ahead of them. Therefore, in order to respond to the social needs of the countries, they are preparing solid discipleship programs with the principles of the gospel that are preparing the church for the future. They also know that transformation will eventually happen during the course of time. They will have to invest strategically in younger generations.[34] True peace and justice will occur under the lordship of Christ in the new societies.

---

[33] Carlos F. Cardoza-Orlandi and Justo L. Gonzalez, *To All Nations from All Nations: A History of the Christian Missionary Movement* (Nashville, TN: Abingdon Press, 2013), p. 389.

[34] Enrique Pinedo, 'Mission and the Children of Latin America: A Historical Perspective from the Latin American Congress of Evangelization – CLADE', in Miguel Álvarez (ed.), *The Reshaping of Mission in Latin America* (Oxford, UK: Regnum Books International, 2015), pp. 103-16.

Concluding Remarks

In this presentation, we have seen a historical approach to the manifestation of God's grace in Latin America. Christian leaders of this region seem to understand that there is more work to be done by the church in order to reach true transformation in society. They realize that the initiative of grace comes from God himself. He loves the Latin American people and wants all of them to experience redemption through Christ. Many people have responded to God's offer, yet the work of redemption and transformation remains unfinished.

Fortunately, the implementation of the grace of God among the Latin American people continues to expand. God's gift of grace faces opposition from the forces of evil that have been in positions of authority and in control of the economy. Nonetheless, God's people continue to take a stand against all of them in the power of the Holy Spirit, which makes that grace relevant to the communities. At this point, I think that the key to succeed in this endeavor is to endure hardship, be patient, and trust God and his grace on behalf of the people that he so loves in Latin America.

5

EXPLORING THE TEACHING OF SOCIAL ACTION

As we have seen, for the past 500 years, the RCC has been active in the culture, spiritual formation, traditions, and mindset of most Latin Americans. For a Latino, becoming an Evangelical or Pentecostal includes a process of transition from Catholicism, even if it is nominal Catholicism to another Christian stream.

A responsible researcher will have to acknowledge more than 500 years of historical influence of the RCC on most Latin Americans. Pentecostals or other evangelical groups may no longer adhere to the RCC, but in their culture, history, and mind-set they reflect a strong Catholic mentality. Thus, the study of Pentecostal missiology in Latin America will have to recognize this variable.[1] For that reason, this study evaluates the historical influence of the RCC on Pentecostal thinking about issues such as the common good, subsidiarity, solidarity, and the values of social life. Having had a RCC background in their early Christian formation, Latin American Pentecostals are able to understand and handle common ideas with RCC theologians for the solution of some of the most difficult

---

[1] On the influence of Catholic theology over some Pentecostal thinkers see José María Tojeira, *Historia de la Iglesia en Honduras* (La Ceiba, Honduras: Talleres Claret, 1987), pp. 24-32. Not that Pentecostals are preaching or teaching Catholic theology. However, it is fair to acknowledge that most Pentecostals are former Catholics. Therefore, some Catholic teaching is still reflected at least in certain attitudes, especially in ministry and the approach to the Christian disciplines, such as prayer, fasting, and so on.

socio-economic, political, and spiritual problems of the region. Consequently, the discussion of this section ties these three cords together in order to understand current mission trends among Pentecostals in Latin America.

When Catholics become Pentecostal, they still carry with them elements of their Catholic background. This is evident in their general approach to life and religion.[2] Such RCC flavor can be observed in most religious practices and congregational activities. Even when Pentecostals become critical of the RCC, this inherited background is expressed in different forms of resentment against the RCC for having kept them confined in ignorance for so long.

In order to comprehend part of the influence of Catholicism on Pentecostal thinking, I reviewed some documents, which help to clarify the issues discussed as follows.

The Common Good

Historically, RCC mission has guarded the principle that the 'common good to which every aspect of social life must be related if it is to attain its fullest meaning, stems from the dignity, unity, and equality of all people'.[3] According to Leonardo Boff, 'the common good indicates the total sum of social conditions which allow people, either as groups or as individuals, to reach their fulfillment more fully and more easily'.[4]

In recent years there was a fine line between what was theologically ideal and what was politically inclined to socialism.[5] The Catholic theology of the common good came close the point of sharing the same ideal with the philosophy of socialism, although it is fair to say that socialism comes in all sorts of different forms and

---

[2] On the influence of Catholic theology over Pentecostals in Latin America, see Oscar Corvalán, 'Pentecostalismo, Ecumenismo y Cristiandad', in Daniel Chiquete and Luis Orellana (eds.), *Voces del Pentecostalismo Latinoamericano* (Concepción, Chile: RELEP, 2011), IV, pp. 357-76 (368).

[3] Leonardo Boff, 'Comunidades Eclesiais de Base e Teologia da Libertação', *Convergência* 16.145 (1981), pp. 430-40.

[4] Van Engen, *Footprints of God: A Narrative Theology of Mission*, p. 76.

[5] Rubem Alves, *A Theology of Human Hope* (Washington, DC: Corpus Books, 1985), p. 64.

guises.[6] Catholic scholars like Leonardo Boff argued in the early 1980s:

> The common good does not consist in the simple sum of the particular goods of each subject of a social entity. Belonging to everyone and to each person, it is and remains common, because it is indivisible and because only together is it possible to attain it, increase it and safeguard its effectiveness, which is also tied to the future.[7]

Sergio Bernal also argued:

> Just as the moral actions of an individual are accomplished in doing what is good, so too the actions of a society attain their full stature when they bring about the common good.[8]

The common good, in fact, can be understood as the social and community dimension of the moral good.

Pentecostals realized that if they wanted to remain active in their service to every person, they also had to keep the common benefit of the gospel active in the community as one of the main goals for all members.[9] It is clear that the human person cannot find fulfillment in isolation from others. Cecilia Loreto Mariz also states, 'this is a truth that has to be lived in community and Pentecostals instill it in every individual not only to seek his or her own benefit but also with other members'.[10] This is also expressed in the society of Pentecostal life and ministry.

---

[6] Jon Sobrino, *Jesús en América Latina* (Santander, España: Editorial Sal Terrae, 1997), pp. 47, 82; and Juan Luis Segundo, *Masas y Minorías* (Buenos Aires, Argentina: Editorial La Aurora, 1993), p. 34.

[7] Boff, *Comunidades Eclesiais de Base e Teologia da Liberação*, p. 436 and Jon Sobrino, *No Salvation Outside the Poor: Prophetic-Utopian Essays* (Maryknoll, NY: Orbis Books, 2008), pp. 23-38. See also Jon Sobrino, *Challenge to Christian Theology* (Maryknoll, NY: Orbis Books, 2008), pp. 62-79.

[8] Sergio Bernal Restrepo, *La Iglesia del Brasil y el Compromiso Social: El Paso de la Iglesia de la Cristiandad a la Iglesia de los Pobres* (Rome: Pont University Gregoriana, 1986), pp. 33-39.

[9] See for instance, David Bueno, 'The Struggle for Social Space: How Salvadoran Pentecostals Build Communities in the Rural Sector', *Transformation* 18.3 (2001), pp. 6-14.

[10] Celia Loreto Mariz, 'Perspectivas Sociológicas Sobre el Pentecostalismo y el Neopentecostalismo', *Revista de Cultura Teológica* 3.13 (1995), pp. 7-16.

RCC theology states, 'no expression of social life can escape the issue of its own common good, in that this is a constitutive element of its significance and the authentic reason for its very existence'.[11] Except for the political implications included by the RCC scholars, this notion is very close to what Pentecostals teach about being together in one accord and serving one another.[12] As a matter of fact, this is the condition among believers that propels the outpouring of the Holy Spirit who enables believers to serve the community using the charismatic gifts in their service.

Responsibility for the Common Good

It is clear that the demands of the common good will depend on the dynamics and social conditions of a community. These conditions are connected to the levels of respect for all people and the integral promotion of humanity intentionally designed by the leaders of the community. Concerning this matter, Rubem Alves states:

> These demands concern above all the commitment to peace, the organization of the state's powers, a sound juridical system, the protection of the environment, and the provision of essential services to all, some of which are at the same time human rights: food, housing, work, education, access to culture, transportation, basic health care, the freedom of communication and expression, and the protection of religious freedom. The common good therefore involves all members of society, no one is exempt from cooperating, according to each one's possibilities, in attaining it and developing it. The common good must be served in its fullness, not according to reductionist visions that are subordinated by certain people to their own advantage; rather it is to be based on a logic that leads to the assumption of greater responsibility.[13]

---

[11] Marcelo de Carvalho Azevedo, 'Opción por los Pobres y Cultura Secular en América Latina', *Razón y Fe* 10.2 (1983), pp. 147-61.

[12] George W. Harper, 'Philippine Tongues of Fire? Latin American Pentecostalism and the Future of Filipino Christianity', *Journal of Asian Mission* 2.2 (2000), pp. 225-59. Also, Harold D. Hunter, 'Full Communion: A Pentecostal Prayer', *Ecumenical Trends* 37.1 (January 2008), pp 1-7.

[13] Alves, *A Theology of Human Hope*, p. 13.

Likewise, Pentecostals have their own theology of the common good, which corresponds to the highest redemption of the life for the common good of all members of the community.[14] Juan Sepúlveda had realized that this common good is very 'difficult to attain because it requires dedication to holiness and love to develop the constant ability and effort to seek the good of others as though it were one's own good'.[15]

Tasks of the Political Community

Both Pentecostal and catholic scholars agree that the 'responsibility for attaining the common good, besides falling to individual persons, belongs also to the state, since the common good is the reason that the political authority exists. So the state must guarantee the coherence, unity, and organization of the civil society of which it is an expression, in order that the common good may be attained with the contribution of every citizen'.[16] In this case, the individual or family group may not be able to obtain their full development by themselves. Hence, it requires community efforts to help them to be in position to live a dignified human life.

---

[14] López, *La Misión Liberadora de Jesús*, p. 78. The author makes a practical application to the needs of the community in Perú, where Pentecostals are invited to share public responsibilities for the sake of society.

[15] Although Pentecostal scholarship does not seem to interested in the teachings of the common good as stated by RCC, scholars such as Juan Sepúlveda and José María Mardones have shown interest in the theme. See for instance Juan Sepúlveda, 'Overcome the Fear of Syncretism: A Latin American Perspective', in Lynne Price, Juan Sepúlveda, and Graeme Smith (eds.), *Mission Matters* (Frankfort: Peter Lang, 1997), pp. 157-68. See also José María Mardones, *Nueva Espiritualidad: Sociedad Moderna y Cristianismo* (México, DF: Universidad Iberoamericana, 1999), pp. 16-24. A number of non-Latino scholars have also written about the matter. One of them is Lynne Price, *Theology Out of Place: A Theological Biography of Walter J. Hollenweger* (JPTSup 23; London, UK: Sheffield Academic Press, 2002). The other scholar who sees the teachings on the common good in the Pentecostal tradition is Scandinavian theologian Veli-Mati Käkkäinen. From his teaching post at Fuller Theological Seminary, he has observed Latino Pentecostalism at both the USA and Latin America. See Veli-Mati Käkkäinen, 'Culture, Contextualization and Conversion: Missiological Reflections from the Catholic-Pentecostal Dialogue (1990–1997)', *Journal of Asian Mission* 2.2 (2000), pp. 262-75.

[16] Käkkäinen, 'Culture, Contextualization and Conversion', pp. 262-75.

This need creates the necessity to develop political institutions with the purpose of providing opportunities to help a person's progress. This helps those who are limited with spiritual, material, cultural, and moral goods. Through these teachings, Pentecostals are now learning that the goal of life is to provide every individual with the opportunity to avail themselves of the good of society in a way that is deemed fair to every person. This is also God's goal for humanity, and He takes pleasure in the well-being of every individual.

Governments have the duty to design and apply specific regulations that will ensure every citizen access to the good of society. This action must harmonize with laws that implement assistance and justice for all. The proper action to reconcile the interests of individuals and particular groups is one of the most difficult and delicate tasks of the public authority. This is why some liberation theology scholars insisted,

> The state must not forget that in democracy, where decisions are usually made by the majority of representatives elected by the people, and those responsible for government are required to implement the common good of their country. Not only according to the guidelines of the majority but also according to the effective good of all the members of the community, including the minorities.[17]

Now, for Pentecostals the common good of society is not an end in itself. It has value only in reference to attaining the ultimate ends of the person and the universal common good of the whole of creation.[18] For Pentecostals, 'God is the ultimate end of his creatures. The common good may not be deprived of its transcendent dimension for any reason. It moves beyond the historical dimension

---

[17] Sobrino, *No Salvation Outside the Poor*, p. 64.

[18] López, *La Misión Liberadora de Jesús*, p. 84. See also Daniel Chiquete, 'Healing, Salvation and Mission: The Ministry of Healing in Latin American Pentecostalism', *International Review of Mission* 93.370-371 (2004), pp. 474-85. This opinion however, has been affected by the context of a dialogue between Catholic and Pentecostal scholars, which takes place at international level, but it reflects, in part, the intention of finding a common ground in the approach to the common good. See also J. Reginaldo Prandi, *A Realidade Social das Religiões no Brasil* (São Pablo, Brasil: Hucitec-Edusp, 1992).

while at the same time fulfilling it'.[19] Therefore, this teaching becomes increasingly relevant to the faith in the sacrifice of Jesus. It offers a clear understanding of the rights of every human to the common good that God made available to them.

Pentecostals also think that human history begins and ends in Jesus. Thanks to him, every reality including human society can be brought to its supreme goal—to its fulfillment by means of him and in light of him.[20] Thus, a purely historical and materialistic vision would end up transforming the common good into a simple socio-economic well-being. However, contrary to this, Pentecostals look towards the supernatural empowerment of the Holy Spirit to overcome human limitations. The same Spirit fills them with love to care for the common good of the people they serve.[21]

The Principle of Subsidiarity

Another matter of revision between Pentecostal and catholic scholars is the issue of subsidiarity. For catholic scholars, the principle of subsidiarity is one of the most constant directives of social responsibility to the community of faith. For them,

> It is impossible to promote the dignity of the person without showing concern for the family, groups, associations, and local territorial realities. To this they add social, cultural, recreational, professional, and political expressions by which effective social growth and transformation of the culture is made possible.[22]

Moreover, 'this is the realm of civil society, understood as the sum of the relationships between individuals and intermediate social groupings, which are the first relationships to arise and which

---

[19] Guillermo Cook, 'Informe: Consulta Pentecostal Sobre la Teología de la Liberación', *Pastoralia* 7.15 (1985), pp. 107-11.

[20] López, *La Misión Liberadora de Jesús*, pp. 78-86.

[21] E.g., see Land, *Pentecostal Spirituality*, pp. 92-97, who highlights the power of love, which operates through believers full of the Holy Spirit. The integration of both power and love is what makes the gospel effective.

[22] See Leonardo Boff, *Jesucristo y la Liberación del Hombre* (Madrid, España: Ediciones Cristiandad, 1995), p. 285. The author argues that regardless of the political affiliation or the religious identity, if a person looks for the good of the other, he or she is manifesting the works of the Redeemer.

come about thanks to the creative subjectivity of the citizen'.[23] Therefore, this network constitutes the basis of a true community. This level of corporate relationships strengthens social responsibilities, making it possible for individuals to recognize one another in higher standards of social work and activity.

On the basis of this principle, communities of a higher order would have the opportunity to adopt healthy attitudes to assist with respect to the lower socio-economic levels of people who are part of their societies. Concerning this Jon Sobrino argues,

> In this way, intermediate social entities can properly perform the functions that are entrusted to them. They are not required to give them up to social entities of a higher level. That way the intermediate social entities do not suffer the risk of being absorbed or substituted and in the end, being denied their dignity and essential place.[24]

Latin American Pentecostals do not have a teaching of subsidiarity as the RCC. However, in their ethics and actions on behalf of the community, they seem to practice similar principles. Hence to the interest of the well-being and progress of the community, Pentecostals add a spiritual dimension that enhances the ethics and moral values of the people. It is only when they overemphasize the spiritual dimension to the detriment of social participation that Pentecostals fail to fulfill the purpose of a holistic gospel.

Indicators of Public Participation

Pentecostals have taken a different approach to the teaching of subsidiarity compared to Catholics. They acknowledge the need to protect people from the abuse of social authority, but they are willing to communicate with those in authority to assist people. However, they do not seem to be passionate about making significant efforts to force the issue of social justice with authorities. Latin American Pentecostals longingly pray that government officials will practice fairness and equality in their endeavors. They understand that this principle is necessary because every individual, family, and

---

[23] Boff, *Jesucristo y la Liberación del Hombre*, p. 260.

[24] Sobrino, *Jesús en América Latina*, p. 82.

group has something good, original, and unique to offer for the benefit of the community. Therefore, they must be respected and appreciated for that.[25]

Pentecostals may very well realize that by neglecting the principle of subsidiarity, they limit the freedom and the genuine initiative of people. This is perhaps one of the perils Pentecostals now face. They cannot continue to grow without coming to an understanding of their social responsibilities to the community. Pentecostals tend to remain indifferent to the world and its unjust powers. However, their growth has permeated practically every group that there is in Latin American society. This pronounced visibility imposes a delicate and crucial responsibility on behalf of the people they serve. Furthermore, they seem to have taken steps to work with the civil authority, the educational system, and cultural entities.

In RCC circles, the principle of subsidiarity is opposed to certain forms of centralization, bureaucratization, welfare assistance, and the unjustified presence of the state in public mechanisms. Gerard Hughes argues 'by intervening directly and depriving society of its responsibility, the state's social assistance leads to a loss of human energies and an inordinate increase of public agencies. They are dominated more by bureaucratic ways of thinking than by concern for serving their clients, which are accompanied by an enormous increase in spending'.[26] He also adds that an insufficient recognition of private initiative and the failure to recognize its public function contribute to undermine the principle of subsidiary as monopolies do as well.[27]

For Pentecostals to practice the principle of subsidiarity they would have to assume responsibility for the need to promote social justice and respect for every family in their own right to develop spiritually and socio-economically. They have to appreciate local associations of individuals and intermediate organizations that are expressing their choices. Pentecostals are learning to encourage the

---

[25] A report on this matter appeared in Jean Pierre Bastian, *La Mutación Religiosa de América Latina: Para una Sociología del Cambio Social en la Modernidad Periférica* (México, DF: Fonda de Cultural Economical, 1997), pp. 21-33.

[26] Gerald J. Hughes, *Authority and Morals: An Essay on Christian Ethics* (Washington, DC: Georgetown University Press, 2002), p. 32.

[27] Hughes, *Authority and Morals*, p. 56.

power of private enterprise and initiative.[28] They are recognizing every entity that remains committed to serving the common good of the people. These individuals and organizations have their own distinct contributions to the common good and deserve to be respected. They are recognizing that the presence of socio-economic pluralism is necessary in society. Its vital components are indispensable to the function and stability of the community. They are also learning to safeguard human rights and the rights of minorities.

Balance is necessary in the public and private actions of civil service. These decentralized methods help citizens become more responsible and actively involved in the political and social reality of their country. These principles of subsidiarity offer vision and viable methods that generate Christian participation in social, economic, and political matters that affect the community. In any case, the common good correctly understood is to defend the promotion of humanity and the way this is understood in the community. It must preserve the objective of making social decisions connected with the principle of subsidiarity. This RCC contribution is causing Pentecostals to revisit their principles related to the promotion of the human individual and social justice.[29]

Public Service

Within the context of subsidiarity there are some significant differences between Catholics and Pentecostals. The discrepancies are

---

[28] With regards to public involvement in the political arena, Pentecostals have not done much, except for isolated efforts, which have not been documented appropriately. See Fumero, *La Iglesia Enfrentando el Nuevo Milenio*, pp. 86-89. Some Pentecostals are now interested in running for office and working on behalf of the community in the public arena. See López, *Pentecostalismo y Transformación Social*, p. 46.

[29] In reference to the promotion of humanity and the community by Pentecostals in Latin America, see Cecilia Castillo Nanjarí, 'Imágenes y Espiritualidad de las Mujeres en el Pentecostalismo Chileno', in Daniel Chiquete and Luis Orellana (eds.), *Voces del Pentecostalismo Latinoamericano* (Concepción, Chile: RELEP, 2009), III, pp. 183-98; Also see Pablo A. Deiros, *La Acción del Espíritu Santo en la Historia: Las Lluvias Tempranas* (Miami, FL: Editorial Caribe, 1998); and Juan Sepúlveda, 'Reflections on the Pentecostal Contribution to the Mission of the Church in Latin America', *Journal of Pentecostal Theology* 1.1 (1992), pp. 4-14.

mostly observed in the moment of execution. Catholics are guided by pragmatic actions while Pentecostals tend to examine the biblical and spiritual principles that determine their actions.

For RCC scholars the

> characteristic implication of subsidiarity is public participation, which is essentially expressed in a series of activities by which the citizen, either as an individual or in association with others, contributes to the cultural, economic, political, and social life of the civil community to which he belongs, either directly or through representation.[30]

For instance, Ignacio Ellacuría sees public participation as a duty 'to be consciously fulfilled by all, with responsibility and with a focus on the common good'.[31]

However, Pentecostals are now seeing that public participation is not restricted to certain individuals or community groups. The utility of information and the value of culture are significant areas of growth amongst the masses. Public officials are therefore called upon to guard the integrity and transparency of these valuable and dynamic instruments.[32] For Pentecostals, it is important to work in cooperation, whereby all people become involved in the building of a strong community that preserves and defends the principle of subsidiarity. With this principle in mind, Narciso Sepúlveda suggests that it is necessary to encourage Pentecostal public participation amongst the most marginalized and disadvantaged people.[33]

It is also important to rotate political leaders in order to preserve and forestall the establishment of unhealthy privileges. Sepúlveda also adds 'strong moral pressure is needed from Pentecostals so that

---

[30] An extensive analysis of Christian participation in the cultural, economic, political, and social life appears in José Míguez Bonino, *Toward a Christian Political Ethic* (Philadelphia, PA: Fortress Press, 1983), pp. 112-18.

[31] Ignacio Ellacuría, *Freedom Made Flesh: The Mission of Christ and His Church* (Maryknoll, NY: Orbis Books, 1996), pp. 41-42.

[32] See for instance, N. Sepúlveda, 'How the Pentecostal Mission Church of Chile had Become a Member of the WCC and What It Means to Them', in *Consultation with Pentecostals in the Americas* (San José, Costa Rica: World Council of Churches, 1996), pp. 68-70.

[33] Sepúlveda, 'How the Pentecostal Mission Church of Chile Had Become a Member of the WCC', p. 70.

the administration of public life will be the result of the shared responsibility of each individual with regards to the common good'.[34]

Participation in Democracy

For both Catholics and Pentecostals, 'citizens are called to freely and responsibly exercise their civic role with and for others in the community context. It is one of the pillars of all democratic orders and a major guarantee of the democratic system's permanence.'[35] According to Koson Srisan,

> A democratic government is primarily defined by the distribution of power in the interests of the people. This power is exercised in their regard and on their behalf. Therefore, it is clearly evident that every democracy must be participative.[36]

Ideally, this 'means that the different subjects of civil community at every level must be informed, heard, and involved in the exercise of different functions'.[37] However, this is still a struggle for Latin American Christians.

Some Catholics find it appropriate to take action on behalf of freedom, whereby they could go on the streets to combat sinful structures responsible for poverty and social evils.[38] Some Pentecostals think it is better to pray about the circumstances and to look for the guidance of the Holy Spirit, in order to determine whether or not it is right to participate in the democratic processes of their countries.[39]

The next discussion on this matter is about how both Catholics and Pentecostals foster participation in all the different fields of

---

[34] Sepulveda, 'How the Pentecostal Mission Church of Chile Had Become a Member of the WCC', p. 72.

[35] Sepúlveda, 'How the Pentecostal Mission Church of Chile had Become a Member of the WCC', p. 70.

[36] Koson Srisang, *Perspectives on Political Ethics: An Ecumenical Inquiry* (Washington, DC: Georgetown University Press, 2006), p. 143.

[37] Srisang, *Perspectives on Political Ethics*, p. 143.

[38] Hughes, *Authority and Morals*, p. 52.

[39] This matter of Pentecostal participation in public service was discussed by Käkkäinen, 'Culture, Contextualization and Conversion', pp. 263-69.

relationships between people and civil institutions. To understand this issue, special attention has to be paid to the historical context and the social relationships that have been built up in the community. According to Hughes, 'the overcoming of cultural, juridical, and social obstacles that often constitutes barriers calls for work in the areas of information and education'.[40]

In relation to this matter, Pentecostals still seem to be in disadvantage, for they still show limited resources pertaining to information and education. However, they are now encouraging enabled citizens to practice informed participation in public service.[41]

Solidarity

Another matter of concern in Latin America is the understanding and appropriation of the principle of solidarity by Catholics and Pentecostals. The second half of the twentieth century witnessed the participation of Christians from both backgrounds in the social, economic, and political life of Latin America. Liberation theology and the II Episcopal Conference of Medellin[42] in 1968 provided the basis for RCC scholars to encourage solidarity with those who suffer. However, Pentecostals have made some isolated efforts that have led them to start looking at their society with a more proactive attitude and to create programs of evangelization and transformation on behalf of the poor.[43]

---

[40] Hughes, *Authority and Morals*, p. 50.

[41] See how a Chilean Pentecostal began to encourage public participation in the account recorded by Richard Waldrop, 'The Social Consciousness and Involvement of the Full Gospel Church of God of Guatemala', *Cyber Journal of Pentecostal-Charismatic Research* (1997). http://www.pctii.org/cyberj/cyberj2/waldrop.html. Accessed 10 October 2009.

[42] Liberation theologians considered the II Episcopal Conference of Medellin, in 1968, as the Latin American answer to the changes proposed by Vatican II. They evaluated the cultural, social, economic, and political situations from the dominant countries point view, and instead, they adopted the position of the prophetical peoples, who are willing to assume their own suffering and aspirations. See Gutiérrez, *Teología de la Liberación*, p. 57.

[43] Believers eventually took the name charismatics partly to distinguish this movement of better-educated, higher-income Christians from that of Pentecostals such as those belonging to the Assemblies of God, Church of God, the Foursquare Gospel, and the Church of God in Christ. See John Dart, 'Charismatic and Mainline', *The Christian Century* 123.5 (March 7, 2006), pp. 22-27.

Equality and Dignity of the Human Being

For the purpose of this study, solidarity focuses on the 'social nature of the human person, the equality of all in dignity and rights, and the common path of individuals and peoples towards an ever more committed unity'.[44] This can be accomplished thanks to the current expansion of technology and the rapid use of live communication. The extraordinary advances in computer technology as well as the increased volume of commerce and information exchange all bear witness to this possibility. 'For the first time, since the beginning of human history, it is now possible to establish relationships between people who are separated by great distances'.[45]

However, for both Catholic and Pentecostal scholars, even in the 'presence of the current phenomenon of interdependence and its constant expansion, there persists stark inequalities between developed and developing countries'.[46] These inequalities are stoked by different forms of oppression, exploitation, and corruption which produce destructive attitudes in the life and behavior of many communities.[47] Juan Sepúlveda also insists, 'the acceleration of interdependence between persons and peoples needs to be accompanied by equally intense efforts on the ethical-social plane, in order to avoid the dangerous consequences of perpetrating injustice on a global scale';[48] and missiologists from both RCC and Pentecostal traditions concur that this would carry very negative repercussions not only in some underdeveloped countries but also in those societies that seem to be socio-economically advantageous.

Solidarity as a Social Principle

In the 1980s, Enrique Russell studied the principles of solidarity in the social context of Costa Rica. He found that the 'new relation-

---

[44] Srisang, *Perspectives on Political Ethics*, p. 140.

[45] Srisang, *Perspectives on Political Ethics*, p. 143.

[46] See for instance, Bueno, *The Struggle for Social Space*, p. 10; and Kärkkäinen, 'Culture, Contextualization and Conversion', p. 266.

[47] Bueno, *The Struggle for Social Space*, p. 9.

[48] Sepúlveda, 'How the Pentecostal Mission Church of Chile Had Become a Member of the WCC', p. 70.

ships of interdependence between individuals and peoples, which are forms of solidarity, have to be transformed into relationships tending towards genuine ethical-social solidarity'.[49] RCC scholars see this as a moral requirement inherent within all human relationships. Thus 'solidarity is understood under two complementary aspects: that of a social principle and that of a moral virtue'.[50]

This principle of solidarity has served as foundational for liberation theology. Its exponents saw its value and moral virtue as determinant in the order that institutions operated. Thus, based upon this principle, these structures of sin must be overcome. They cannot continue to pre-determine or condition the relationships between individuals or groups in society.[51] Moreover, institutional structures 'must be purified and transformed into structures of solidarity through the creation or appropriate modification of laws, market regulations, and juridical systems'.[52]

According to these ideas, Pentecostals are looking at solidarity as a moral virtue and not as 'a feeling of vague compassion or shallow distress at the misfortunes of so many people, both near and far'.[53] To some extent, they attach the notion of the common good to their practice of ministry. The principle of 'solidarity rises to the rank of fundamental social virtue since it places itself in the sphere of justice'.[54] Solidarity can be taken as a virtue 'directed to the common good, and is found in a commitment to the good of one's

---

[49] E.D. Russel, 'Un Análisis Contextual de la Iglesia Católica en América Latina', *Pastoralia* 2.3 (1989), pp. 32-44.

[50] Russel, 'Un Análisis Contextual de la Iglesia Católica en América Latina', p. 44.

[51] Alfonso López Trujillo, 'Medellín: Una Mirada global', *Medellín Reflections en el CELAM* (Madrid, España: Biblioteca de Autores Cristianos, 1997), p. 12; also, José Miguez Bonino, 'El Nuevo Catolicismo', in C. René Padilla (ed.), *Fe Cristiana y Latinoamérica Hoy* (Buenos Aires, Argentina: Ediciones Certeza, 1994), p. 91.

[52] Bonino, 'El Nuevo Catolicismo', p. 91.

[53] Pentecostalism is known for acting by feelings and experience. Their solidarity in social concerns is a spontaneous expression, rather than an intentional effort. See Carmelo Álvarez, *Pentecostalismo y Liberación: Una Experiencia Latinoamericana* (San José, Costa Rica: DEI, 1992), p. 50; Benjamín G. Gutiérrez, *En la Fuerza del Espíritu; Los Pentecostales de América Latina: Un Desafío de las Iglesias Históricas* (Ciudad Guatemala, Guatemala: CELEP, 1995), p. 67; and Carlos Tapia, 'Adiós a las Armas: La Guerra del Fin del Mundo', *La República Lima, Perú* (1994), p. 23.

[54] Gutiérrez, En la Fuerza del Espíritu, p. 10.

neighbor with the readiness, in the sense of the Gospel, to lose oneself for the sake of the other'.[55]

Human Growth and Transformation

The social doctrine of solidarity of the RCC shows that there is a close relation between solidarity and the common good, between solidarity and the universal destination of goods and between the common good of the people and solidarity. It is only through the basis of equality that people care for each other and work for peace in the world.

Hugo Assmann views the term solidarity as the 'need to recognize the ties that unite men and social groups among themselves and the space given to human freedom for common growth in which all share and participate'.[56] Thus, the commitment to this goal is translated into the positive contribution of seeing that nothing is lacking in the common cause.[57] When this action and attitude is transferred to the will of people, then they will realize the importance of working towards the good of the neighbor. In the case of Pentecostals, this attitude of service may go beyond the interest of an individual or a group.

Currently, the Pentecostal approach to this principle of solidarity prompts men and women to exercise a

> spiritual awareness that they are debtors of the society of which they have become part. They are debtors because of those spiritual conditions that make human existence liveable and because of the indivisible and indispensable.[58]

Additionally, they are spiritual debtors in their influence over culture, science, and knowledge, whether they are material or immaterial goods that the human condition has produced.

---

[55] Samuel Solivan, *The Spirit, Pathos and Liberation* (JPTSup 14; Sheffield: Sheffield Academic Press, 1998), pp. 22-30.

[56] Hugo Assmann, *Opresión-Liberación: Desafío de los Cristianos* (Montevideo, Uruguay: Tierra Nueva, 1991), p. 79.

[57] Assmann, *Opresión-Liberación: Desafío de los Cristianos*, p. 82.

[58] Pentecostals are quick to evaluate social, economic, and political scenarios based upon their spiritual radar. They tend to offer spiritual explanations to most phenomena that happen in society. Part of this discussion is found in Villafañe, *El Espíritu Liberador*, pp. 52-61.

Healing and Reconciliation

Both Catholics and Pentecostals agree that the unsurpassed apex of the perspective of mission is the example of the life and ministry of Christ Jesus. He is the New Man united with God but with such humanity that he suffered 'death on a cross'.[59] In Jesus it is possible to understand the transcendent love and recognize he is the living resource for humanity to obtain healing and reconciliation with God and fellow individuals. His atoning sacrifice is sufficient to overcome the weaknesses of humanity, and it is strong enough to bring about faith and love for those who believe and follow Him.

Life in society can also be rediscovered despite human contradictions and social ambiguities. There is hope for those who receive him as Lord, Savior, and Redeemer. That is a provision of grace continuously granted to those who repent. It also carries an invitation to participate in higher levels and forms of sharing in fraternal love as the Holy Spirit indwells the believer.

Catholics and Pentecostals agree that Christ Jesus makes the connection between solidarity and fellowship. The Holy Spirit illuminates the entire meaning of this connection. 'When solidarity operates with faith it could go beyond itself. It could change society with the Christian dimensions of total gratuity, forgiveness, and reconciliation.'[60] Catholics and Pentecostals see their neighbor not only as a human being who has his or her own rights, but also a living image of God the Father once that individual has surrendered his or her life to Christ. He or she is now placed under the continuous action and protection of the Holy Spirit. 'So one's neighbor must therefore be loved, even if an enemy, with the same love with which the Lord loves him or her. And for that person's sake one must be ready for sacrifice.'[61]

---

[59] Solivan, *The Spirit, Pathos and Liberation*, p. 30.

[60] That is the argument of Samuel Solivan in his dialogue with the Catholic theology of mission and the work of the Holy Spirit. See Solivan, *The Spirit, Pathos and Liberation*, pp. 22-30.

[61] Villafañe, *El Espíritu Liberador*, pp. 52-56.

Spiritual Values

This comparative study between Catholics and Pentecostals ends with an overview of the virtues of truth, freedom, and justice. Catholic scholars argue that besides the principles that constitute the foundations of society, there are social responsibilities that also indicate some foundational values on the part of the community of Christians.

Thus, the reciprocity between Christian principles and sound human values determines the level of relationships held in society.[62] For instance, Julio de Santa Ana states that in social values there is 'an expression of appreciation to be attributed to those specific aspects of moral good that these principles foster. These principles serve as points of reference for the proper structuring and ordered leading of life in society'.[63] However, this practice requires that the principles of social life and personal virtue become associated with healthy moral attitudes in order to strengthen these values.

Meanwhile, Pentecostals understand that social values are part of the dignity of the individual whose human development is fostered by the work of the Holy Spirit. These values are known as freedom, truth, justice, and love. A person may obtain spiritual and social perfection by putting them into practice.[64] These 'values constitute the indispensable point of reference whereby public authorities will identify their call to promote the good of economic, political, cultural, and technological structures and the necessary changes in institutions'.[65] Pentecostals are also learning that respect for the autonomy of earthly matters leads the community of believers into healthy relationships. They are also satisfied to have the opportunity to pray for their authorities and those in public office.

---

[62] Hughes, *Authority and Morals*, p. 56.

[63] Julio Santa Ana, *Protestantismo, Cultura y Sociedad* (Buenos Aires, Argentina: Editorial La Aurora, 1990), pp. 125-26.

[64] Bernardo Campos seems to get near the Catholic theology of mission when he writes about spiritual and social action among Pentecostals. See Campos, *De la Reforma Protestante a la Pentecostalidad de la Iglesia*, pp. 32-43.

[65] Campos, *De la Reforma Protestante a la Pentecostalidad de la Iglesia*, pp. 32-43.

The Truth

RCC scholars and Pentecostals also agree that men and women, as members of their communities, have the responsibility to seek, learn, and move towards that which is truthful. Therefore, they show respect for others and creation. They bear responsible witness to all of these. Leonardo Boff states, 'living in the truth has special significance in social relationships. In fact, when the coexistence of human beings within a community is founded on truth, it is ordered and fruitful, and it corresponds to their dignity as persons.'[66] He also adds, 'the more people and social groups strive to resolve social problems according to the truth, the more they distance themselves from abuses and act in accordance with the objective demands of morality'.[67]

Twenty-first century reality calls for intensive educational efforts and strong corresponding commitments practiced intentionally by all involved, so that those who are seeking truth will not be ascribed to a simple sum of opinions that may become confusing. This matter involves the community of faith and the world of public communications as well as those who control the economy. These areas may fall under an unscrupulous use of wealth and may raise even more pressing questions. Therefore, it demands transparency and honesty in personal activity and social involvement. Both Catholics and Pentecostals are working now in order to affect Latin America with the benefit of the truth as taught by the gospel.

Freedom

Catholics and Pentecostals value freedom as a sign of progress. Freedom is God's divine image inherited by humanity, so it is considered a sign of dignity for every person. Freedom is exercised in relationships between human beings. Every individual has the right

---

[66] See Leonardo Boff, *La fe en la Periferia del Mundo* (Santander, España: Editorial Sal Terrae, 1981), p. 145; and Sepúlveda, 'Reflections on the Pentecostal Contribution to the Mission of the Church in Latin America', pp. 93-108.

[67] Boff, La Fe en la Periferia del Mundo, p. 145.

to be accepted and recognized as a free, worthy, and responsible person.[68]

> The right to the exercise of freedom, especially in moral and religious matters, is an inalienable requirement of the dignity of humanity. The meaning of freedom must not be restricted, considering it from a purely individualistic perspective and reducing it to the arbitrary and uncontrolled exercise of one's own personal autonomy.[69]

Freedom exists where there are reciprocal bonds, which are governed by justice and truth, and these are the links that connect people with one another. For Catholics, understanding freedom becomes far deeper and broader, especially when this affects the social level involving different dimensions.[70] Furthermore, for Pentecostals, according to Angela Pollack, the term becomes deeper and broader when believers are filled with the Holy Spirit and enabled to serve efficiently under the guidance of the Spirit.[71]

Both Catholics and Pentecostals respect the uniqueness of humanity in the expression of freedom. Both agree that every individual of the community must have the right to fulfill his or her personal potential and vocation. Every individual must seek the truth and have the right to profess his or her faith as well as cultural and political preferences. Members of society should have the freedom to express their opinions concerning government and have the liberty to decide on their state of life and line of work.

> They should be free to pursue initiatives of economic, social, or political nature. This must take place within a strong juridical

---

[68] On a general approach to human freedom, see Moltmann, *God for a Secular Society*, p. 79. The author discussed the situation of a person between personal liberty and social faithfulness.

[69] Moltmann, *God for a Secular Society*, p. 77.

[70] Heinrich Muhlen, *Espíritu Carisma Liberación* (Salamanca, España: Don Bosco Verlag, 1974), p. 275.

[71] See Angelina Pollak Eltz and Yolanda Salas de Lecuna *El Pentecostalismo en América Latina entre Tradición y Globalización* (Quito, Ecuador: Docutech, 1998), p. 116. This work is very important for it suggests a sincere dialogue between two permanent residents of Latin America, Catholics and Pentecostals. Dialogue is the way to agree on the approach to order, common good, public order, and social responsibility.

framework, within the limits imposed by the common good and public order, and, in every case, in a manner characterized by responsibility.[72]

Most Pentecostals, however, are still learning about this value of faith. Their discourse is not strong enough to be heard in the circles of socio-economic and political powers.[73] Nevertheless, this notion of freedom continues to grow in their community of faith.

Freedom is also expressed as 'the capacity to refuse what is morally negative, in whatever guise it may be presented. People must have the capacity to distance themselves effectively from everything that could hinder personal, family, or social growth'.[74] Catholics see the fulfillment of freedom in the capacity of the individual to decide for the good. Pentecostals see this fulfillment of freedom when believers live in the Spirit. It is the Holy Spirit who guides them to genuine peace, goodness, and freedom.

Justice

RCC theologians take justice as a value that shows one of the virtues of moral integrity. Justice is the firm and continuous will that recognizes God's sovereignty and the fulfillment of all human rights. 'From a subjective point of view, justice is translated into behavior that is based on the will to recognize the other as a person, while, from an objective point of view, it constitutes the decisive criteria of morality in the inter-subjective and social sphere'.[75]

Historically, Catholics have called

For the most classical forms of justice to be respected: commutative, distributive, and legal justice. They have given greater importance to social justice, which represents a real development

---

[72] Hughes, *Authority and Morals*, p. 62.

[73] Bastian, *La Mutación Religiosa de América Latina*, p. 24.

[74] Moltmann, *God for a Secular Society*, p. 78.

[75] Robert D. Lupton, *Compassion, Justice and the Christian Life* (Ventura, CA: Regal Books, 2007), pp. 52-55.

on justice in general, which regulates social relationships according to the criterion of observance of the law'.[76]

They see social justice as a requirement that is always related to social questions. Social justice today is a worldwide matter in its scope and demands. It concerns the socio-economic and political affairs of society, 'together with the structural dimension of problems and their respective solutions'.[77]

In the case of Pentecostals, some scholars agree that the practice of justice is important. They recognize the individual value of the person. Human dignity must be protected and promoted against exclusive criteria of utility and ownership.[78] Justice requires an authentic meaning in Christian anthropology. Justice is not merely a simple human condition that demands attention. What is known as just is not determined by simple human laws but by an inherent understanding deep in the identity of the human being with what is right and just.[79] Latin American Pentecostals are participating in ecumenical dialogues where RCC scholars are also present.[80] Such ecumenical initiatives could help them to find grounds of common understanding. They may set principles for peaceful coexistence in a large but promising continent.

We have approached social responsibility and its influence on church mission. During the course of the study, I realized Pentecostals are often asked about their participation in the development of society. They are also prompted to respond to issues related to peace and justice. Hence, I decided to explore the recent history of

---

[76] See Daniel G. Groody, *Globalization, Spirituality, and Justice: Navigating the Path to Peace* (Maryknoll, NY: Orbis Books, 2007), pp. 26-27.

[77] Groody, *Globalization, Spirituality, and Justice*, p. 27

[78] See Anthea Butler, 'Facets of Pentecostal Spirituality and Justice', *Consultation with Pentecostals in the Americas* (San José, Costa Rica: World Council of Churches, 1996), pp. 28-44.

[79] Butler, 'Facets of Pentecostal Spirituality and Justice', p. 32.

[80] A dialogue between Catholic and Pentecostals has taken place since 1972. It includes representatives from both sides and from different geographical zones. So Pentecostals from Latin America have been invited to participate on a personal basis. Those participations have begun to develop awareness about the need to extend the Catholic-Pentecostal dialogue for Latin America, only. However, no action seems to have been taken toward this purpose. See Käkkäinen, 'Culture, Contextualization and Conversion', pp. 268.

Pentecostal participation in social action and concerns particularly in Latin America. I even looked into their participation in social work during the days of the Cold War as this took place in Latin America.

Pentecostals did not seem to have a solid theology of integral mission. That was the main reason for having ambivalent opinions and theological positions toward socio-economic, cultural, and political participation. Consequently, at some point they refrained from participating in these fields perhaps for not having adequate knowledge about mission theology in times like these or for not having adequate training for significant participation in social action. Other Pentecostals, especially the most conservative, spiritualized the matter and decided that it was not biblical to become involved in the affairs of the world. The reaction varied from church to church, for they did not appear to have a common consensus in their role as agents of change in society.

Since most Pentecostals in Latin America are former Catholics, I also decided to explore the influence of the theological principles of social responsibility, as proposed by the RCC, on the Pentecostal understanding of social action. Most catholic schools in Latin American teach the RCC teachings of the common good, political participation, solidarity, and the fundamental values for social life. Moreover, as I studied these principles, I found that Pentecostals in Latin America also tend to look at these principles as valid models for responding to social concerns.[81]

Therefore, in the dialogue between Pentecostals and RCC theology, I found that in the back of their minds, Pentecostals favor most of these teachings although in their shift toward Pentecostal theology they have become more biblically oriented in their approach to mission. Pentecostals recognize the validity of public participation in democratic processes. They may not have the proper training for it, but they support Christians who become involved in public service. I arrived at the same conclusion in matters that work on behalf of the equality and dignity of the human being.

---

[81] For instance, Benjamaín Guerrero Bravo, *El Fruto del Espíritu: El Carácter del Cristiano y la Misión de la Iglesia* (Lima, Perú: Ediciones Puma, 1997), pp. 86-92; studied how Catholic theology affects Pentecostal mission in context. Most Pentecostals come from that tradition so when they become Pentecostals they carry their theological roots with them.

Although Pentecostals will not recognize it publicly, it is evident by their teachings that they still support the RCC teaching of solidarity for the common growth of humanity. Of course, Pentecostals are strict in observing the values of truth, freedom, justice, and love in order to foster the common good. They want to make sure all of these principles fulfill the purpose of God for society. Subsequently, they preach and teach about staying faithful to the principles of the gospel in order to accomplish these purposes.

What is very significant here is the possibility of a dialogue between Pentecostals and RCC theologians in Latin America. Both streams have common concerns for the development of society and the common good of people. Both traditions have embraced the historical responsibility for the human growth and transformation of the Latin American societies. Pentecostals and Catholics are against violence and social injustice. These fields of common interest could serve as future scenarios for a significant dialogue between these streams of Christianity.

6

MISSION AND THE ECONOMY

On the matter of poverty versus riches, there seems to be at least two ways to approach economic success and wealth found in the teachings of Pentecostalism. On the one hand, there is an indication of an attitude of gratitude that makes material provision available for the needs of life. At some point, abundance is seen as a sign of blessing from the Lord. As a matter of fact in the Wisdom Literature poverty is seen as one of the consequences for infidelity to the will of God[1] and also as a natural fact.[2]

On the other hand,

> Economic prosperity and wealth are not condemned in themselves. What God disapproves is the misuse of the economic goods. Pentecostals testify against fraud, oppression, exploitation, usury, and injustice, especially when these evils affect the poor and marginalized.[3]

They also see the conditions of poverty and marginalization as consequences of human degradation that offend God from whom

---

[1] On this topic, see Elizabeth Salazar Sanzana, 'Touching the Master's Cloak: Women in Chilean Pentecostalism', in Vinson Synan, Amos Yong, and Miguel Álvarez (eds.), *Global Renewal Christianity: Latin America* (Lake Mary, FL: Charisma House, 2016), II, pp. 295-311.

[2] Carmelo Álvarez, *Alborada en Tiempos Fecundos: Una Teologica Ecumenica y Pentecostal* (Quito, Ecuador: Consejo Latinoamericano de Iglesias, 2007), p. 30.

[3] Gamaliel Lugo, 'Etica Social Pentecostal: Santidad Comprometida', in Carmelo Álvarez (ed.), *Pentecostalismo y Liberación. Una Experiencia Latinoamericana* (San José, Costa Rica: DEI, 1992), pp. 101-22.

humanity has access to every good gift. All He wants is for those in charge of wealth to deliver it rightly and fairly.

Concerning this theological approach, there are some scholars like Beltzasar Núñez who question this position of poverty as a consequence of sin, for it looks simplistic and in opposition to God's plan for humanity.[4] René Peñalba also states, 'There is no such thing as some people being punished with poverty as a consequence of their sin. That would open the affirmation that those who please God will necessarily be blessed with wealth.'[5] Following this line of argument, one would think that poverty is related to other issues that affect human societies.

There is also the position based upon the teachings of Jesus, which recognizes one's own poverty regardless of the individual's personal or spiritual condition in life. Due to their humility, Jesus promised that God would pay particular attention to the poor. Thus, when the poor cry out to the Lord for help, God listens and answers them. The divine promises are addressed to the poor. In reference to the situation of poverty in Honduras, Adrianne Pine stimulates hope among some churches by stating,

> The poor, oppressed, and marginalized will inherit the benefits of God's covenant with His people through the saving work of Jesus. For His work is a plan to establish a new covenant with His people and write the new laws for His kingdom in the hearts of all believers.[6]

However, there is also room to think that when poverty is taken with an attitude of humility, this opens the way to understanding God's purpose for creation. Here God shows the vanity of the

---

[4] If poverty contravenes God's intention for humankind, then surely it is largely due to human sin against the purposes of God. However, the question is also, the sin of whom? Fraud, exploitation, injustice is all part of human sin, surely. See Belsazar Núñez, *Quiero Vivir mi Vida* (Tegucigalpa, Honduras: Editorial Arte Creativo, 2006), p. 65.

[5] René Peñalba, *Metamorfosis del Creyente: El Proceso de Transformación en la Vida Cristiana* (Tegucigalpa, Honduras: CCI, 2001), p. 48. Peñalba defends that every person has the right to live a life according to God's plan. His plan is that of well-being for each individual. To think otherwise is to fall into deception and accept that alienation is normal.

[6] Adrienne Pine, *Working Hard, Drinking Hard: On Violence and Survival in Honduras* (Los Angeles, CA: University of California Press, 2008), p. 167.

wealthy putting their trust in their own resources.[7] It is obvious that God despises the person who puts his or her trust in his or her own works. When wealth grows, a person's greed and pride increases, and the purpose of God's provision of resources is defeated. Some Pentecostals even teach that God sees the other side of poverty, whereby an individual decides to remain humble, serving the poor in spite of the privilege brought about by money and power.[8]

The gospel takes on the status of a moral value when it becomes an attitude of availability and openness to God and of trust in Him. This statement is in concordance with Ignacio Alonzo who argues, 'This attitude makes it possible for people to recognize the relativity of economic goods and to treat them as divine gifts to be administered and shared, because God is the first owner of all goods'.[9]

Justice and the Economy

On the matter of money or material goods, Jesus took the tradition of the Old Testament and made it clear how his disciples should handle themselves in regards to these.[10] He came to establish the Kingdom of God, and this can only be established on the conversion of the hearts of people and the action of the gifts of the Holy Spirit.[11] This is the new manner by which social relationships would be established. This is the condition that makes a new society possible. Such a society must reflect justice, solidarity, brotherhood, and cooperation.

---

[7] Lugo, *Etica Social Pentecostal: Santidad Comprometida*, p. 110.

[8] See Peñalba, *Metamorfosis del Creyente*, p. 56.

[9] Ignacio Alonzo and Iris Barrientos (eds.), *Fe y Política* (Tegucigalpa, Honduras: Editorial SETEHO, 2006), pp. 45-52. This volume registers the position of pastors who propose a biblical approach to the issue of poverty and the possession of wealth, not from a socialist point of view, but from Christian one. Now from a Pentecostal perspective, see Gilberto Alvarado López, *El Poder Desde el Espíritu. La Visión Política del Pentecostalismo Contemporáneo* (Buenos Aires, Argentina: Publicaciones Científicas para el Estudio de la Religiones, 2006), pp. 56-58. The author argues that Pentecostals recognize economic goods as part of the blessings from God, but the purpose of those goods is to serve humanity, with a humble spirit.

[10] Alonzo and Barrientos, *Fe y Política*, p. 46.

[11] This is the argument of Alvarado López, *El Poder del Espíritu*, p. 54. That the goal of the Spirit is to convert the heart of people, so that economic goods could accomplish their purpose in society.

Christ inaugurated a new kingdom, which is originated in the goodness of human activity as originally designed by God. In this new reality, humanity is placed in communion with God once again, and with the help of the Holy Spirit believers work out the purpose of Jesus for the world. According to Mario López,

> In Jesus, man is called to render justice to the poor, releasing the oppressed, consoling the afflicted, actively seeking a new social order in which adequate solutions to material poverty are offered and in which the forces thwarting the attempts of the weakest to free themselves from conditions of misery and slavery are more effectively controlled.[12]

This is the evidence of the presence of the kingdom of God in the world.

Honduran economist Mario López claimed in the early 1990s that 'economic activity is to be considered and undertaken as a grateful response to the vocation, which God holds out for each person'.[13] Regarding this matter, Lugo says that historically, 'men and women were placed in the garden to live in it and to keep it, using every resource available for their benefit, but within very well specified limits;'[14] and, as López suggests, with a spiritual commitment to perfecting it. By assuming this responsibility, 'they were bearing witness to the goodness of the Creator.[15] That way, they moved towards the fullness of freedom to which God called them.[16] Thus, 'good administration of the gifts and of physical goods was also a work of justice towards humanity. What had been received had to be used properly, preserved and increased as suggested by Jesus in the parable of the talents.'[17]

Therefore, it is clear that every economic effort and material prosperity should serve for the advancement of humanity. 'If peo-

---

[12] Mario René López, *Historia y Misión del Protestantismo Hondureño* (San José, Costa Rica: Editorial Visión Mundial Internacional, 1993), pp. 28-32.

[13] López, *Historia y Misión del Protestantismo Hondureño*, p. 36.

[14] Lugo, *Ética Social Pentecostal: Santidad Comprometida*, p. 112.

[15] López, *Historia y Misión del Protestantismo Hondureño*, p. 41.

[16] López, *Historia y Misión de Protestantismo Hondureño*, p. 33.

[17] See Wesley D. Balda, *Heirs of the Same Promise* (Monrovia, CA: MARC, 1984), pp. 100-102. The author advocates for the proper use of material goods. Contemporary Christians should not fall into the temptation of accumulating goods selfishly. See also, López, *Historia y Misión del Protestantismo Hondureño*, p. 33.

ple dedicate themselves with faith to this purpose, even the economy and human progress can be transformed for the good of humanity'.[18] Lugo states that 'solidarity and love can be expressed in these areas that affect all people, especially the poor and the marginalized'.[19]

It is this faith in Christ that makes a correct understanding and approach to social development possible. With their natural ability, Pentecostals could contribute to the discipline of theological reflection which is based upon their action in the life of the community. In effect, 'faith in Christ the Redeemer is brought to life by the Holy Spirit, who illuminates human nature to development and guides believers in the task of collaboration'.[20]

In his approach to the letter to the Colossians, Carmelo Álvarez thinks that the apostle Paul deliberately emphasized that Christ is 'the firstborn of all creation' and that 'all things were created through him and for him'.[21] In fact, 'all things hold together in him,' since 'in him dwells the fullness of God and through Him God reconciles to himself all things'.[22] This is part of God's plan that in the eternity of Christ the image of God as the Father has been perfected. Carlos Garma also adds that God culminated as the Son the mission of the first-born who was raised from the dead in all His humanity.[23] Through Christ's death and resurrection, humanity was conquered and redeemed. Thus, the way of reconciliation amongst people was made possible in the sacrifice of Jesus Christ.[24]

Fairness in the Distribution of Wealth

There is always a legitimate purpose for the access and accumulation of goods. Improper use or selfish accumulation of goods contradicts such a purpose and falls into immorality. God provides all goods, and people are to keep this principle in mind for the right

---

[18] López, *Historia y Misión del Protestantismo Hondureño*, p. 45.

[19] Lugo, *Ética Social Pentecostal: Santidad Comprometida*, p. 119.

[20] See Álvarez, *La Palabra, El Espíritu y la Comunidad de Fe*, p. 64.

[21] See Álvarez, *Pentecostalismo y Liberación*, p. 32.

[22] Álvarez, *Pentecostalismo y Liberación*, p. 30.

[23] See Carlos Garma Navarro, *Buscando el Espíritu: Pentecostalismo en Iztapalapa y la Ciudad de México* (Doctoral Dissertation, University of El Paso, 1999), p. 123.

[24] Garma, *Buscando el Espíritu*, p. 122; also Lugo, *Etica Social Pentecosta*, p. 112.

attitude towards material possessions. Christian redemption includes the freedom from greed and selfishness. This is particularly valid in the attitude of Christians toward wealth, 'for the love of money is the root of all evils; it is through this craving that some have wandered away from the faith'.[25]

Historically, one finds that even the early church fathers paid more attention to the transformation of hearts rather than emphasizing the need to change the political and social structures of their day. They insisted that those who worked in public office should see themselves as servants of the community. In light of this, the purpose of riches is to assist humanity. They are to be used to produce benefits for the people and for the entire society. 'How could we ever do good to our neighbor,' asked Clement in Alexandria, 'if none of us possessed anything?'[26] Hence, in the preaching of John Chrysostom,

> Riches belong to some people so that they can gain merit by sharing them with others. Wealth is a good that comes from God and is to be used by its owner and made to circulate so that even the needy may enjoy it. Evil is seen in the immoderate attachment to riches and the desire to hoard.[27]

Likewise, Basil the Great invited the powerful and the wealthy to open their store houses, and he exhorted them with these words, 'a great torrent rushes, in thousands of channels, through the fertile land: thus, by a thousand different paths, make your riches reach the homes of the poor'.[28] Thus, for Basil wealth is like the water that comes out of the fountain: 'The greater the frequency with which it is drawn, the purer it is, while it becomes foul if the fountain remains unused'.[29] Gregory the Great, a very rich man, is quoted as having said, 'The rich are only administrators of what they possessed. Giving what was required to the needy is a task that was to

---

[25] Álvarez, *Alborada de Tiempos Fecundos*, pp. 30-31.

[26] P.M. Barnard, *Early Church Classics* (Cambridge: Cambridge Texts and Studies, 1901), IX, p. 456.

[27] John Chrysostom, *On Wealth and Poverty* (Crestwood, NY: St. Vladimir's Seminary Press, 1984), p. 143.

[28] George S. Bebis, 'Introduction to the Liturgical Theology of St. Basil the Great', *Greek Orthodox Theological Review* 42.3-4 (1997), pp. 273–85.

[29] Bebis, 'Introduction to the Liturgical Theology of St. Basil the Great', p. 278.

be performed with humility because the goods do not belong to the one who distributes them.'[30] These cases are historical evidence of those who also affirmed that retaining riches selfishly is not innocent. Moreover, they made it possible to think that giving and assisting those in need is a way of paying a personal or social debt.

Justice and Morality

In today's world of global economy, a Christian stance might be opposed and even disqualified at some point. Some economists and business leaders may argue that economics work according to certain internal laws that have nothing to do with morality. Nonetheless, current economic trends suggest that Christians (and not just Christians) are affected by the systems of this the world order.

After reviewing Pentecostal scholarship, we could not find written documents addressing the issue of morality in the economy. The only time the matter is addressed is verbally and from the pulpit. This action may satisfy those who attend weekly services, but very little evidence is documented.[31] Consequently, Pentecostals will have to find ways to address social teaching properly and insist on the moral connotations of the economy. One Honduran writer who discusses the morality of the economy is Beltzasar Núñez. He states, 'even though economics and moral science employ each of their own principles in their own sphere, it is an error to say that economics and moral orders are so distinct from and alien to each other that the former depends in no way on the latter'.[32] Thus, for

---

[30] Barnard, *Early Church Classics*, p. 457.

[31] A Honduran author whose studies addressed the issue of morality in the economic structures of Honduras is Alberto Amaya. His aim is to study the cause of poverty and suffering in the country. He clearly introduces the concept of appropriation of resources of foreign people who arrived after World War II, with the advantage of having superior access to money and resources against the disadvantage of the local people who could not compete with them. Thus the newly arrived people eventually held the power and control of the country. See Jorge Alberto Amaya, *Los Árabes y Palestinos en Honduras 1900-1950* (Tegucigalpa, Honduras: Editoriales Guaymuras, 1997), pp. 91-99.

[32] Belsazar Núñez, *Identidad y Misión* (Tegucigalpa, Honduras: Editorial Benugra, 1995), pp. 62-68. The author also tags the economic discrepancies among the Honduran society. See also, Núñez, *El Ministerio Pastoral* (Tegucigalpa,

Núñez, 'the laws of economics determine the limits of what productive human effort can do or achieve, and what it can attain in the productive field of goods'.[33]

The moral responsibility of men and women in the field of economics carries spiritual and material consequences. There is the potential to produce goods for the wellbeing of individuals and the community, or alternatively, to produce destructive elements that work to the detriment of people. Alberto Amaya states, 'industry is natural to humanity. Yet it has to be undertaken in accordance with those ethics that are compatible with the purpose of God for society.'[34] Thus, there is an unavoidable moral responsibility to adhere to God's design for the world when involved in economic production. Such industries as pornography and drug trafficking are instruments of corruption and contradict the purpose of God for humanity.

There cannot be healthy economic activity without moral integrity. Moral responsibility determines the purpose of economic activity. The motives of those involved in industry will have to be evaluated according to God's purpose for humanity.[35] For instance, Raúl Zaldívar has suggested a distinction that is necessary between morality and the economy, which does not entail the separation of these two spheres, but rather he points out that they operate in common reciprocity. Thus, in the economic and social realms, the dignity and complete vocation of the human person and the welfare of society as a whole are to be respected and promoted.[36]

Honduras: Editorial Benugra, 1992), pp. 93-96. From a pastoral perspective, these teachings make strong emphasis on the morality of the economy in the country.

[33] Núñez, *El Ministerio Pastoral*, p. 86.

[34] Amaya, *Los Arabes y los Palestinos en Honduras*, p. 96.

[35] See also William I. Robinson, *Transnational Conflicts: Central America, Social Change, and Globalization* (New York, NY: Verso, 2004), p. 86. The author claims that fairness will be achieved when all parties involved will assume the benefits of industry's common interest.

[36] One author that helps understand this position is Raúl Zaldívar, *La Doctrina de la Santidad* (Barcelona, España: Editorial CLIE, 2001), pp. 206-21. This book addresses the demands of the gospel for holiness in the way people handle themselves with regards to goods and money. The loss of balance, which equals justice, causes people to fall under the power of money – that is the root of evil as stated in 1 Tim. 6.10. See also Zaldívar, *Crítica Bíblica* (Barcelona, España: Editorial CLIE, 1994), pp. 62-70.

Humanity is the source, the center, and the purpose of all economic and social life. Giving the proper and due weight to the interests that belong specifically to the economy does not mean rejecting all considerations of a meta-economic order as irrational. This is so because the purpose of the economy is not found in the economy itself but rather in its being destined for humanity and society. The economy, in fact, whether on a scientific or practical level, has not been entrusted to men and women with the purpose of bringing proper human coexistence. Thus, the production, distribution, and consumption of material goods and services must benefit all people in the community.

As previously stated, the development of the economy carries a moral responsibility. It has to do with the efficiency of the promotion of humanity. Solidarity with the individual and the community will have to be observed at all levels of the production of wealth and goods. Morality, which is a necessary part of economics, is neither opposed to it nor is it neutral. Alexis Pacheco stated in the early 1990s: 'If morality is inspired by justice and solidarity, this in itself represents a positive factor for social efficiency within the economy'.[37] He also argued,

> The production of goods is a duty to be undertaken in an efficient manner, otherwise resources are wasted. On the other hand, it would not be acceptable to achieve economic growth at the expense of human beings, entire populations or social groups, condemning them to indigence.[38]

The virtues of solidarity, human growth, transformation, and assistance to the poor and the needy are intrinsically linked to the production of goods, services, and structures for the benefit of society. God gave men and women the ability to generate wealth. This capacity can serve the purposes of God for humanity. Therefore, it is the responsibility of those who participate in the production of the economy to consider ways in order to conduct themselves accord-

---

[37] Alexis Pacheco and Guillermo Jiménez, 'Hacia una Pastoral de las Personas Amenazadas por la Pobreza', in *CLADE III: Tercer congreso Latinoamericano de evangelización* (Quito, Ecuador: Fraternidad Teológica Latinoamericana, 1992), pp. 120-36.

[38] Pacheco and Jiménez, 'Hacia una Pastoral de las Personas Amenazadas por la Pobreza', pp. 128-32.

ing to the principles and moral values of the gospel. Any activity contrary to this purpose will bring about the destruction and rejection of God's moral plan for the economy.

Moral character must be exercised at every action in the world of economics. Such an action has to keep the interest of people in its purpose. Hence, every individual or people group has the right to participate in the industrious production of the economy. People respond positively when they can use their capacity or receive the opportunity to contribute and to produce. This action provides every individual with the opportunity to contribute in the development of the family and the community. That is why Euraque said, 'If everyone is responsible for everyone else, then each person also has the duty to commit himself to the development of all'.[39] Then he adds, 'this is a duty in solidarity and in justice, but it is also the best way to bring progress to all of humanity'.[40]

When economics is practiced with a high level of morality, 'the service rendered by the production of goods and the services is useful for the growth of each person and becomes an opportunity for every individual to embody solidarity'.[41] This effort to generate social projects and goods for the purpose of lifting the levels of human growth and transformation of society is difficult. It takes intentionality by those in a position of advantage in relation to the access of resources and control of economic production.

The 'economy that is generated by industrious people has as its object the development of wealth and its continuous increase'.[42] Hence, this activity is right when it focuses on the development of community projects. According to Raúl Zaldívar, 'development cannot be reduced to a mere process of accumulating goods and services. Accumulation of wealth without having the common good

---

[39] Darío A. Euraque, *Estado, Poder, Nacionalidad y Raza en la Historia de Honduras: Ensayos* (Tegucigalpa, Honduras: Ediciones Subirana, 1996), pp. 113-15.

[40] Euraque, *Estado, Poder, Nacionalidad y Raza*, p. 115.

[41] Euraque, *Estado, Poder, Nacionalidad y Raza*, p. 113.

[42] Some would argue that this aim is incompatible with that of caring for the environment, that the elimination of poverty will create an unsustainable degradation of the natural world. See M. Carley, *Policy Management Systems and Methods of Analysis for Sustainable Agriculture and Rural Development* (Rome and London: FAO IIED, 1994); see also G.E. Carlson, D. Zilberman, and J. Miranowsky (eds.), *Agricultural and Environmental Resource Economics* (Oxford, UK: Oxford University Press, 1993), pp. 87-112.

in mind does not bring about authentic human happiness'.[43] Therefore, it is the responsibility of the community of faith to denounce
evil purposes that work against the purpose of God for the economy. The church is called to guard the principles of faithful morality
in the approach and use of wealth.

It is possible to evaluate the role of economy in society.
Although the secular world may take the voice of the church as one
opinion only, nonetheless it must assume its moral responsibility in
providing instruction to those who have direct access to wealth.
The church has to exercise its prophetic ministry in calling society
to order. The role of the economy is one of the most debated issues in current times.

The church recognizes a system that practices free enterprise and
human creativity in economic activity. However, if such an economic dynamic is not circumscribed to a healthy juridical framework,
such activity is polluted and is, therefore, out of order and punisha-
ble. Thus, a healthy Christian perspective of the economy is defined
regarding the social and political benefits that enhance the conditions of society. These are the values that are to be observed in the
activity of a community committed to the moral principles of the
economy.

Solidarity with the People

Achieving integral development is fundamental in the world of
economics. This has to be performed in solidarity with the needs of
people. The goal is to promote the good of every person and of
the whole person. Achieving this goal requires vision for an economic system that guarantees equality in the distribution of resources. Villafañe argues: 'This attitude is concomitant with that of
solidarity, born out of the principles of the gospel. Such an attitude
generates awareness to the matter of interdependence, which affects the economic, social, and political community.'[44] He also suggests that this is an attitude that brings about unity and cooperation

---

[43] Raúl Zaldívar, 'Relación Estado-Iglesia y su Apertura al Protestantismo en
Honduras', *Revista Vida y Pensamiento* 1 (1996), p. 92.

[44] See Villafañe, *El Espíritu Liberador*, p. 52.

amongst people and makes them feel united by a common destiny in their own context.[45]

When social and economic problems pervade the life of society as a whole, this leads to the recognition that the state alone may not be able to solve such problems. People then will understand that solidarity will help the community move forward in developing the potential of all its members. Individualism is defeated and mutual cooperation takes on the social and political behavior of the people.[46] Eventually, society enhances the building of partnerships that pave the way for better conditions of life. By fostering every individual's capacity and dignity, the community receives the benefit of creativity amongst all its members.

Greater participation in human development will help society become aware of individual needs and the different capacities of all community members. This awareness may also benefit the rich in their use and distribution of their wealth. Abundance of resources and money could evolve into corruption and confusion, not only amongst those who produce it but also with those who benefit from it. In some societies known for their abundance of wealth, existential problems are frequently observed in the inability of the rich to handle the material goods available to them. Some people are unable to experience an adequate meaning of life.[47] They either become alienated or are reduced to simple machines for production. They are unable to affirm or build their dignity as persons created in the image of God. Developed societies have been able to generate an abundance of material goods, but many times these are obtained at the expense of people and often to the detriment of the poor.

The differences between the wealthy and the poor are made manifest in human society. One can find poverty and misery even in rich societies just as selfishness and misuse of wealth in the poor

---

[45] Villafañe, *El Espíritu Liberador*, p. 56.

[46] This view is also supported by Darío A. Euraque, *Reinterpreting the Banana Republic: Region and State in Honduras, 1870-1972* (Chapel Hill, NC: University of North Carolina Press, 1996), p. 198.

[47] Juan Gelman, 'El Grito Silencioso', *El Nuevo Diario* (2007), p. 8. The author argues that development has to start by meeting the basic needs of people. Rich societies do not seem to understand the magnitude of the poverty in countries such Nicaragua.

communities. Obviously, the work of God is to change the hearts of people, so they can follow the principles of solidarity in the economy as taught by the gospel.

Indicators of a Healthy Economy

In the social teachings of the gospel, the economy is an important theme since it is part of human productivity. Production of goods should not become the aim of life. The social and economic systems should not ignore the ethical and spiritual values of the gospel. A system that reduces the economy to production and consumption of goods has weakened the moral and ethical purpose of the human production of wealth. This attitude limits humanity to mere instruments of economic activity. After observing the social conditions and cultural values of some Pentecostals in Brazil, Robert Chestnut concluded, 'the importance of an individual should never be limited to a materialistic value, even when that person depends on material goods for survival or for improving his or her quality of life'.[48] In light of this thought, an increased sense of God and self-awareness are fundamental to any development of human society.

Faced with the rapid advancement of technological and economic progress and with the equally rapid transformation in the processes of production and consumption, 'Pentecostal mission is now proposing new projects for educational and cultural formation'.[49]

Raúl Zaldívar argues that the community of faith knows, 'believers are called to a life, which is qualitatively dignifying, and to assume mutual responsibilities that will face dangers together and in unity'.[50] Therefore, believers are to be guided to assist one another by a comprehensive picture of human and fraternal solidarity.

This approach respects all the dimensions of his or her being, which subordinates their material and instinctive dimensions to their interior and spiritual ones. An economic system does not possess criteria for correctly distinguishing new and higher forms of

---

[48] Chesnut, *Born Again in Brazil*, p. 132.
[49] Chesnut, *Born Again in Brazil*, p. 145.
[50] Zaldívar, 'Relación Estado-Iglesia', p. 14.

satisfying human needs from new artificial needs that hinder the formation of a mature personality. Thus, a great deal of educational and cultural work is urgently needed, such as the education of consumers in the responsible use of their power of choice. This includes the formation of a strong sense of responsibility among producers and among people in the mass media in particular as well as the necessary intervention by public authorities.

Humanity in God's Mission

It is clear that Christ has revealed the mystery of the Trinitarian love of God for humanity. Therefore, the vocation of love which has been bestowed upon Christians is also based upon this revelation of God in His Incarnated Son. This is the revelation that lightens the dignity and the freedom of humanity. Benjamín Bravo says:

> That revelation also shows the importance of healthy relationships, which can only be experienced through life in a community. That Trinitarian relationship of God is also the basis for the relationship between individuals who have been created in the likeness of God.[51]

Humanity has the privilege of extending God's community through a community life that reflects His love for all people.

Humanity has been called to live in the communion of the Trinitarian God. Just as the three Divine members of the Trinity are in fellowship with one another, so humans discover the purpose of their existence by loving, respecting, and appreciating one another as a foundational aspect of a healthy society. Pentecostalism has rediscovered a fundamental part of the new emphasis in many traditions of the church such as koinonía. These horizons are open to human reason, for there is a connection between God and humanity when the people of God are in fellowship with one another in the bonds of God's love. It is clear then that humans are the only creatures in the world that can relate with one another as God re-

---

[51] See Benjamín Bravo, *El Fruto del Espíritu* (Lima, Peru: Ediciones Puma, 1997), pp. 72-75. The author makes the case for the dynamic role of the Holy Spirit in the Trinity and the promoter of healthy relationship with regards to humanity.

lates in the Trinity. That is how humans discover the fullness of love and fulfill God's purpose for their existence.

The destiny and the vocation of human society are established in the revelation of Christ. It is Christ in the individual who instills a true identity for the person. Thus, when humans promote integral relationships that raise dignity and enhance the quality of life, solidarity and mutual appreciation are experienced. In this kind of society, the providence of God is manifested in all His children.

Christians affirm that in the book of Genesis there is a description of the creation of humanity in the image of God. This likeness with God allowed men and women to have fellowship with Him. Genesis also describes the identity of people as well as the vocation of every individual. This book narrates the creation of humanity as a free act of God, which also reveals the wisdom of the Creator when He made them with the freedom to decide and the capacity to obey.

These characteristics provided men and women the capability to relate with God and with other fellow individuals in love and respect. These relationships gave them the ability to discover and fulfill an authentic social life and the capability to understand the integral meaning of their mission in the world. In their union with Christ, believers are capable of understanding the role and the importance of reciprocity in their approach to the Trinitarian love that has been offered to the universe in the person of the Son of God. This is all part of God's design for the happiness and wellbeing of humanity.

The book of Genesis also provides the anthropological foundations for the existence of humanity. Herein, Christian anthropology finds the basis for human dignity. It gathers evidence that describes the design of God for His creation. The creation account is performed by divine social beings that created persons with the capability to socialize in fellowship with one another. Hence, they are capable of having communion which is the basis of respect not only for other humans but also for the entire creation that God has made for the benefit of the human race. In that way men and women could live in a healthy environment and take good care of the creation according to the will of God. Moreover, this reality of humanity in society and history is rooted in the redemptive plan of

God, which takes place in the life and ministry of Jesus Christ, the Son of God, who becomes the salvation for the world.[52]

The Individual in God's Plan of Redemption

It was God the Father who offered salvation in its fullness to humanity in his only Son, Jesus Christ. It was the Father's initiative that was carried out and transmitted to humanity by the Holy Spirit. It was an integral salvation for the individual and for his or her whole person. On this subject, Vaccaro says,

> Salvation is both universal and integral. It reaches out to the individual in all his or her dimensions. It is an integral salvation that is experienced personally and socially. It affects the spiritual and material realities of men and women. This redemption is historical and also transcendent for it affects the spiritual realm of humanity.[53]

Vaccaro also adds that salvation

> becomes a reality in human history, because everything that was created continues to be good and fits the perfect will of the Creator. It is also real because the Son of God became flesh. He was a true human being who was willing to obey in order to accomplish an integral redemption for those who receive him.[54]

This plan of redemption will be completed in the future when God will judge men and women on account of their response to the redemptive plan of salvation.[55] As a result, the redeemed will share in Christ's resurrection and in the eternal communion of life with the Father in the fellowship of the Holy Spirit.

The salvation offered by God to humanity requires a free response. Humans can accept or reject Christ's offer of redemption. 'This is what faith is about and it is through faith that men and

---

[52] Peñalba, *Metamorfosis del Creyente*, p. 56.

[53] Gabriel Vaccaro, 'Reseña Histórica del Movimiento Ecuménico: Desarrollo, Opciones y Desafíos', in Carmelo Álvarez (ed.), *Pentecostalismo y Liberación: Una Experiencia Latinoamericana* (San José, Costa Rica: Departamento Ecuménico de Investigaciones, 1992), p. 218.

[54] Vaccaro, 'Aportes del Pentecostalismo,' p. 230.

[55] Vaccaro, 'Aportes del Pentecostalismo,' p. 228.

women commit their entire self to God, responding to God's su-
perabundant love'[56] and 'with concrete demonstrations of love for
their brothers and sisters in Christ and with solid hope knowing
that 'he who promised is faithful'.[57] In fact, as Juan Sepúlveda states,
'the design of the plan of salvation never consigns humans to a
condition of passivity in relation to their Redeemer. The Holy Spirit
reveals the plan of salvation to men and women who freely make
their decision to accept or reject God's redemptive plan,'[58] and just
as Jesus is a Son to his Father, the Holy Spirit also moves believers
to experience the same relationship with God the Father.[59]

The universality and integral nature of the plan of redemption
given to humanity by Christ establishes a direct link between the
redeemed and the Redeemer. He or she is now responsible for his
or her neighbor in all circumstances of life. It is clear that the description of God's covenant with Israel reveals His purpose for
humanity. All universal quests for truth and the meaning of life that
were attested by the commandments, the law of God and the ora-
cles of the prophets are completely explained in the life and ministry of Jesus Christ.

This plan of salvation finds a clear explanation and a precise expression in the teachings of Jesus Christ.

> The supreme witness of his sacrifice on the cross confirms it.
> His obedience to the Father and his love for humanity made him
> the perfect offering demanded by sinners. This evidence of love
> enabled him to respond to the scribe who asked him, 'which
> commandment is the first of all'[60]

Jesus answered with authority:

> The first is: 'Hear, O Israel: the Lord our God, the Lord is one;
> and you shall love the Lord your God with all your heart, and
> with all your soul, and with all your mind, and with all your

---

[56] Euraque, *Reinterpreting the Banana Republic*, p. 198.

[57] Peñalba, *Metamorfosis del Creyente*, p. 56

[58] Juan Sepúlveda, 'Theological Characteristics of Indigenous Pentecostalism',
p. 52.

[59] Vaccaro, 'Aportes del Pentecostalismo al Movimiento Ecuménico', p. 235.

[60] Sepúlveda, 'Theological Characteristics of Indigenous Pentecostalism,' p.
45.

strength'. The second is this: 'You shall love your neighbor as yourself'. There is no other commandment greater than these.[61]

The human heart was designed to experience a relationship with God. Believers in Christ are open to give and receive concrete love. In Christ humans are open to another individual, even when that other person may be an enemy.[62] This is so because a human's inner dimension is rooted in the commitment to justice and solidarity and to the building of a social, economic, and political life that corresponds to God's plan.

Disciples of Christ in Latin America

Evil has always threatened personal life and social relationships in the world. However, with his sacrificial death, Jesus Christ gave his followers the example of how to behave and relate with one another in the community. Samuel Solivan suggested that if believers follow Jesus' example, the meaning and the reality of life and death become important in the redemption of the community. The testimony of Christians committed to the principles of the gospel assures a new way of life in society.[63] As a new creation, believers are enabled by grace to 'walk in newness of life'.[64]

This new life has the power to influence even those outside the Christian way, for they also participate in the new society made available by God in Christ to all people. Robert Moffitt also recognizes that 'Christ died for all humanity and all people are made participants of the benefits originated in his provision'.[65] However, for the fulfillment of God's purpose, it is necessary for all persons to make a decision regarding their relationship with Christ by accepting or rejecting his offer of salvation.

---

[61] Peñalba, *Metamorfosis del Creyente*, p. 52.

[62] Villafañe, *El Espíritu Liberador*, p. 54.

[63] Solivan, *The Spirit, Pathos and Liberation*, p. 112.

[64] Peñalba, *Metamorfosis del Creyente*, p. 58.

[65] Robert Moffitt, *Si Jesús Fuera Alcalde* (Buenos Aires, Argentina: Editorial Peniel, 1997), pp. 40-54. The author argues that just as Jesus died for all humanity, in the same way his followers ought to give themselves for the sake of the good of all people. He claims that that is compatible with the redemption of God to society.

The Holy Spirit is the divine agent that reveals the real meaning of Christ to every individual, but each person is free to choose either to accept and follow Christ or to reject him. This decision will have spiritual consequences and will also affect social relationships. The Spirit makes the difference among members of the community.

It is the inner transformation that occurs in the individual that develops identity with Christ and enhances healthy relationships amongst fellow individuals. Therefore, as Benjamín Bravo says, 'the offer of the gospel appeals to the spiritual virtues and moral values and capacities of individuals who have made a permanent commitment to abide by the principles taught by Jesus Christ to his followers'.[66]

The priority of conversion is fundamental for the inner transformation that takes place in the heart of people. After conversion, men and women are called to conform to the principles of justice and move forward to the truth.[67] They are to promote this new condition of life among those who have not experienced it yet. Believers also grow in maturity, for they are able to reject evil and seek holiness instead.

It is a genuine conversion to Christ that makes it possible to love others as oneself. This new nature enables believers to persevere in this Christian conduct with a determination to work and serve the good of all members of the community. The followers of Christ become instruments of peace. They promote a new world order for everyone. In Christ there is no more room for violence and discrimination among humans. Instead, he enables believers to promote good, honest, and responsible relationships in the community. This is the evidence of the good life instilled by the Spirit of God amongst those who follow Christ.[68]

The new life in Christ also equips believers to appreciate the universe and take good care of creation. They are caretakers of the environment and become responsible for promoting a good quality of life. Evidence of redemption is in the complete restoration of all

---

[66] Bravo, *El Fruto del Espíritu*, p. 74.

[67] Bravo, *El Fruto del Espíritu*, p. 70.

[68] An account of this determination of God's people to be in solidarity with the reality of those suffering can be found in Luis Bush, 'Greater Glory Yet to Come', in Daniel Rickett and Dotsey Welliver (eds.), *Supporting Indigenous Ministries* (Wheaton, IL: Billy Graham Center, 1997), pp. 7-8.

things related to humanity, which includes spiritual, cultural, social, and economic conditions of a life worth living. Once redeemed by Christ and made a new creature, believers can love the things that God created. They recognize that those goods are made possible by the providence of God. The attitude then has to be transformed into appreciating, caring, guarding, and protecting the creation and the goods provided by God for the benefit of humanity.

Believers also thank their Divine Benefactor for all these things. They use them and enjoy their benefits in a spirit of humility and freedom. Thus, men and women are brought to a true possession of the world, as having nothing yet possessing everything: 'All (things) are yours, and you are Christ's, and Christ is God's'.[69]

The Gospel to Humanity

Most Pentecostals see the church as the sign and defender of the transcendence of the human person. They see the community of those who have been brought together by the risen Christ as the sign and safeguard of the transcendent dimension of the witness to all people in their human and spiritual condition. The community of faith is a sign and instrument of fellowship with God in Christ and of harmony, unity, and love amongst all men and women. The mission is to proclaim and communicate the salvation brought to the world by Jesus Christ, which the Bible calls 'the Kingdom of God'.[70] That is the communion that God wants to have with those who receive Him. The kingdom of God welcomes all believers who have Christ and are willing to abide by His teachings through discipleship.

The mission of the church is to proclaim the good news of God for the world in the salvation wrought by Jesus. The church also fosters the kingdom of Christ and ministers the benefits of the gospel to humanity. Moreover, the church becomes the seed for the beginning of the Kingdom of God on earth.

Based upon his experience, Leonardo Boff presents the church as the community of all believers that places herself in position to serve the kingdom of God by announcing the gospel and com-

---

[69] Peñalba, *Metamorfosis del Creyente*, p. 56.
[70] Peñalba, *Metamorfosis del Creyente*, p. 50.

municating the will of God for the new Christian communities.[71] Moreover, the community of believers serves this kingdom by spreading the gospel. This activity is an expression of God's love inherited by the church by which believers are motivated to communicate and express the blessings of the kingdom to those who accept Christ. This action of the church prepares people to accept God's redemptive in Christ Jesus his Son.

Pentecostals do not seem to be open to the ideal that this kingdom may be found even beyond the limits or confines typically assigned to the church in the history of salvation. However, they believe it is the Holy Spirit who instills individuals to believe in God. It is He who breathes God's knowledge and understanding to individuals when and where He wills.[72] Such standards include repentance and acceptance of God's redemptive work, which ends in the provision of Christ to the world.[73]

Pentecostals also agree that the political community and the church will have to remain independent from each other and autonomous in their own service. Although both are devoted to the service of humanity, there is a difference between those who work socially and those are occupied with spiritual matters. Gabriela Llano Sotelo states that for Pentecostals,

> There is a clear distinction between those who affirm that religion and politics are included in the plan of salvation. Pentecostals see religious freedom as a specific achievement obtained by

---

[71] Leonardo Boff, *When Theology Listens to the Poor* (San Francisco, CA: Harper & Row, 1984), pp. 65-66. See also José Comblin, *The Holy Spirit and Liberation* (Maryknoll, NY: Orbis Books, 1989), p. 89.

[72] Solivan, *The Spirit, Pathos and Liberation*, p. 110.

[73] José Míguez Bonino, *Poder del Evangelio y el Poder Político* (Buenos Aires, Argentina: Editorial Independiente Rúcula, 2001), pp. 64-65. Although Bonino did not speak for Pentecostalism, his expanded approach to salvation in the grace of God is significant, for he concludes that all individuals are measured in Christ, who is the beginning and the end of salvation. Bonino also speaks about the relationship between Christians and the political entities. 'Although the church is not to be confused as political system, it does affect the political system.' This has validity in regards to the political definitions presented by Pentecostals as observed after a century of Pentecostalism, particularly in Latin America, where the extremes between right and left has emerged in different contexts or in every country.

historical Christianity, and this is one of its contributions to humanity.[74]

Religious freedom is not a goal in itself but a state achieved in favor of humanity during the course of proclaiming the gospel to the world.

In reference to the plan of salvation, Pentecostals believe that Christ brought about a saving purpose and an eschatological end, which can be received by those who accept him and will be fully attained in the life to come. According to Roberto Dominguez,[75] the community of faith offers a significant concern for humanity, which impels believers to work for the benefit of humankind. This contribution is important because it makes history even more human and also motivates Christians to offer themselves as safeguards against all forms of totalitarianism.[76] When believers get involved in this endeavor, they are capable of showing men and women their integral vocation and definitive mission on earth.

The preaching of the Gospel, the living in the Spirit, and the experience of fraternal communion are common distinctions that identify a typical Pentecostal community. These virtues contribute to elevate the individual's dignity and his or her society. It consolidates noble social purposes and endows sound activities, whereby men and women will enter into a deeper sense of human meaning and responsibility.

When it comes to concrete historical facts, most Pentecostals argue that the coming of the kingdom of God cannot be merely reduced to the level of social, economic, or political activity. Rather, it is seen in the level of developing a human social life that is integral in its meaning and reality. At this level, humanity is able to attain

---

[74] See Gabriela Llano Sotelo, *Pentecostalismo y Cambio Social: El Caso de la Colonia Emiliano Zapata en Hermosillo, Sonora* (México, DF: INHA, 1995), p. 108. Another significant source is the work of Silvie Pedron Colombani about the transformation of Pentecostalism in Guatemala. See Silvie Pedron Colombani, 'Pentecostalismo y Transformación Religiosa', in Jean Pierre Bastian (ed.) *La Modernidad Religiosa Latinoamericana* (México, DF: Fondo de Cultura Económica, 2004), pp. 133-59; See also Cleary and Stewart-Gambino, *Power, Politics, and Pentecostals in Latin America*, pp. 112-13.

[75] See the work of Roberto Dominguez, *Pioneros de Pentecostés en el Mundo de Habla Hispana: México y Centro América* (Barcelona, España: CLIE, 1990), p. 114.

[76] See Sepúlveda, 'Un Puerto para los Náufragos de la Modernidad', pp. 261-78.

justice, peace, wholeness, and solidarity, which become doors that have to remain open in order to access the transformational work of the Holy Spirit in favor of society.

This chapter, theological in nature, explored the Pentecostal approach to mission among the poor and marginalized. In the first part, I dialogued with Pentecostal scholars in Latin America who write with regards to the theology of social responsibility. I started with the assumption that most Pentecostals take on their mission service from the poor to the poor. This context is unique. The mission work is studied as being carried by missionaries who initiated their service in their own context of poverty.[77] They are the ones who know how to approach the poor and marginalized.

With this framework in perspective, I explored this Pentecostal approach to integral mission. The secondary question had to do with how Pentecostals perceive themselves as missionaries to their world, so this study was necessary in order to see how they perceive themselves as mission workers. In their response, one could observe a commitment to evangelize and to serve those who are socio-economically disadvantaged.

Pentecostals realize their commitment to mission goes far beyond spiritual redemption. They are becoming involved in socio-economic and political decisions that affect not only their communities but also the entire society.[78] Perhaps among different challenges, Pentecostals are now learning to document their own history of their participation in the development of their community.

In the second part of this chapter I examined the Pentecostals' theological attitude toward matters related to morality and the economy. Since I had initiated a dialogue with the RCC teachings on social responsibility in chapter three, in this chapter I contrasted the RCC concept of integral development to explore the levels of solidarity in the community to the understanding and practice of integral mission by the Pentecostal churches. I argue that this dialogue proposes significant insights for the debate on integral mission in Latin America as a whole.

---

[77] On the matter of integral mission among the poor, see David Ruiz, *La Transformación de la Iglesia* (Bogotá, Colombia: COMIBAM, 2006), p. 23.

[78] See for instance Alexis Pacheco, 'Let Those Who Have Never Been Heard, Be Heard', *World History Archives* (Washington, DC: World Bank, 1998), pp. 2-4.

Although morality and the economy are themes continually used in RCC circles, Pentecostals are also learning to handle such issues as they affect their own communities. As I said earlier, they are now participating in forums where transparency, decency, and trust are being implemented on all levels in the community. This approach may challenge Pentecostals to teach issues such as peace and justice in the moral fields and the socio-economic affairs of the nation.

In the third part of the chapter, I explored Pentecostals' notion toward the development of the human person in God's plan of love. At this point, I realized it was necessary to study the Pentecostal approach to salvation for the individual, the community, and the whole person in order to develop an integral understanding of the practice of mission. Moreover, since Pentecostals appear to be mostly community oriented, I decided to look also at the Pentecostal motivation toward common areas related to mission such as education and cultural formation. However, a significant number of Pentecostal organizations are now promoting education in order to transform the culture.

The study organized material discovered through participant observation and literature search. It highlights what is considered to be the distinctive marks of Pentecostal mission in Latin America. It includes a discussion of current trends of mission thinking and practice. In addition, it is important to recognize that there may be some similarities and differences found with regard to traditionally known patterns of holistic mission practiced by other evangelical groups in Latin America.

7

WIDENING THE STUDY OF *MISSIO DEI*

In this section we build the case for a broader perspective of mission, so for that purpose we will refer to the Pentecostal community in general. This study intends to input mission information that will inform the understanding of mission among Pentecostals in general.

Donald E. Miller and Tetsunao Yamamori have already done a significant work in the field of social action as observed in their study on progressive Pentecostal theology. Miller and Yamamori have moved out from that stream of Pentecostalism that emphasizes personal salvation to the exclusion of any attempt to transform the community. Instead they have adopted a new field of action in Christian service. They are calling it Progressive Pentecostalism.[1]

Miller and Yamamori define Progressive Pentecostals 'as Christians who claim to be inspired by the Holy Spirit and the life of Jesus and seek to holistically address the spiritual, physical, and social needs of people in their community'.[2] These emerging Pentecostals are known by their contemporary and expressive praise and worship. They empower lay people for ministry. They also show genuine compassion to the holistic needs of people. Progressive Pentecostals serve the individual and the community. They perceive

---

[1] Donald E. Miller and Tetsunao Yamamori (eds.), *Global Pentecostalism: The New Face of Christian Social Engagement* (Los Angeles, CA: University of California Press, 2007), p. 2.

[2] Miller and Yamamori, *Global Pentecostalism: The New Face of Christian Social Engagement*, p. 3.

the move of the Holy Spirit individually and in the worshipping community.[3]

With Miller and Yamamori's definition in mind, we have organized new ideas and insights that arise from the previous sections. Once we have classified the issues, we will proceed to analyze them with the purpose to establishing creative proposals, which may be useful to understand Pentecostal integral mission. During the course of the discussion, we make reference to some points that require further research and reflection. Nevertheless, those issues pointed out here are useful to this work.

We discuss finally the reason why Pentecostals seem to be successful in building communities referred to here as communities of faith. Such communities base their faith and action around spiritual principles, values, and virtues. Pentecostal communities have been established mostly among the poor and marginalized. As we have seen, in recent decades, the RCC and other Christian organizations have assumed the position of opting for the poor in their approach to mission.[4]

The difference between mission service provided by Christian entities and the Pentecostal church could be explained this way: Pentecostal mission starts from and within the poor. Pentecostals did not have to go to the poor. They are the poor and their missiology comes from within as a movement of the poor. Poverty is part of their historical background. Their faith and commitments taught them to overcome poverty with the transforming work of the Holy Spirit, which is initiated by the practice of the gospel from the inside out. Liberation theologians may argue that they also come from the poor. The difference lies in the spiritual approach. Pentecostals act out of spiritual conviction, while liberation theologians seem to

---

[3] Miller and Yamamori, *Global Pentecostalism*, p. 3.

[4] The preferential option for the poor is one of the significant teachings for social service in the Roman Catholic Church of Latin America. Pedro Arrupe used the phrase 'option for the poor' in 1968 in a letter to the Jesuits of Latin America. As a developed theological principle, Gustavo Gutierrez, first articulated it in his landmark book on liberation theology. See Gutiérrez, *A Theology of Liberation*, pp. 67-72. See also Gerald S. Twomey, 'The Preferential Option for the Poor', *Catholic Social Thought from John XXIII to John Paul II* (Vatican: Edwin Mellen Press, 2005), pp. 278-90.

have acted out of socio-political and religious convictions which were not compatible with Pentecostals.[5]

Some Pentecostal churches, however, still struggle in their understanding of mission because they tend to spiritualize social ills. Poverty, injustice, and illness are seen as direct consequences of evil activity in human nature. Pentecostals may find it beneficial to learn how to address the issue of institutional sin and recognize that social evils could also be produced by evil structures of power that work against God's purpose for humanity. However, Pentecostals seem to be expanding their faith beyond beliefs and committing to more faithful practicalities. Although current Pentecostal churches are paying more attention to church growth, such numbers are also generating the ability to affect the community by transforming old paradigms into new life standards that will complete the fullness of God's purpose for the community. To meet such demands, Pentecostals may have to re-focus their attention to areas of service such as community development and integral assistance to the poor that are social responsibilities that do not seem to be intentionally included in most contemporary Pentecostal ministries.

Evangelism and Social Concern

As we have seen, Pentecostals understand the community of believers as God's dwelling place with men and women. With regards to community life David Bosch states,

> Pentecostal believers share their joys and hopes, their anxieties and sadness, stand with every man and woman of every place and time, to bring them the good news of new life in the Kingdom of God. Christ Jesus manifested the signs of God's king-

---

[5] One significant contributor to understanding integral mission among the poor in Latin America is René Padilla. From his integral approach to mission he would probably describe himself as an Anabaptist, i.e. a Baptist in the tradition of the intentional Christian community, although the theological influences that he has imbibed are quite eclectic. Padilla has edited several books, as well as written articles in influential academic journals. Although this affirmation is yet to be proven, Padilla has also influenced Pentecostals with his teachings on integral missional. See for instance C. René Padilla, 'A Message for the Whole Person', *Transformation* 9.3 (1993), p. 1. See also Padilla, 'Evangelism and Social Responsibility', p. 27.

dom. This has come and continues to be present among those who believe.[6]

Bosch also suggests that it is in the present world where the church serves as the agency, whereby

> God shares his love and hope. God's love inspires and sustains every commitment to human freedom and advancement. The church is present amongst mankind as God's dwelling place. In it men and women find support and solidarity, which is an expression of the redeeming love of Christ.[7]

This idea leads to the assumption that the community of faith is neither an abstract ideal nor a simple spiritual teaching. The church was designed to serve people in the context of human history and in the real world. Thus, believers are inspired by the Spirit of love to serve the community. That way, believers show their willingness to cooperate with God's divine redemptive plan for humanity.

Darío López states that every person is unique in his or her individuality and that every individual establishes his or her relationships in a free society with others.[8] With this framework in mind, Valerio Gerber suggests that human life was designed in a way that individuals could network with people who also have the capability to relate to other individuals and social groups. Pentecostals could also assist their 'people to invest in the formation of social communities for the advancement of their personal and family groups'.[9] These are some of the factors that 'originate and shape society with structures that express its political, economic, juridical, and cultural constructs'.[10] Then rightly so, Pentecostals affirm that the Holy

---

[6] On this issue, see David J. Bosch, *Transforming Mission: Paradigm Shifts in Theology of Mission* (Maryknoll, NY: Orbis Books, 1996), pp. 99-113. Although not cited as a Pentecostal scholar, Bosch's classic volume has been translated into Spanish and consulted at most training programs across Latin America.

[7] Bosch, *Transforming Mission*, p. 92. On the same topic, see also López, *El Nuevo Rostro del Pentecostalismo Latinoamericano*, p. 68.

[8] López, *El Nuevo Rostro del Pentecostalismo Latinoamericano*, p. 56.

[9] Vergil Gerber, *Missions in Creative Tension: The Green Lake '71 Compendium* (Pasadena, CA: William Carey Library, 1971), p. 56. The author discusses the way Christians work through natural networks built on relationships that occur in the context of the local church. Basically the same experience happens among the Pentecostal communities in different contexts.

[10] Gerber, *Missions in Creative Tension*, p. 56.

Spirit is the agent who enables the church to become efficient in serving the community. Therefore, in David Harley's words at the end of one of his works, 'the church is therefore able to understand humanity in his or her vocation and aspirations, limits and misgivings, in his or her rights and duties, and to speak a word of life that reverberates in the historical and social circumstances of human existence'.[11]

Permeating Society with the Gospel

Pentecostal churches seem to be successful at proclaiming the gospel. The high number of believers testifies that; however, they seem to show limitations in the presentation of the redemptive and transformative mission of the gospel. Because of that, they seem to be limited in the advancement of the community. For example, the field of education still seems to be one of the major challenges for them to overcome. Pentecostals may have to revise their understanding and practice of integral mission if they are to enrich and permeate society with the transforming mission of the gospel.

The way Pentecostals serve the community could indicate their levels of spirituality and commitment to transform the life of every individual affected by their ministry. The deficiency may lie in their instruction as agents of social transformation. They do not have a theology of integral mission incorporated into their teachings. In reality, Pentecostals have not been indifferent to the suffering of the poor and the marginalized. They are aware of these difficult situations that negatively affect society.

Pentecostals have been attentive to the moral conditions of the community. In their own way, Pentecostals have promoted the human aspects that enrich people's lives. For them

> Society is not simply a secular and worldly reality, and therefore, foreign to the message of salvation. Instead, Pentecostals understand that the best of the community is accomplished when the principles of the gospel are observed. For Pentecostals, society is

---

[11] David Harley, *Preparing to Serve: Training for Cross-Cultural Mission* (Pasadena, CA: William Carey Library, 1995), p. 89.

made up of men and women who are the primary subjects to be served by the church.[12]

What Pentecostals need is to develop a solid teaching of integral mission that will strengthen their current efforts in the community.

Through their current teachings, Pentecostals realize that it is the Holy Spirit who inspires believers to proclaim the message of redemption wrought by Christ in the gospel. Redemption also carries the purpose of transforming human history. However, in the back of their minds Pentecostals seem to view this transformation as a secondary goal as one of the blessings of being redeemed. Therefore, since social transformation is not considered part of the core of redemption, those who advocate for integral mission would notice something missing in the Pentecostal teachings. 'The community of faith proclaims the gospel in the power of the Holy Spirit and in love, bearing witness to men and women, in the name of Christ Jesus, to the dignity and fellowship with persons'.[13]

Another area of concern is the teaching of peace and justice in conformity with the principles of the gospel. Carmelo Álvarez advocates for these teachings to be openly taught not only at seminaries but also studied at the local church level by all members of the congregation. Álvarez asks Pentecostals to leave their comfort zone of the neighborhood and proceed to defend and speak boldly in favor of peace and justice.[14]

In reality, social justice and peace are part of the core of integral mission. For Lopez these are also Pentecostal concerns because they deliver a message that brings spiritual, moral, and social freedom to humanity.[15] This means, 'the gospel has the effectiveness of truth and grace that comes from the Spirit of God, who penetrates

---

[12] Bosch, *Transforming Mission*, p. 96.

[13] For more information on the theology of power and love, see Daniel L. Migliore, *Faith Seeking Understanding: An Introduction to Christian Theology* (Grand Rapids, MI: Eerdmans, 2004), pp. 312-21.

[14] See Carmelo Álvarez, *Santidad y Compromiso: El Riesgo de Vivir el Evangelio* (México, D.F.: Casa Unida de Publicaciones, 1985), pp. 25-34. This debate on holiness, peace, and justice was initiated at Pentecostal circles at a slow pace, but it continued to draw more attention, particularly in the most recent scholarship. Unfortunately, the topic continues to be omitted or avoided at denominational leadership levels. Nevertheless, the theme seems to gain more ground at schools and seminaries where the new leaders are trained.

[15] López, *El Nuevo Rostro del Pentecostalismo Latinoamericano*, p. 61.

hearts, predisposing them to thoughts and designs of love, justice, freedom, and peace'.[16] By transforming society with the gospel, Pentecostals will have to

> infuse freedom, which is found in the gospel, into the human heart. That is the gospel that promotes a society befitting humanity in Christ Jesus. They ought to build a community that is more human because it is a society in greater conformity with the purpose of God for the world.[17]

Through their involvement in community service, Pentecostals will have to carry out their mission at a local level. There they will serve as instruments of social transformation. Hence, in the redemptive mission that Christ entrusted to them, there is also room for the supernatural to take place, especially in attending to the poor, the weak, and the marginalized. The supernatural dimension is also an expression of the unlimited power of Pentecost to transform people's lives. This dimension is also an expression of the integral power of the gospel.[18] It is good though that 'Pentecostals do not understand the supernatural as an entity or as a place that begins where the natural ends. Instead they see it as the union of the supernatural with the natural, whereby the natural is lifted a higher level through holiness.'[19] For Norberto Saracco, it is clear that 'for Pentecostals everything that belongs to the human order is also part of the supernatural, for in the exercise of the supernatural the human condition is also found within it,'[20] and that is so because the person is living in the Spirit. Thus, the gifts of the Holy Spirit are delivered in order to assist the limitations of humanity, and because of that, those who participate in the love of God are able to exercise them. Likewise, Jesus Christ is also the fulfillment of all things in the present social order.[21] Through him, humanity is able to recover its original connection with the Creator of life, wisdom,

---

[16] See Bueno, 'The Struggle for Social Space', pp. 171-91.

[17] Bueno, 'The Struggle for Social Space', p. 172.

[18] Chandler Russell, 'Fanning the Charismatic Fire', *Christianity Today* 12.4 (1967), pp. 39-40.

[19] Russell, 'Fanning the Charismatic Fire', p. 39.

[20] Saracco, *The Word and the Spirit in the Evangelizing Community*, p. 12.

[21] Dayton, *Raíces Teológicas del Pentecostalism*, pp. 26-30.

and love.[22] Indeed, 'God so loved the world that he gave his only begotten Son'.[23] Since this connection was lost with the first Adam, God has re-connected with humanity through the last Adam, Jesus his Son.[24]

The Pentecostal teaching of redemption begins with the Incarnation, by which the Son of God takes on all that is human except sin according to the solidarity established by the wisdom of the Creator and embraces everything in His gift of redeeming love.[25] Humanity then is touched by this love in the fullness of his being, which is corporeal and spiritual, in solidarity with others. Hence, the whole person is involved in the mission of the gospel. The community of believers follows a path enlightened with a mission that is integral involving an effective action in favor of the poor and the weak. Pentecostal believers understand that they are faithful to the gospel when they offer themselves as instruments of transformation in the hands of God. They become agents of integral redemption to those who receive Christ as Lord and Savior.[26] This is one of the marks of Pentecostalism, especially in the condition of human suffering. The combination of the proclamation of the gospel to the poor and marginalized with the action and assistance of the supernatural generates new life and gives hope to people.

Evangelism and Human Advancement

The discussion starts here by affirming that social service will have to be embraced by Pentecostals as an integral part of their ministry. They are becoming aware that there is a profound relationship between evangelization and human advancement. They are also aware that this relationship is part of an anthropological condition be-

---

[22] Padilla, *A Message for the Whole Person*, p. 2.

[23] See Jn 3.16 and the comment of López, *El Nuevo Rostro del Pentecostalismo Latinoamericano*, p. 65.

[24] Russell, 'Fanning the Charismatic Fire', p. 39.

[25] David Burrell states that the Pentecostal doctrine of mission embraces solidarity with the human needs, which are included in the gift of redemption. See David Burrell, *Freedom and Creation in Three Traditions* (Notre Dame, IN: University of Notre Dame Press, 1994), p. 210.

[26] Roger Cabezas, 'Despertar Ecuménico del Pentecostalismo Latinoamericano', in CEPLA, *Jubileo: La Fiesta del Espíritu. Identidad y Misión del Pentecostalismo Latinoamericano* (Maracaibo, Venezuela: CEPLA, 2001), pp. 78-91.

cause the individual who connects with the gospel also forms part of a social environment and a particular economic situation.[27] At this point we are ready to say that Pentecostals may have to incorporate these teachings in their theological foundations.

Comblin also argues 'since the proclamation of the gospel is an activity that cannot be disassociated from the plan of God for the creation and the redemption of humanity, both proclamation and social responsibility must stick together in mission'.[28] Therefore, it is fair to affirm here that God's redemptive plan reaches the human condition in concrete circumstances such as poverty, suffering, and injustice.

Daniel Chiquete also emphasizes, 'God's purpose is to restore and transform that which has been disfigured or distorted by the power of evil'.[29] Thus, the community of believers is also aware of its responsibility and participation in the redemptive mission, which is manifested in the Incarnation of Jesus Christ. Accordingly, Pentecostals may need to adjust their approach to evangelization by integrating social responsibility in mission. Together with proclamation of the gospel, they may benefit by learning to promote peace and justice for the advancement of humanity.

Social Responsibility

This debate of social responsibility is born out of the relationship between the gospel message and the community. Understood in this way, social responsibility is the distinctive whereby Pentecostals may commit themselves to carrying out the proclamation of the gospel and assuming a prophetic role. This proposal is for Pentecostals to recognize that teaching and spreading the gospel with social responsibility is essential to ministry by the community of faith.

This concept of integral mission takes into consideration the consequences of the message proclaimed and social actions in-

---

[27] From his Catholic charismatic background, José Comblin describes how the base communities of Brazil have linked redemption to the social and economic situation of the community. José Comblin, 'Brazil: Base Communities in the Northeast', in Guillermo Cook (ed.), *New Face of the Church in Latin America: Between Tradition and Change* (New York, NY: Obis Books, 1994), pp. 205-25.

[28] Comblin, 'Brasil', p. 218.

[29] Chiquete, 'Healing, Salvation and Mission', p. 12.

volved. Evidently the message will initiate spiritual change, which will affect the community's daily work and struggles for justice in the context of bearing witness to Christ as the Savior. At this point, Burrell's argument is valid; he says 'social mission is also part of the very heart of Christian service'.[30] This teaching may offer refreshing ideas to Pentecostals as they effectively engage in social responsibility. Pentecostals may now see the mystery of salvation as a service that stems not only from the proclamation of the gospel but also from leading in the transformation of the community.

It is clear that the Pentecostal community cannot assume all responsibility for what happens in the community, but it could speak with authority and competence against social evils and in favor of what is good for the people. When these matters are integrated to the proclamation of the gospel, then the community is benefited. On this subject, Donald Dayton has written,

> Jesus did not bequeath to the church a mission merely in the political, economic, or social order. The purpose Christ assigned to his followers was holistic and included both the physical and spiritual realities of people.[31]

Dayton also adds, 'this mission of evangelization can be the source of commitment, direction, and vigor to establish and consolidate a community according to the law and purpose of God for humanity'.[32] As we have seen, Pentecostals do not intervene directly in technical questions with regards to social concerns, but their Christian principles enable them to act as the Holy Spirit guides them in any given political or socio-economic circumstance. They seem to be skillful to implement their principles and have the ability to propose systems or models of social organization that benefit the common interest of people. This is more relevant in the most marginalized areas where the local church usually takes the initiative to find solutions to problems of common interest for the people.

Although Pentecostals realize that this is not the only mission entrusted by Christ to their community of faith, some still insist that 'the church's competence comes from the principles of the gospel — believers are to proclaim the truth that sets individuals

---

[30] Burrell, *Freedom and Creation in Three Traditions*, p. 208.
[31] Dayton, *Raíces Teológicas del Pentecostalismo*, p. 129.
[32] Dayton, *Raíces Teológicas del Pentecostalismo*, p. 129.

free, which is the message proclaimed and witnessed to by the Son of God made human'.[33] Yet a new generation of Pentecostals is becoming involved in the principles of integral mission, which may lead to a more significant presentation of the gospel.

Confronting Evil in Socio-Political Structures

Some Pentecostals still adhere to the traditional teaching that the ministry of believers is to assist individuals to find the path of salvation. This seems to be their primary and sole purpose for ministry. This action provides them with an overall idea that the social teaching is not needed in the church. If the church becomes involved in social action, it may miss its goal that is proclaiming the gospel of salvation to the lost.[34] These Pentecostals believe that the community of faith has the responsibility to teach the truth and the way of integrity to people. They also understand that believers need to serve their fellow citizens in order to make Christian principles real to humanity. They teach that the purpose of the gospel is to put its principles into practice.[35] For them true faith and sound behavior will be manifested in the field of practice, which involves believers sharing their lives with other individuals in the community. Whether or not these responsibilities seem spiritual, their purpose remains focused on the human being whom God calls by means of the Christian community to participate in his gift of salvation.

Other Pentecostals see missiology as the discipline that teaches to embrace the idea that

> people will not respond to the gift of salvation through partial, abstract or merely verbal acceptance, but with the whole of their lives. Men and women leave their old lifestyle to initiate anew,

---

[33] A theological explanation to the matter of church participation in changing social structures is found in Paul Freston, 'Pentecostalism in Latin America: Characteristic and Controversies', *Social Compass* 45.3 (1998), pp. 335-58.

[34] For a better understanding of the development of social doctrine in the evangelical church of Latin America, see Hong In Sik, *¿Una Iglesia Posmoderna? En Busca de un Modelo de Iglesia y Misión en la Era Posmoderna* (Buenos Aires, Argentina: Ediciones Kairós, 2001), pp. 72-86.

[35] Russell, 'Fanning the Charismatic Fire', p. 40.

which is also relevant and testifies of their redemption in Christ.[36]

These Pentecostals do not see mission as a privilege, but instead 'they think of it as the right and responsibility that believers have to proclaim the gospel in the context of community'.[37] That will make the liberating Word of the gospel transforming in the complex worlds of production, labor, business, finance, trade, politics, law, culture, and social communications, where men and women live and work'.[38] For these Pentecostals mission is not restricted to a purely private sphere, and the Christian message is not relegated to a purely spiritual salvation incapable of shedding light on human earthly existence.

Therefore, it is significant that some Pentecostals are interested in learning that they cannot remain indifferent to social matters. These believers are aware that mission is to instill spiritual and moral principles in the community including those pertaining to social order and to denounce prophetically any human injustice.

Political Participation

Pentecostals view God's mission not as a simple participation in activities of benevolence. Instead, they think of it as part of a mission that was formed over the course of time to participate in social solutions using diverse actions according to the teachings of the gospel.[39] Nevertheless, Pentecostals realize that there are adjustments that have to take place in their mission thinking in order to continue with their ministry successfully. Such adjustments have to do with methods and epistemological definitions of integral mis-

---

[36] A good source to understand the wholeness of Pentecostal mission is found in Allan H. Anderson, 'Towards a Pentecostal Missiology for the Majority World', in Grant McClung (ed.), *Azusa Street and Beyond* (Gainesville, FL: Bridge-Logos, 2006), pp. 169-89.

[37] See Allan H. Anderson, 'Structures and Patterns in Pentecostal Mission', *Missionalia* 32.3 (2004), pp. 233-49.

[38] Anderson, 'Structures and Patterns in Pentecostal Mission', pp. 233-49.

[39] This line of thought is shared by Quentin Schultz, 'Orality and Power in Latin American Pentecostalism', in Donald E. Miller (ed.), *Coming of Age: Protestantism in Contemporary Latin America* (Boston, MA: University Press, 1994), pp. 65-88.

sion, theology, and practice. At the moment, Pentecostals associate social responsibility (which also includes political participation) with the experience of Christian life.

However, according to Juan Sepúlveda, 'theology and particularly, mission theology cannot be defined by socio-economic parameters only'.[40] Thus, the gospel does not present mission as an ideology nor as a pragmatic political or socio-economic system that intends to change or create new political structures or socio-economic patterns aligned to particular interests. On the contrary, Sepulveda adds, 'Pentecostals are looking at mission as an instrument of reflection and practice of socio-economic and political justice, which ought to be exercised in accordance with the principles of the gospel'.[41] Therefore, Pentecostal mission is also looking at ways to interpret and implement Christian principles to the reality of the community. Sepulveda also acknowledges that Pentecostals are also

> determining how they will approach human vocation, which once was considered earthly and transcendent. They want to guide believers to choose wisely with their participation in Christian service in order to fulfill the purpose of the gospel in the community.[42]

Pentecostal churches interpret social doctrine as theological in nature, specifically theological and moral, since it is a doctrine aimed at guiding people's spiritual and moral behavior. Regarding this matter Doug Peterson said,

> Pentecostals find this teaching at the crossroads where Christian life and conscience come into contact with the real world. They see it in the efforts of individuals, families, people involved in evangelism, cultural and social life, as well as politicians and statesmen to give it a concrete form and application in history.[43]

---

[40] Sepúlveda, 'Pentecostalism as Popular Religiosity', pp. 80-88.

[41] Sepúlveda, 'Pentecostalism as Popular Religiosity', p. 82.

[42] Sepúlveda, 'Pentecostalism as Popular Religiosity', p. 93.

[43] Although Douglas Petersen did not specifically address the matter of Pentecostal theology of moral behavior, he does seem to imply that Pentecostal mission is generally focused on the behavioral change when the person is inducted into the community of faith. See Douglas Petersen, 'Pentecostals: Who

Brian Smith also states,

> Pentecostal mission observes at least three areas of interest in social service: (1) the theological basis that motivates mission into action; (2) the principles that drive believers to transform society and (3) the spiritual intentionality that generates the power and the ability to face any given situation for the good of people.[44]

These areas of interest help the church define the method and motivation that believers use in the transformation of society.

In principle, Pentecostals' social responsibility finds its strength in biblical and spiritual revelation on the practice of the faith by great-commission-committed Christians. The Holy Spirit is the source of inspiration and understanding of the gospel. He drives believers into social service and inspires them to understand human needs and to guide individuals to enhance human life. In God's plan for humanity, He created men and women with the capacity of fellowship with one another. The practice of this principle is important in the transformation of the community.

Smith also said, 'Christians receive the divine Word by faith and put it into practice when it is activated by the Holy Spirit, who also interacts with reason in the practice of mission'.[45] Reason structures the understanding of faith and leads it into practical action. For Smith, 'mission is accomplished when it is driven beyond knowledge and understanding into practical circumstances of human life. Mission deals with the typical difficulties and the needs of people in their context of their life.'[46]

As long as Pentecostal mission remains centered on the teachings of Christ, there is no danger of weakening its transformative ability. Eldin Villafañe also points out that since 'the revelation of Christ by the Holy Spirit illuminates the ministry of believers

---

are They?' in Vinay Samuel and Chris Sugden (eds.), *Mission as Transformation: A Theology of the Whole Gospel* (Oxford, UK: Regnum Books, 1999), pp. 76-111.

[44] Both Catholics and Pentecostals in Latin America could find these three levels of missiological teaching in the Pentecostal community in the descriptive approach of Brian Smith to the matter of social concerns. Brian Smith, *Religious Politics in Latin America: Pentecostal vs. Catholic* (Notre Dame, IN: University of Notre Dame Press, 1998), pp. 86-112.

[45] Smith, *Religious Politics in Latin America*, p. 92.

[46] Smith, *Religious Politics in Latin America*, p. 98.

through service, they find understanding of the meaning of human dignity and the ethical requirements inherent to it'.[47] Pentecostal mission, then, is the ability to transform society through faith and obedience to Jesus Christ. By faith they also develop a greater capacity to impart knowledge and to transform people with the truth that affirms solidarity with those who remain marginalized by the negative circumstances of life.

Mission in Dialogue with other Sources of Knowledge

The teaching of integral mission should also be able to draw information from other sources of knowledge. It should have the ability to dialogue with interdisciplinary and academic scholarship. This Pentecostal mission could become capable of discussing themes such as the incarnation of the truth in a changing society continually affected by political and social ingredients that require interdisciplinary discussions in order to present the cause effectively.[48] It should be able to understand and dialogue with those disciplines concerned with humanity and look for options that could contribute to the well-being of humanity.

According to Villafañe, this theology of integral mission could be capable of making significant use of the various disciplines that build their structures of knowledge on the principles of philosophy. 'Pentecostal integral mission should be capable of using descriptive analysis and reports that come out of the human sciences'.[49] However, Pentecostal missiologists are aware of the fact that neither philosophy nor the social sciences are neutral. They have their own structures and core values that determine, to a considerable degree, what they describe and the conclusions they deduce from their observations. Nonetheless, dialogue is necessary and has to be done in accordance with scriptural and spiritual principles that are natural to missiology as well as to Pentecostalism.

Although Pentecostals may not have dialogued with the social sciences, it may be valuable to recognize that a significant contribu-

---

[47] Villafañe, *El Espíritu Liberador*, pp. 123-30.

[48] See for instance, Cleary, 'Latin American Pentecostalism', pp. 131-45.

[49] Villafañe, *El Espíritu Liberador*, p. 121.

tion to the development of mission theology could also be obtained from an objective dialogue with them. In a way Cleary admits,

> The church could receive valuable ideas from the social sciences, which could facilitate missiological and anthropological understanding of humanity. There is a wider range and complexity of knowledge that derives from the networking activity experienced through social relations.[50]

This attentive and constant openness to other branches of knowledge could make Pentecostal mission relevant and reliable in contemporary ministry. The contributions of the various disciplines of the social sciences could add valuable elements that would enhance a theology of Pentecostal integral mission. This approach to knowledge could also open opportunities for Pentecostal believers to speak to individuals in more convincing manners. It would allow them to be more effective in fulfilling the task of incarnating the revelation of the Word of God in the conscience of people, thus making social responsibility relevant in integral mission theology.[51]

Moreover, social sciences will have to recognize the relevance of theology of integral mission. This could validate an interdisciplinary dialogue that challenges the social sciences to study Christian mission from another angle. Theology of integral mission aims at serving humanity from a biblical and spiritual perspective. The incarnation of the gospel in society could provide the opportunity for believers to promote and work for the benefit of society with the principles of the gospel.

Mission in the Community of Faith

A theology of integral mission belongs to the community of believers. This is so because local congregations are the agents that propose and formulate its objectives as well as the dissemination of its principles and teachings. Integral mission is not the prerogative of a specialized group in the church. Instead it is the objective and

---

[50] Cleary, 'Latin American Pentecostalism', p. 140.

[51] Concerning the interdisciplinary dialogue of Pentecostalism, Jorge Soneira wrote an article that focuses on the field of missiology. See Jorge Soneira, 'Los Estudios Sociológicos Sobre el Pentecostalismo en América Latina', *Sociedad y Religión* 8.1 (1991), pp. 60-67.

goal of all believers who are part of a community of faith. For Vaccaro, integral mission also expresses the way the congregation understands and approaches social structures and community attitudes towards social, economic, and political responsibility.[52] Pentecostals could benefit to learn how to stimulate the community of faith to participate in the planning, definition, and purpose of integral mission. Leaders could trust believers to assume different and specific tasks that make use of gifts and natural abilities available to the community of faith.

These contributions would be expressions of the commitment made by believers associated with God. They also bear witness to the appreciation for the supernatural found among Pentecostals. This combination of natural and supernatural activities enables believers to appreciate their Pentecostal faith and stimulates unity in the church to promote missional teachings as part of the nature of church. It also affirms Christian education, which carries the responsibility to form people capable of exercising the ministry of teaching in the areas of faith and morals with the authority received from the Holy Spirit. The church's mission is not only the thought or work of qualified persons but also the thought of the congregation insofar as it enables believers in the work of ministry.

Therefore, in the Pentecostal community if social responsibility is taught intentionally, one required component is the teaching and acceptance of the priesthood of all believers. That understanding determines the direction of the development of mission. This teaching, in turn, is integrated into the general ministry of the church in the concrete and particular situations of the many circumstances. This integration gives a precise definition to this teaching, translating it and putting it into practice. Snell states, 'understanding mission, in its most extensive meaning, helps the validation of the contributions and emphasis put on the concept of mission practiced in the community of faith'.[53] Let us also bear in mind that

---

[52] See for instance, Vaccaro, *Identidad Pentecostal*, p. 40. Also, Cornelia Butler Flora, *Pentecostalism in Colombia* (Rutherford, NJ: Farleigh Dickinson University Press, 1976), pp. 31-36.

[53] For some insights about Pentecostal care and social responsibility, see Jeffrey T. Snell, 'Beyond the Individual and Into the World: A Call to Participation into the Larger Purposes of the Spirit on the Basis of Pentecostal Theology', *Pneuma: The Journal of the Society for Pentecostal Studies* 4.1 (1992), pp. 45-46.

mission education also focuses on the integration of the body of believers in the process of service.

Pentecostals also seem to be paying attention to the corrective measures of their approach to the church's teaching of mission. For decades they have integrated their mission mandate integrally to the needs of the community. By conferring the same dignity and authority to these fields of service, they have taken an essential step in the development of the community at large. Concerning this matter, Murray Dempster has said,

> The Pentecostal weight of mission teaching requires solid involvement from the part of leaders, who also model mission to their students. Mission has to be taught all the time and it should be the object of support by all members of the community of faith.[54]

Mission of Reconciliation

Essentially, the object of Pentecostal mission is to reach out to the individual with the offer of salvation, which is integral to its purpose and scope. The person is also entrusted to the church to care for him or her with spiritual and human responsibility. By virtue of its mission, the community of faith is enabled by the Holy Spirit to show integral concern for every individual. The community of faith is made aware of the importance of enhancing the quality of life and social relationships, which are built upon integral justice and godly love.

The convergence of these elements becomes the very fabric of human society. For Anthea Butler, 'mission depends decisively on the quality of protection and promotion offered to humanity. In the end, this mission seeks the promotion and implementation of this condition in every community that has come to exist in the world'.[55]

---

[54] Murray Dempster, 'Christian Social Concern in Pentecostal Perspective: Reformulating Pentecostal Eschatology', *Journal of Pentecostal Theology* 2 (1993), pp. 52-53.

[55] Anthea Butler, 'Facets of Pentecostal Spirituality', *Consultation with Pentecostals in the Americas* (San José, Costa Rica: World Council of Churches, 1996), pp. 28-44. Butler defends the promotion of human growth and transformation as the main reason for the existence of the church in the community. Any other kind of spiritual formation will be a distortion of Christian mission.

Therefore, the dignity of humanity and the right of every individual constitute the basic components of healthy relationships between individuals, communities, and nations. These are missional objectives that Pentecostal communities may have to incorporate when implementing their service to the community.

Integral mission also carries a prophetical duty or responsibility that is to denounce evil when it is present in human relationships. For instance, violence and injustice are social evils that are continually working against God's purpose for society. Believers are responsible for denouncing them and the community of faith is called upon to assume a prophetic role to uncover the forces of evil that violate human rights. The gospel pays special attention to the mission of protecting the poor and the weak. The rights of the poor and the weak are not to be ignored or trampled upon. Societies that allow this kind of evil are becoming strongholds for a greater expansion of violence and cycles of injustice. People under these categories eventually rise up against the abuses and imbalances that lead to significant social upheaval.[56] A large part of the social responsibility of the church comes about in response to important questions to which social justice provides the proper answers.

Pentecostal integral mission understands that humanity has to be liberated from everything that oppresses men and women. He or she has to be given the opportunity to fulfill the purpose of God designed for all human beings. Thus, mission has the purpose to indicate the path in establishing harmony and the way that a reconciled society should follow in order to experience love, justice, and harmony in the community. Plutarch Bonilla states, 'Mission works in a society that anticipates with its ethics and moral standards the new heavens and new earth in which righteousness dwells'.[57] And rightly so, Pentecostals will have to anticipate the coming of that

---

[56] On the matter of upheaval and social imbalances, see Antonio González, *El Evangelio de la Paz y el Reinado de Dios* (Buenos Aires, Argentina: Ediciones Kairós, 2008), pp. 56-63. González argues that the gospel of peace may also be understood observing the social realities. This helps to understand the authentic Christian position against violence as it is seen in the present world order. The non-violence approach is an ethical and strategic option inspired by the example of Jesus, Gandhi and other peacemakers who fought for human freedom. Thus, it is necessary to check on our theological options in the kingdom of God and ask ourselves the real meaning of that peace carried by the gospel.

[57] Bonilla, *La Misión de la Iglesia Según el Libro de los Hechos*, p. 76. See also Russell, 'Fanning the Charismatic Fire,' p. 36.

new humanity by working integral mission through society in the power of the Spirit.

Mission to the Community

In the case of Pentecostals, the first recipient of mission is the community, so all believers are expected to live their faith in community. The call for Pentecostals is to teach that social responsibility is a critical part of that mission because social responsibility plays a significant role in the obligations of peace and justice in society.[58] This mission calls for a moral truth that inspires people in the community to respond to the assistance offered by believers committed to social work. Some congregations have gifted members who are capable of serving the community with a great deal of success.

This awareness of social responsibility in Pentecostal mission also includes the assumption of responsibilities that affect the design and organizational functions of the community. The practice of an integral mission makes significant contributions to political structures, economic systems, and administrative skills implemented in society. With this idea in mind, Bonilla states, 'the community of faith, not only pastors, is to take these variables into consideration when it plans and executes its mission to society'.[59] Thus, social responsibility as practiced by the church is not only sensitive to the needs of the individual but also to the corporate needs and group limitations.

Historically, Pentecostals have thought of social responsibility specifically as the natural change that happens to individuals after conversion. They have assumed that redemption and social uplift occur naturally to those who believe. However, there is a new generation of Pentecostals who know that social responsibility also has a universal destination and has to be implemented with an intelligently designed plan of action. Anthea Butler wrote:

> The gospel mission must affect the entire society and ought to serve all people. Mission raises consciousness about the needs of society and assumes an active disposition to tackle human diffi-

---

[58] Villafañe, *El Espíritu Liberador*, p. 125.
[59] Bonilla, *La Misión de la Iglesia Según el Libro de los Hechos*, p. 64.

culties in the way of the Spirit, which is manifested in the works of the gospel expressed by God's people.[60]

Butler is right in the extension of social mission to all people, which is something that Pentecostals do not seem to have included in their mission theology yet. Nevertheless, the positive argument is that Pentecostals continue to add new insights to their mission thinking. Eventually they may include integral mission in the structure of their theology of social responsibility.

To accomplish the above, Pentecostals may have to adjust to the fact that the ultimate design for mission is to affect all people of the community. Integral mission works on behalf of humanity, highlights the dignity of people and promotes the well-being of the community. Hence, integral mission gives everyone the opportunity to decide for or against Christ's gift of redemption and to become the persons that God intended for him or her to be when He created him or her. Therefore, Pentecostals may have to incorporate the teaching that mission is also designed to reach out to the benefit of all people groups. That integral mission ought to be practiced by all followers of Christ in order to reach individuals and community needs.

Mission, Spirituality, and Renewal

There is evidence that Pentecostals are now self-studying their mission, which shows significant advances related to the continuity of their faith commitments and the renewal of their principles and practices of ministry.[61] One point in their favor is that they could justify this self-critique as guided by the perennial revelation of the Holy Spirit. For this reason, Pentecostals claim that their commitments do not depend on arguments related to cultural differences or to political ideologies prevailing in certain contexts. Rather, they make sure that their service remains faithful to the Pentecostal in-

---

[60] Butler, 'Facets of Pentecostal Spirituality and Justice', p. 29.

[61] This self-study for significance and continuity of the Pentecostal movement in the new millennium was clearly documented by Grant McClung, at the turn of the Century. See his article Grant McClung, 'Pentecostals, the Sequel: What Will It Take for This World Phenomenon to Stay Vibrant for Another 100 years?' *Christianity Today* 50.9 (April 1 2006) pp. 29-30.

spiration that moves mission into practicing principles of ministry that are biblical and consistent with theologically sound reflection.[62] Méndez also claims, 'this exercise helps believers to identify criteria of discernment and understanding of social action. It also links the ministry of the congregation with the gospel message and principles revealed by the Holy Spirit.'[63] Being like this, one would expect that this continuous revelation that is foundational in Pentecostal theology would also be permanent in their approach to integral mission.

This continuity of revelation may cause Pentecostalism to move consistently in expanding its mission in contemporary history. This is one of the reasons David Bosch said, 'Pentecostals are neither conditioned by having to comply with historical demands nor limited in their potential and capability to be creative'.[64] Then, they should not be afraid of this new approach to service because we have seen how the Holy Spirit renews the church in its mission and purpose continually.

Having discussed it, we can now say that Pentecostal mission could also teach social responsibility as a work in progress, where the work of the Holy Spirit in the life of society is always on-going. That mission is backed by the fact that truth is capable of penetrating human circumstances, indicating the path to social justice and the road to peace in society. This is why Méndez states: 'Pentecostals realize that the gospel's message cannot be confined to the convenience of changeable socio-economic circumstances or to political realities within a particular historical context'.[65] This is true because this kind of teaching takes a dynamic approach to mission through reflection and continues to create the ideal approach to changing negative situations that harm people in the community. It is this approach to mission that drives believers to serve society by presenting a message that is relevant in the transformation of the community.

---

[62] Méndez, *La Iglesia: Fuerza del Espíritu*, p. 112. The author defends the continuity of the Pentecostal faith and mission in the midst of cultural change and new theological arguments coming from other Christian streams.

[63] Méndez, *La Iglesia: Fuerza del Espíritu*, p. 110.

[64] Bosch, *Transforming Mission*, p. 109.

[65] Méndez, *La Iglesia: Fuerza del Espíritu*, p. 88.

As we have seen, the Pentecostal congregation is not retreating within itself from its social responsibility. On the contrary, it has always been driven to reach out to the suffering and assist the needs of the poor and marginalized. Very often they do this as a personal initiative, or sometimes they even act together as a congregation. Pentecostals have always served in the midst of people, and they have been considered as a model in living the gospel with the community. According to Anthea Butler, 'Pentecostals think that the Holy Spirit sends them to serve people wherever they are, with their existential difficulties and human circumstances that carry them away from God's purpose for their lives'.[66] Thus, for Pentecostals the community of faith is the first point of contact with the gospel. The next step is to witness to those who are not part the community. This witnessing includes using all of the resources made available to them by the Holy Spirit. The aim is to transform the lives of people and the community. According to Butler, Pentecostal believers are initiated in a process 'that leads them into understanding the message of reconciliation with God and the following freedom that is experienced through love, justice and peace for those who believe'.[67] Therefore, the potential for integral mission is there. It will only take intentional promotion and teaching among the churches for this model to succeed.

Social Transformation

Historically, Pentecostals have identified their mission service with the person of the Holy Spirit, who is the transformational Agent of individual, as well as cultural and social realities. They have also become instrumental in building human communities by virtue of bringing out the social significance of the gospel to the community. It is commonly accepted that early in the twentieth century, Pentecostals began to address social questions typical of that time, thus creating a new paradigm in the understanding and practice of mission.[68]

---

[66] Butler, 'Facets of Pentecostal Spirituality and Justice', p. 31.

[67] Butler, 'Facets of Pentecostal Spirituality and Justice', p. 27.

[68] See the historical account of Charles W. Conn about early Pentecostals during the first decade of the 20th Century around the East Coast of the United States. He pays particular attention to the simplicity of life and to the community

In Latin America, Pentecostals learned that they had a message with spiritual and social implications concerning human situations that affected the individual and the community. Although they did not feel capable of formulating biblical doctrine of church mission, they acted with their conscience and in good faith in order to confront social evils in the community.[69] These efforts also enabled the church to analyze and think about practical solutions to social problems and to indicate directions to follow peace and justice for all the people involved.

In its approach to social responsibility, Pentecostal mission may be capable of understanding the importance of the sort of social service that focuses on the well-being of people in the community. Pentecostals also seem to be able to articulate a reliable theological understanding of the social condition of people in their communities. According to Luis Orellana, Pentecostals also seem to be learning to cooperate with Christian anthropology by revealing the inviolable dignity of every individual.[70]

Chuck Kraft states: 'Pentecostals have the potential to understand the human perspective of economics and analyze the political realities of work in the original design for the community'.[71] Guerrero also writes: 'Pentecostals are capable of learning to promote and inspire genuine human values, which are sustained through the implementation of the principles of the gospel to individual needs, cultural practices and community life'.[72]

Then, we can speak for a Pentecostal anthropology that is in support of the various pastoral tasks that care for the individual and his or her well-being in the community. Such care incorporates the principles of Pentecostal faith, whereby the believer is filled and

---

service that they provided even to those referred to as unbelievers, but were the center of their mission and ministry. Charles W. Conn, *Like a Mighty Army* (Cleveland, TN: Pathway Press, 2000), p. 26.

[69] Orellana, 'El Futuro del Pentecostalismo en América Latina', pp. 141-56. The author describes the historical foundations of Pentecostal thought and clearly describes the development of mission in the Latin American contexts of ministry.

[70] Orellana, 'El Futuro del Pentecostalismo en América Latina', pp. 141-56.

[71] Chuck H. Kraft, *Anthropology for Christian Witness* (Maryknoll, NY: Orbis Books, 1996), p. 6. In the very first section of his book, Kraft discusses the dignity of the human person and the purpose of God for humanity.

[72] Guerrero Bravo, *El Fruto del Espíritu*, p. 46.

empowered by the Holy Spirit. That experience cleans the inner life of believers and enables them to work for the good of people. Carmelo Álvarez states,

> Through the inspiration of the Holy Spirit, Pentecostals are able to guide the mind and heart of individuals through sound judgment. In this guidance, new and healthy values precede their decisions and the way they conceive and build new models and patterns for their lives.[73]

Concerning this matter, Luis Orellana also writes: 'the present society is confronted by the need to understand the difference between the principles of the gospel and the cultural values assimilated by people'.[74] Thus, Pentecostals make the gospel relatable and available to every individual. The gifts of God are made available to every person in the community by the ministry of believers. This approach to mission is important because a secularized understanding of salvation could reduce the gospel to a merely human philosophy. That approach will look for social solutions to the needs of humanity instead of those solutions dispensed by the experience of an integral gospel.

In the case of Pentecostals, Juan Driver argues, 'they are now taking a step forward not only in the evangelization effort but also into a new stage of history in their mission work and that social responsibility is present in the process of evangelization'.[75] It is remarkable that in their own way, Pentecostals have found that society is in need of a proclamation of the gospel, which also focuses on the solution of the human needs. They just need a theology of integral mission that may enhance the quality of their service.

Spirituality and Social Action

As stated earlier, social action is still new to Pentecostals as part of their theological formation. It is true that they have significant involvement in social service, which is taken as part of their spiritual

---

[73] Álvarez, *Pentecostalismo y Liberación*, p. 56.

[74] Orellana, 'El Fuego y la Nieve', p. 143. The author describes the internal struggles of Pentecostals in Chile. At some point they were challenged to abide by the principles of the gospel or by the cultural values of the moment.

[75] Driver, *La Fe en la Periferia de la Historia*, p. 67.

discipline, but that is done on an informal basis. Hence, until they have a formal teaching on integral mission incorporated into their curriculum and doctrinal commitments, we may not see a fully developed mission theology among them. Early in their history Pentecostals realized that the church exists to work in favor of human growth and transformation, and their actions needed to comply with this portion of ministry.

With regards to this matter Bernardo Campos states, 'The Pentecostal church is able to interact with society and culture. Its mission is to ensure that people experience hope in concrete situations especially in times of difficulty and despair.'[76] Campos adds,

> Social action works in concrete realities and prepares believers to experience the human awareness of evangelization. For example, serving the poor and the weak makes the experience of the gospel complete and builds awareness of redemption to the community in general.[77]

If Pentecostals want to be socially responsible, they will have to guide believers into a two-fold exercise: helping them to discover the truth and to discern the path to success in their service. Furthermore, they will encourage Christians to bear witness to people with an authentic spirit of service, and that way the gospel will be effective in the field of social action. Bernardo Campos argues, 'this is pure Pentecostal mission, for they understand that once they are filled and empowered by the Holy Spirit they are enabled to efficiently proclaim the full gospel to the poor, the weak, and the marginalized'.[78] Their service is accompanied by the witness of spiritual gifts, which are operated by believers committed to Christ. Pentecostal mission also makes social action credible because in its practice, one can see the internal logic and consistency of ministry that is endorsed by the Holy Spirit.

---

[76] Bernardo Campos, 'Pentecostalism: A Latin American View', in *Consultation with Pentecostals in the Americas* (San José, Costa Rica: World Council of Churches, 1996), p. 62.

[77] Campos, 'Pentecostalism', p. 63.

[78] Campos, 'Pentecostalism', p. 45.

Formation of Social Responsibility

One recommendation for Pentecostal churches is to embrace the formative value of social responsibility. As we have seen, Pentecostals recognize that the blessing of a new life is the result of the combined effort of the Holy Spirit and the believers. This combined experience enables them to pursue integral redemption for the individual and the community. Bosch says,

> This fraternal solidarity takes place in the search for social justice and peace, whereby the fullness of Christian service is presented in actual history. This could be found in the content of the message and methodology of mission employed by Pentecostals.[79]

This approach to mission enriches the reception and application of the gospel by virtue of the dynamic contribution to the areas of community reached by service.

In regards to Christian formation, Pentecostals may not find it difficult to understand that the teaching of social action is directed towards enabling believers to evangelize and promote the humanization of temporal realities. This is similar to what Newbigin states:

> The community of faith is the bearer of a spiritual ability and practical understanding of ministry, which provides support to the mission of transforming community life. Such action helps Christian service to conform its actions to the plan of God.[80]

Thus, Pentecostals may have to start training believers to understand and appreciate the moral order. This attitude could motivate them to promote freedom that is constructed when people approach social responsibility with the truth. It would help individuals to become socially responsible. Then, they would strive for truth and justice in cooperation with other members of the community. Evidently, this is a new contribution to Pentecostal mission but once embraced, this could carry significant formative value.

---

[79] Bosch, *Transforming Mission*, p. 355.
[80] Newbigin, *Foolishness to the Greeks*, p. 138.

Promotion of Dialogue

Social responsibility is also instrumental in the dialogue between the community of faith, the civil authority, and the political community. Dario Lopez refers to the importance of dialogue as an appropriate instrument for the promotion of attitudes modeled after the teachings of the gospel.[81] However, like in Western societies he argues, 'such actions promote authentic cooperation and productive collaboration in the redemptive process of humanity'.[82] Pentecostals also seek to strengthen civil and political authority in their call to serve society. Many times pastors approach local authorities with the purpose to support their service. This attitude also reveals the level of commitment on the part of Pentecostals toward social concerns and political responsibility.[83]

If we observe the social interaction that takes place in the Pentecostal communities, we can see that they are actively participating in multiple dialogues that foster collaboration with the various groups of society. In addition, since the Pentecostal communities are made up largely of the poor and marginalized, such dialogue could be enriched by the experience of marginalization and oppression that most Pentecostals suffered in their mission contexts. Such dialogues continue to broaden their range of service. For example, a group of Pentecostals is now defending the dignity of the people and promoting peace and justice.[84] They are speaking on behalf of those in poverty and marginalization. They are combating poverty and hunger in the world. They are promoting equal distribution of the goods of God's earth as well as providing housing and literacy.[85] Thus, it is fair to say that Pentecostals are also learning to focus on the holistic development of the children and the youth. They are

---

[81] López, *Los Evangélicos y los Derechos Humanos*, p. 102.

[82] Newbigin, *Foolishness to the Greeks*, p. 95.

[83] Newbigin, *Foolishness to the Greeks*, p. 76.

[84] This is the Pentecostals and Charismatics for Peace and Justice Movement, which unites scholars and practitioners around a table to reflect on issues pertaining to such matters. See PCPJ, 'Charismatics Peacemakers and Peacemaking', *Pentecostals for Peace and Justice* (2009). http://www.pcpj.org/index.php/resources-topmenu-45/86-charismatic-peacemaking-and-peacemakers. Accessed 10 November 2009.

[85] Cf. B. Battaini-Dragoni, Panel on 'Social Justice and Security', World Youth Conference; León, Guanajuato: México, Aug. 23-27, 2010.

participating in national, regional, and global consultations that promote ministries on behalf of the emerging generations.[86]

It is not surprising that because of their Christian experience, Pentecostals have the tendency to emphasize the need for a powerful and regenerating work of the Holy Spirit to overcome the influence of evil in society. This is perhaps one of the reasons they seem to proclaim a message that changes the individual first, then the family, friends and the world.

The Community of Faith

Pentecostals believe that the entire community of faith has a role to play in the fulfillment of God's mission. Nevertheless, their definition of mission has historically been narrowed to proclamation and teaching only. However, Pentecostals have begun to understand and practice mission in various ways through each member according to the gifts and the manner of each person's calling. Mario Méndez thinks that Pentecostals are now responding to the responsibility to proclaim and bear witness to the gospel with the understanding that every mission effort involves all who believe and are willing to obey the call of the Holy Spirit to service.[87] Christian mission is biased to the poor. It is mindful that, in the story of Jesus, God becomes vulnerable with the poor and marginalized. It is aware, moreover, that God undertakes a mission of transformation from that position of weakness. This is the meaning of the cross. Today most church members are not found among the wealthy and powerful but rather among the poor and vulnerable. What does it mean for mission when its agents come mainly from contexts of poverty and exclusion?

As for Pentecostals, they seem to be aware of the pastoral work that is needed in the social context. This way of ministry fits them well because they involve all believers. They become active agents of transformation in the community. They also know that one of their responsibilities is to bear pastoral witness to the poor and marginalized. In this we concur with Mario Méndez who thinks that

---

[86] See for example Enrique Pinedo, *Niñez, Adolescencia y Misión Integral: Nuevos Desafíos de la Educación Teológica en America Latina* (Buenos Aires, Argentina: Kairós, 2012), p. 24.

[87] Méndez, *La Iglesia: Fuerza del Espíritu*, pp. 24-26.

Pentecostals may be on the way to becoming successful not only in the proclamation of the gospel but also in the defense of human dignity.[88] They seem to be spiritually furnished to act individually or associated with groups that participate in this endeavor.

This ministry in the community context involves the service of devoted believers who are capable of using their spiritual and natural gifts.

> Their faithful witness and service is needed particularly in times of intense condition of poverty. Situations like these open significant opportunities to serve people and reminds believers about their principles of holiness and sincere love to the poor and marginalized.[89]

Here we realize that Pentecostals could be easily found at the service of the incarnated Christ. It is this Christ whose love for people shown through Christians suggests some aspects of the new humanity that His mission is encouraging among believers.

---

[88] Méndez, *La Iglesia: Fuerza del Espíritu*, p. 22.
[89] López, *Pentecostalismo y Transformación Social*, p. 38.

8

SPIRITUALITY, SOCIETY, AND MISSION

In this section we study the Pentecostal theology of public service and political participation. The approach to these matters may seem too close to Roman Catholic theology and the discussion may become controversial in some Pentecostal circles. However, more than 500 years of RCC culture and theology has presided in Latin America. Since Pentecostals have been here for about 100 years, a dialogue between Pentecostals and RCC scholars seems to be in order. However, this dialogue is made possible only under the possibilities allowed by an ecumenical point of view.

Fortunately, there are some Pentecostals who are willing to dialogue and reflect on issues related to public life and social concerns. Nevertheless, these issues are neither recognized by the Pentecostal establishment nor found in the syllabi of most academic courses. From this point on the discussion will focus on these controversial and often overlooked themes.

In the study, I build on matters such as public service, the value of democracy, and political participation. Some of the issues discussed here may appear foreign to some Pentecostals, but that does not mean I am 'Pentecostalizing' someone else's mission theology of public service and political participation. On the contrary, these issues are intentionally presented as input for a Pentecostal idea of public service and political participation.[1]

---

[1] The impact of Pentecostals in the community can only be observed through the lifestyle and behavioral change occurred in the believers. Community transformation takes place as a result of the spiritual change in the life of Christians.

Moreover, I selected some issues that are incipient or non-existent among most Pentecostal networks in Latin America. These statements are derived from research that examined the RCC doctrine of social and public service in an open dialogue with Pentecostal scholarship. Most of my observations are based upon themes that have been neglected or ignored by some Pentecostals mainly due to their theological approach to mission and practice of public service.

Public Service

With their service among the poor and the marginalized, Pentecostals have emphasized that the human person is the foundation and purpose of Christian mission, humanity, and political life. They have understood that the human person is responsible for his or her own choices and able to pursue projects that give meaning to life at the individual and social level.[2] On this matter, Christopher Wright writes, 'only in relation to the reality and to others does the human person reach the total and complete fulfillment of himself'.[3] This means that for the human person, a naturally social and political being, social life is not something that is added, but it is part of an essential and indelible dimension.

For Pentecostals the political community originates in the nature of persons, whose conscience reveals and commands them to obey the order that God has imprinted in all His creatures. This order must be gradually discovered and developed by humanity.[4]

Hence, this transformation is concurrent with the doctrinal definitions of most Pentecostal denominations. One example is the Church of God (Cleveland, Tennessee, USA). In its doctrinal commitment, the Church of God teaches about the 'baptism with the Holy Ghost subsequent to cleansing, the enduement of power for service'. Cf. Mt. 3.11; Lk. 24.49, 53; Acts 1.4-8. See also Church of God *Minutes of the 71st General Assembly* (Cleveland, TN: Pathway Press, 2008), p. 14.

[2] On the impact of an individual over the community, Susanna Hoffman did an extensive study that is presented in the work where she is a co-author. See, Susanna Hoffman, Alejandra Massolo, and Martha Schteingart, 'The Worst of Times the Best of Times', in *Participación Social, Reconstrucción y Mujer: El Sismo de 1985* (México, México: Colegio de México, 1985), pp. 206-207.

[3] Chris Wright, *La Misión de Dios: Descubriendo el Gran Mensaje de la Biblia* (Buenos Aires, Argentina: Ediciones Certeza, 2006), p. 434.

[4] Wright, *La Misión de Dios*, p. 231.

Therefore, the political community, a reality inherent in human-kind, exists to develop the full growth of each of its members called to cooperate steadfastly for the attainment of the common good under the impulse of their natural inclinations towards what is true and good. This notion is present in most members of the Pentecostal community, but it is mostly observed among scholars who are now thinking about political, social, and economic matters pertaining to the community at large.

For an evangelical theologian such José Míguez Bonino, the political community finds its authentic dimension in its reference to people. The term 'a people' does not mean a shapeless multitude, let alone an inert mass to be manipulated and exploited, but a group of persons: each in their proper place and in their own way.[5] This way they are able to form their own opinion on public matters and have the freedom to express their own political sentiments and bring them to bear positively for the common good of people. Therefore, a people exists in the fullness of the lives of the men and women by whom it is made up. Each is a person aware of his or her own responsibilities and convictions. 'Those who belong to a political community, although organically united among themselves as people, maintain an irrepressible autonomy at the level of personal existence and of the goals to be pursued'.[6]

The primary characteristic of a people is the sharing of life and values, which is the source of communion on the spiritual and moral level. We could learn from Pope John XXII, who argues that human society must primarily be considered as something pertaining to the spiritual.

> Through it, in the bright light of truth men should share their knowledge, be able to exercise their rights and fulfill their obligations, be inspired to seek spiritual values, mutually derive genuine pleasure from beauty of whatever order it be, always be readily disposed to pass on to others the best of their own cultural her-

---

[5] This paradigm is addressed by Bonino, *Faces of Latin American Protestantism*, pp. 122-23. One of the faces is Pentecostal, which is gradually becoming aware of its strategic role in transforming the Latin American culture.

[6] Bonino, *Faces of Latin American Protestantism*, p. 124.

itage and eagerly strive to make their own the spiritual achievements of others.[7]

Unfortunately, most Pentecostals have been reluctant to be open to
this idea because they tend to spiritualize the social and political
content of the gospel.[8] Instead, they will have to see that the benefits of the gospel not only influence but also give aim and scope to
all that has bearing on cultural expressions, economic and social
institutions, political movements and forms, laws, and all other
structures by which society is outwardly established and constantly
developed.

In reference to the difference between the rich and the poor,
Richard Niebuhr states,

> The community of faith affirms that the poor shall be seen as a
> group with precise rights and duties, most of all, the right to ex-
> ist, which can be ignored in many ways, including such extreme
> cases as its denial through overt or indirect forms of genocide.[9]

In the legitimate quest to have their rights respected, the poor may
be driven to seek greater recognition by all members of society.

Pentecostalism, which generates a new perspective for life, has
provided spiritual and social support for the poor. The poor are
transformed personally and then taught that they have the ability to
transform their community as well. They also know they can accomplish this in an attitude of love and in the power of the Holy
Spirit.

Promotion of Human Rights

In some Pentecostal communities the theme of promoting human
rights is yet to be addressed holistically. However, they are now recognizing that working for the human person as the foundation and
purpose of the political community means laboring to recognize
and respect human dignity through defending and promoting fun-

---

[7] John XXIII, Enclyclical Letter *Pacem in Terris: AAS 55* (1963), p. 266.

[8] Land, *Pentecostal Spirituality*, p. 135.

[9] H. Richard Niebuhr, *Social Sources of Denominationalism* (New York, NY: The
World Publishing Company, 1972), p. 181.

damental and inalienable human rights.[10] Christian responsibility establishes that the common good is chiefly guaranteed when personal rights and duties are maintained. The rights and duties of the person contain a concise summary of the principal moral and juridical requirements that preside over the construction of the political community.[11]

According to José María Ferraro, the political community pursues the common good when it seeks to create a human environment that offers citizens the possibility of truly exercising their human rights and of fulfilling completely their corresponding duties.[12] History has shown that unless these authorities take suitable action with regards to economic, political, and cultural matters, inequalities between citizens tend to become more widespread, especially in today's society. As a result, human rights are rendered totally ineffective, and the fulfillment of duties is compromised. Unfortunately, Pentecostals have not assumed this matter as a ministerial responsibility, for they are still learning about it. Education in political and social issues for the enhancement of the community must take place in the community of faith. The full attainment of the common good requires that the political community develop a twofold and complementary action that defends and promotes human rights. Concerning this, Darío López states,

---

[10] Other that oral information it is difficult to find documents written by Pentecostal sources on the issue of human rights. One of the most reliable sources on the defense of human rights in Honduras is the report of CODEH, *Informe sobre la Situación de los Derechos Humanos en Honduras, Enero 2000 Junio 2008* (Tegucigalpa, Honduras: CODEH, 2008).

[11] See Ramón Custodio, 'The Human Rights Crisis in Honduras', in M.B. Rosenberg and P.L. Shepherd (eds.), *Honduras Confronts its Future: Contending Perspectives on Critical Issues* (Boulder, CO: Lynne Rienner, 1986), pp. 69-72; and Comité para la Defensa de los Derechos Humanos en Honduras (CODEH), *La Situación de los Derechos Humanos en Honduras* (Tegucigalpa, Honduras: CODEH, 1988), p. 20. On that occasion the National Commissioner for the Protection of Human Rights in Honduras offered figures for human rights violations. See Leo Valladares, 'Los Hechos Hablan por Sí Mismos: Informe Preliminar Sobre los Desaparecidos en Honduras 1980-1993', *Comisionado Nacional de Protección de los Derechos Humanos* (Tegucigalpa, Honduras: Editorial Guaymuras, 1994), p. 14.

[12] On the influence of Christians over the political arena, José María Ferrero suggests how believers should engage politics responsibly. See José María Ferrero, 'La Iglesia ante el gobierno del cambio', *Puntos de Vista* 3.1 (1991), pp. 13-25.

It should not happen that certain individuals or social groups derive special advantage from the fact that their rights have received preferential protection, nor should it happen that governments in seeking to protect these rights, become obstacles to their full expression and free use.[13]

The theme of human rights has different connotations depending of the organization that speaks for it. For the sake of my study, I address the matter from the point of view of Human Rights. In this approach I looked into the views and values of the RCC in order to find a link with the Pentecostal communities and their approach to human rights. However, a broader understanding of the philosophy and practice of the human rights is needed. Due to the limits of this research, the matter will have to be addressed in further studies.

Community and Civility

As I look at the RCC approach to social matters, profound meaning of civil and political life does not arise immediately from a list of personal rights and duties expected from community members. Life in society takes on all its significance when it is based on a journey of civil friendship and fellowship. On the one hand, the sphere of rights is that of safeguarded interests, external respect, the protection of material goods, and their distribution according to established rules. On the other hand, the sphere of friendship is that of selflessness, detachment from material goods, giving freely, and inner acceptance of other's needs. If Pentecostals would take advantage of their natural social composition, which is very similar to this meaning of civil and political life, they would be capable transforming the community. Civil friendship, understood in this way, is the most genuine actualization of the principle of fraternal relationships which is inseparable from that of freedom and equality.[14]

Pentecostals are now recognizing that their community of faith has potential foundations that could be significant toward the integral promotion of the person and of the common good. In such cases, civil law could be defined, respected, and lived according to

---

[13] López, *Los Evangélicos y los Derechos Humanos*, p. 46.
[14] López, *Los Evangélicos y los Derechos Humanos*, p. 49.

the manner of solidarity and dedication towards one's neighbor. López insists that justice requires that everyone should be able to enjoy his or her own goods and rights; this can be considered the minimum measure of love.[15]

Pentecostals are realizing that the gospel precept of love enlightens believers on the deepest meaning of political life. In order to make it truly human, political life must foster justice and service for the common good by strengthening basic beliefs about the nature of the political community and instructing about the proper exercise and limits of public authority. The goal that believers must put before themselves is that of establishing community relationships among people.

Political Authority

Pentecostals have adopted similar patterns in understanding and facing authority; however, one common denominator seems clear, they have not taken care of the responsibility to propose and to defend a model of authority that is founded on the social nature of the person.

God made humanity social by nature, and no society can hold together unless someone governs over all by directing all to strive earnestly for the common good. Every civilized community must have a ruling authority, which is intrinsic by nature, and consequently has God for its author. Therefore, political authority is necessary because of the responsibilities assigned to it. In light of these, Pentecostals realize that political authority is a positive component of civil life.

RCC social doctrine states that political authority must not only guarantee an orderly and upright community life without usurping the free activity of individuals and groups but also discipline and orient this freedom while respecting and defending the independence of the individual and social subjects for the attainment of the

---

[15] One Pentecostal scholar who addresses the matter on human transformation is Darío López. His approach to solidarity and respect for the human person is presented from his theological background. See López, *Pentecostalismo y Transformación Social*, pp. 94-98.

common good.[16] Thus, political authority is an instrument of coordination and direction by which many individuals and intermediate bodies move towards relationships, institutions, and procedures that are put to the service of integral human growth. Political authority, in fact, whether in the community as such or in institutions representing the state, must always be exercised within the limits of morality on behalf of the dynamically conceived common good, according to a juridical order enjoying legal status.

Political authority implies that the people are considered as a sovereign body. In various forms, the people transfer the exercise of sovereignty to those whom they freely elect as their representatives, but they reserve the prerogative to assert this sovereignty in evaluating the work of those charged with governing and also in replacing them when they do not fulfill their functions satisfactorily.[17] Although this right is operative in every state and any political regime, a democratic form of government, due to its procedures for verification, allows and guarantees its fullest application. Nevertheless, the mere consent of the people is not sufficient for considering the ways in which political authority is exercised as just. The difficulty with this is that most evangelicals and Pentecostals, in particular, refuse to enter into this discussion because they consider it to be worldly and not part of the ministry of the community of faith thus missing an opportunity to become agents of transformation in the field political authority.

---

[16] Allison A. Bushell, 'The Foundation of Political Authority', *Viewpoint* (2007). http://www.catholicnews-tt.net/v2005/archives/1007/sun28/viewpoint.htm. Viewed 19 April 2011.

[17] Leo Valladares, the Commissioner for the human rights in Honduras, wrote in his annual human rights report about the abusive exercise of political authority in Honduras, particularly against the poor. His document sets the foundation for what he considered to be 'the ideal exercise of political authority on behalf of the people of Honduras'. Cf. Leo Valladares, 'Honduras: The Facts Speak for Themselves', *National Commissioner for the Protection of Human Rights in Honduras* (New York, NY: Human Rights Watch, 1994), p. 225.

Authority as Moral Force

Evangelicals as well as Pentecostals admit that a moral law as proposed by the RCC could guide authority in the right direction[18] but does not go beyond mere principles learned from the gospel. Hence in the practice of mission, they both seem to miss the opportunity to bring transformation in moral authority. All of authority's dignity derives from the exercise of the moral order which in turn has God as its first source and final end.[19] Because of its necessary reference to the moral order that precedes it and on which it is based and because of its purpose and the people to whom it is directed, authority cannot be understood as a power determined by criteria of a solely sociological or historical character. There are some who go as far as denying the existence of a moral order, which is transcendent, absolute, universal and equally binding upon all.[20] Furthermore, where people do not adhere to the same law of justice, they cannot hope to come to an open and full agreement on vital issues. This order has no existence except in God; cut off from God it must necessarily disintegrate.[21] It is from the moral order that authority derives its power to impose obligations and its moral legitimacy, not from some arbitrary will or from the thirst for power, and it is necessary to translate this order into concrete actions to achieve the common good.

True authority recognizes, respects, and promotes essential human and moral values. These innately flow from the very truth of the human being and express and safeguard the dignity of the person. These are values that no individual, majority, or state can ever create, modify, or destroy. These values do not have their founda-

---

[18] Information on how the Catholic Church teaches moral law could be found at The Holy See, 'Man's Vocation Life in the Spirit', in *Catechism of the Catholic Church* (2010). http://www.vatican.va/archive/ccc_css/archive/catechism/p3s1 c3a1.htm. Viewed 2 April 2010.

[19] Padilla, 'A Message for the Whole Person', p. 1. Padilla argues that the gospel of Jesus Christ is an ethical gospel. It has to do with God's infinite love manifest in his Son, but also with the love that he demands from us as his children. It deals with our relationship to God, but also with our relationship to our neighbor.

[20] Padilla, *A Message for the Whole Person*, pp. 2-3.

[21] See also C. René Padilla, 'Latin American Evangelicals Enter the Public Square', *Transformation* 9.3 (1992), p. 2.

tion in provisional and changeable majority opinions but must simply be recognized, respected, and promoted as elements of an objective moral law – the natural law written in the human heart[22] and as the normative point of reference for civil law itself. If, as a result of the tragic clouding of the collective conscience, skepticism were to succeed in casting doubt on these basic principles, the legal structure of the state itself would be shaken to its very foundations; and it could be reduced to nothing more than a mechanism for the pragmatic regulations.

Authority enacts just laws that correspond to the dignity of the human person and do what is required for the right reason. Since the days of enlightenment, human law is law insofar as it corresponds to right reason and therefore is derived from the eternal law.[23]

However, when a law is contrary to reason, it is called an unjust law; in such a case, it ceases to be law and becomes instead an act of violence. Authority that governs according to reason places citizens in a relationship not as subjection to another person but as obedience to the moral order, ultimately submitting to God Himself who is its final source. Whoever refuses to obey an authority that is acting in accordance with the moral order 'resists what God has appointed?'[24] Analogously, whenever public authority fails to seek the common good, it abandons its proper purpose and so delegitimizes itself.

The Right to Conscientious Objection

Conscientious objection against unjust authority is not a subject well-known or spoken among Pentecostal circles. However, I brought the matter up so that believers will have some room for incorporating this matter into their reflection and Christian service. Theologically, citizens are not obligated in conscience to follow the prescriptions of civil authorities if their precepts are contrary to the demands or the teachings of the Gospel. Unjust laws pose dramatic problems of conscience for morally upright people. Besides being a

---

[22] Cf. Rom. 2.15.

[23] C. René Padilla, 'Responses to Democracy – A Christian Imperative', *Transformation* 7.4 (1990), p. 9.

[24] Cf. Rom. 13.2.

moral duty such a refusal is also a basic human right, which as such, civil law itself is obliged to recognize and protect.[25] Those who have recourse to conscientious objection must be protected not only from legal penalties but also from any negative effects on the legal, disciplinary, financial, and professional plane.

It is a grave duty of conscience not to cooperate in practices, which although permitted by civil legislation, are contrary to the Law of God. Such cooperation in fact can never be justified neither by invoking respect for the freedom of others nor by appealing to the fact that it is foreseen and required by civil law. For instance, it is reported that early Pentecostals in the United States were in opposition to carrying weapons. Members of the church were forbidden to serve in the military or organizations that required the use of weapons. It was not until the World War II that Pentecostals decided to leave the matter to the conscience of the individual, and they ruled it on a case-to-case basis.[26]

The Right to Resist

Pentecostals may not even think about such issues as the right to resist politically speaking. Nonetheless, it is useful to examine the recourses utilized by other Christians like those who consider resistance as an instrument to oppose unjust authorities. In the context of political reflection in Peru, Cecilia Blondet writes,

> Recognizing that natural law places limits on positive law means admitting that it is legitimate to resist authority should it violate in a serious manner the essential principles of natural law. Natu-

---

[25] Other than the worker unions and the student organizations, Hondurans Christians are submissive to military forces, particularly in political crisis. Pentecostals are inclined to accept the rulers with an attitude of obedience, as a theological response. See James A. Morris, *Honduras: Caudillo Politics and Military Rulers* (Boulder, CO: Westview Press, 1984), pp. 40-41. Also, Mario Posas, *Modalidades del Proceso de Democratización en Honduras* (Tegucigalpa, Honduras: UNAH, 1988), pp. 84-91.

[26] See Conn, *Like a Mighty Army*, pp. 112-34.

ral law, as portrayed in the RCC teachings constitutes the basis for the right to resistance.[27]

For instance, the Peruvian constitution of 1979 allowed for rebellion against those usurping government in an undemocratic way.[28] There can be many different concrete ways this right may be exercised; there are also many different ends that may be pursued. Charles Drugus even said, 'resistance to authority is meant to attest to the validity of a different way of looking at things, whether the intent is to achieve partial change, for example, modifying certain laws, or to fight for a radical change in the situation'.[29]

According to C.A. Drugus, these are the criteria for taking the right to resistance to extremes:

> Armed resistance to oppression by political authority is not legitimate, unless all the following conditions are met: 1) there is certain, grave and prolonged violation of fundamental rights, 2) all other means of redress have been exhausted, 3) such resistance will not provoke worse disorders, 4) there is well-founded hope of success; and 5) it is impossible reasonably to foresee any better solution. Recourse to arms is seen as an extreme remedy for putting an end to a manifest, long-standing tyranny, which would do great damage to fundamental personal rights and dangerous harm to the common good of the country.[30]

Drugus explained, however, that the gravity of the danger to resist makes the practice of passive resistance preferable, which is a way more conformable to moral principles and having no fewer prospects for success. Although this may not always be the case,

---

[27] Cecilia Blondet, 'Poder y Organizaciones Populares: Estrategias de Integración Social', in Augusto Álvarez (ed.), *El Poder en el Perú* (Lima, Perú: Apoyo, 1993), pp. 189-201.

[28] Blondet, 'Poder y Organizaciones Populares', p. 198.

[29] Among Pentecostals this may be one of the hardest issues to grasp, for they teach submission to political authority. However, Pentecostals are prone to split congregations when disagreement with spiritual authority arises. These contradictions are addressed by Carol Ann Drogus, 'Private Power or Public Power: Pentecostalism, Base Communities, and Gender', in Edward L. Cleary and Hannah W. Stewart-Gambino (eds.), *Power, Politics and Pentecostals in Latin America* (Boulder, CO: Westview Press, 1997), pp. 55-75.

[30] Drogus, *Private Power or Public Power*, p. 58.

there are situations like Mahatma Gandhi in India who show that passive resistance can be a highly effective weapon when used intelligently.[31] However, this is how Drugus explains Gandhi's pragmatic reasons for pursuing strategies of non-violence. On the matter of non-violence, John Howard Yoder stated that there are sufficient Christian reasons for not having to participate in the 'just war tradition'.

Yoder believed that action faithfully in tune with God's rule is likely to be more effective in the case of conflict.[32] Moreover, the term 'non-violence' is often linked with or even used as a synonym for pacifism; however, the two concepts are fundamentally different. Pacifism[33] denotes the rejection of the use of violence as a personal decision on moral or spiritual grounds but does not inherently imply any inclination toward change on a socio-political level. Conversely, non-violence[34] presupposes the intent of (but does not limit it to) social or political change as a reason for the rejection of violence. Moreover, a person may advocate non-violence in a specific context while advocating violence in other contexts.

---

[31] Extensive information on Mahatma Gandhi's passive resistance and his achievements is available at Chris Trueman, 'India's History in the 20th Century', *Indian Stones and Slates* (2000). http://www.historylearningsite.co.uk/mahatma_ghandi.htm. Accessed 18 May 2010.

[32] John H. Yoder, *The Politics of Jesus* (Grand Rapids, MI: Eerdmans, 1972), p. 76.

[33] Some American Pentecostal groups that started around 1917 show evidence of being pacifist movements at some point in their history. Since then there has been a shift away from pacifism in the American Pentecostal churches and towards the support of war. The major pacifist organization for Pentecostal Christians is the Pentecostal Charismatic Peace Fellowship (PCPF). See Paul Alexander, *Peace to War: Shifting Allegiances in the Assemblies of God* (Telford, PA: Herald Press, 2009), pp. 22-37.

[34] Non-violence is a strategy for social change that rejects the use of violence. As such, non-violence is an alternative to passive acceptance of oppression and armed struggle against it. Practitioners of non-violence may use diverse methods in their campaigns for social change, including critical forms of education and persuasion, civil disobedience, and non-violent direct action, and targeted communication via mass media. See Gene Sharp, *Waging Nonviolent Struggle: 20th Century Practice and 21st Century Potential* (Boston, MA: Porter Sargent, 2005), p. 381.

Correction and Punishment

The issue of punishment against the offender could better fit the Pentecostal understanding of moral order. Most Pentecostals would agree that in order to protect the common good, the lawful public authority must exercise the right and the duty to inflict punishments according to the seriousness of the crimes committed. Concerning this matter Daniel Levine has written,

> The civil authority has the twofold responsibility to discourage behavior that is harmful to human rights and the fundamental norms of civil life, and to repair, through the penal system, the disorder created by criminal activity.[35]

Levine also argues, 'in a state ruled by law the power to inflict punishment is correctly entrusted to the courts'.[36] The constitutions of modern states must guarantee the judicial power necessary to define the proper and independent relationships between the legislative, executive, and judicial powers.

Punishment does not serve merely the purpose of defending the public order and guaranteeing the safety of persons. It becomes also an instrument for the correction of the offender; a correction that takes on the moral value of expiation when the guilty party voluntarily accepts his or her punishment. There is a twofold purpose here: on the one hand, encouraging the reinsertion of the condemned person into society; on the other hand, fostering a justice that reconciles which is a justice capable of restoring harmony in social relationships disrupted by the criminal act committed.

In this regard, prison chaplains are called to undertake not only in the religious dimension but also in defense of the dignity of those detained. Unfortunately, the conditions under which prisoners serve do not always foster respect for their dignity. That is why some prisons become places where new crimes are committed. Nonetheless, the environment of penal institutions offers a forum

---

[35] Daniel Levine and David Stall, 'Bridging the Gap Between Empowerment and Power in Latin America', in Susanne Hoeber Rudolph and James P. Piscatori (eds.), *Transnational Religion and Fading State* (Boulder, CO: Westview Press, 1997), pp. 63-103.

[36] Levine, *Bridging the Gap Between Empowerment and Power*, p. 74.

for bearing witness to Christian concern for social issues: 'I was in prison and you came to me'.[37]

In carrying out investigations, the regulation against the use of torture, even in the case of serious crimes, must be strictly observed. Christ's disciples refuse any recourse to such methods, which nothing could justify and in which the dignity of the person is as much debased in his or her torturer as in the torturer's victim. International juridical instruments concerning human rights correctly indicate a prohibition against torture as a principle which cannot be contravened under any circumstances.[38]

Likewise, the use of detention for the sole purpose of trying to obtain significant information for the trial is ruled out. Moreover, it must be ensured that trials are conducted swiftly.[39] Their excessive length is becoming intolerable for citizens and results in a real injustice.

The Democratic System

In their approach to democracy, Pentecostals value the democratic system inasmuch as it ensures the participation of citizens in making political choices and guarantees to the governed the possibility both of electing and holding accountable those who govern them and of replacing them through peaceful means when appropriate. However, in certain moments they have to endorse Christians who encourage the formation of narrow ruling groups, which usurp the power of the State for individual interests or for ideological ends. In

---

[37] Cf. Mt. 25.35-36.

[38] Any act by which severe pain or suffering, whether physical or mental, is intentionally inflicted on a person for such purposes as obtaining from him, her, or a third person, information or a confession is an act of violence against the human rights of the person affected. See for instance Ronald D. Crelinsten, 'In Their Own Words: The World of the Torturer', in Ronald D. Crelinsten and Alex Peter Schmid (eds.), *The Politics of Pain: Torturers and Their Masters* (Boulder, CO: Westview Press, 1994), pp. 35-64.

[39] On the application of justice and rule of law in Honduras, Donald Schulz describes the efforts of the United States to assist the Central American countries. These efforts, however, are a testimony that the rule of law in the area is still defective. See Donald E. Schulz and Deborah Sundloff Schulz, *The United States, Honduras and the Crisis in Central America* (Boulder, CO: Westview Press, 1994), pp. 142-49.

principle, Pentecostals agree that authentic democracy is possible only in a state ruled by law[40] and on the basis of a correct conception of the human person.[41] It requires that the necessary conditions be present for the advancement both of the individual through education and formation in true democratic ideals and of the subjectivity of actively participating in society through the creation of structures of participation and shared responsibility.

Values of Democracy

John H. Yoder was very clear on his understanding of democracy; he said,

> An authentic democracy is not merely the result of a formal observation of a set of rules but the fruit of a convinced acceptance of the values that inspire democratic procedures, such as the dignity of every individual, the respect of human rights and commitment to the common good as the purpose and guiding criterion for political life.[42]

If there is no general consensus on these values, the deepest meaning of democracy is lost and its stability is compromised.

In the political arena, most Latin American Pentecostals do not yet seem to have found universal criteria for establishing the foundations of a correct hierarchy of values in democracy. Although they recognize the importance of the democratic society, they still seem to be undecided on the extension or the depth of their participation. That could be one of the hindrances, which may prevent them from making an impact in the newly emerging democracies, especially in Latin America and particularly in recent political events in Honduras. Nowadays there is a tendency to claim that agnosticism and skeptical relativism are the philosophy and the basic atti-

---

[40] The matter of democracy has become more visible in Pentecostal scholarship in Latin America. One example is Luis E. Samandu, 'El Pentecostalismo en Nicaragua y sus Raíces Religiosas Populares', *Pasos* 17 (1988), pp. 1-9.

[41] On the subject of authentic democracy and the rule of law, see Joan M. Nelson and Stephanie J. Eglington, *Encouraging Democracy: What Role for Conditioned Aid?* (Washington, DC: Overseas Development Council, 1992), pp. 95-96.

[42] Yoder, *The Politics of Jesus*, p. 68.

tude, which correspond to democratic forms of political life.[43] That is the reason Moltmann says,

> Those who are convinced that they know the truth and firmly adhere to it are considered unreliable from a democratic point of view, since they do not accept that the majority determines truth, or that it is subject to variation according to different political trends'.[44]

Thus, if there is no ultimate truth to guide and direct political action, then ideas and convictions can easily be manipulated for reasons of power. As history demonstrates, a democracy without the values freedom, truth, justice, and peace easily turns into thinly disguised totalitarianism. Democracy is fundamentally a system and as such is a means and not an end. Its moral value is not automatic but depends on conformity to the moral law to which it must be subject. In other words, its morality depends on the morality of the ends that pursues and the means that it employs.

Institutions and Democracy

Even though most Pentecostals are still learning how to become involved in democratic systems, they seem to recognize the validity of the principle concerning the division of powers in a state. One example of Pentecostal participation was the recent case of the presidential succession in Honduras on June 28, 2009. Some Pentecostals decided that their support for the new government was necessary. They marched along massive crowds to support the new legally appointed President. They also conducted intensive prayer rallies on behalf of the country and the new government. They were aware of the opposition from the international community against the new political system in place, but they had it clear that international political forces were misguided and mistakenly bullying Honduras.[45]

---

[43] On the matters of agnosticism and relativism over political life, see Moltmann, *God for a Secular Society*, pp. 67-70.

[44] Moltmann, *God for a Secular Society*, p. 92.

[45] The Attorney General of Honduras charged President Manuel Zelaya with violations to the constitution of the country. The Supreme Court issued an arrest warrant against him. After a resignation letter from President Manuel Zelaya was read to the National Congress, this accepted Zelaya's resignation as President, on 28 June 2009. Congress unanimously agreed to: under the Articles 1, 2, 3, 4, 205,

This time some Pentecostals played a strategic role in strengthening the new government and the democratic institutions of the country. They denounced the double standard morality of the international community in their threats against Honduras and stood solidly with the interim President. This political crisis also served some Pentecostals to prove that their mission extends beyond the walls of the church and the limits of their community of faith. They were working in cooperation with many more organizations to defend their democracy. This cooperation was operated at all fronts possible and at all levels of influence. If Honduras survived its most critical political crisis of the 21st Century, a great part of that success had to do with active members of the Pentecostal community who participated actively on behalf of democracy.

In the democratic system, political authority is accountable to the people. Darío López encourages that representative bodies must be subjected to effective social control.

This control can be carried out above all in free elections which allow the selection and change of representatives. The obligation on the part of those elected is to give an account of their work.[46] This is guaranteed by respecting electoral terms, and it is a constitutive element of democratic representation. In their specific areas, like drafting laws, governing, setting up systems of checks and balances, elected officials must strive to seek and attain that which will contribute to making civil life proceed well in its overall course.

Those who govern have the obligation to answer to those governed, but this does not imply that representatives are merely pas-

---

220, subsections 20, 218, 242, 321, 322, 323 of the Constitution of the Republic of Honduras, (1) to disapprove Zelaya's repeated violations of the constitution, laws, and court orders, (2) to remove Zelaya from his post as President, (3) to name the current President of the Congress Roberto Micheletti interim president to complete the constitutional term that ended on January 27, 2010. Micheletti's term in office saw demonstrations for and against him. Domestically his government was supported by 80% of Honduras and by most civil and democratic organizations. See for instance a thorough analysis of the 2009 political crisis of Honduras at G. Rodríguez and E. Sosa, *Honduras Culture and Politics* (Tegucigalpa, Honduras: CESPAD, 2009), pp. 1-3. Most evangelicals and Pentecostal organizations were part of the national mobilization, which was under the continuous attack of the so-called International Community, which was misled by antidemocratic forces in Latin America.

[46] See López, *El Nuevo Rostro del Pentecostalismo Latinoamericano*, pp. 91-97.

sive agents of the electors.[47] The control exercised by the citizens does not exclude the freedom that elected officials must enjoy in order to fulfill their mandate with respect to the objectives to be pursued. These do not depend exclusively on special interests but in a much greater part on the function of synthesis and mediation that serve the common good – one of the essential and indispensable goals of political authority.

Moral Components of Political Representation
Plutarco Bonilla once stated:

> Those with political responsibilities must not forget or underestimate the moral dimension of political representation, which consists in the commitment to share fully in the destiny of the people and to seek solutions to social problems.[48]

In this perspective, responsible authority also means authority that is exercised with those virtues that make it possible to put power into practice as service. For instance, authorities must show patience, modesty, moderation, and efforts to share. This kind of authority is able to accept the common good and not prestige or the gaining of personal advantages as its true goal at work. This statement fits the Pentecostal communities well due to their social and economic background where this lifestyle seems to be common among believers.[49]

Among the deformities of the democratic system, political corruption is one of the most serious because it betrays both moral principles and the norms of social justice. It compromises the correct functioning of the State having a negative influence on the relationship between those who govern and the governed. It causes a growing distrust with respect to public institutions bringing about a progressive disaffection in the citizens with regard to politics and its representatives with a resulting weakening of institutions. Corruption radically distorts the role of representative institutions because they become an arena for political bartering between clients'

---

[47] López, *El Nuevo Rostro del Pentecostalismo Latinoamericano*, p. 28.

[48] Plutarco Bonilla, 'La Misión de la Iglesia según el Libro de los Hechos', *La Biblia en las Américas* 5.53 (1998), pp. 12-16.

[49] Walter Hollenweger, *Pentecostalism: Origins and Developments Worldwide* (Peabody: Hendrickson Publishers, 1997), pp. 110-12.

requests and governmental services. In this way political choices favor the narrow objectives of those who possess the means to influence these choices and are an obstacle to bringing about the common good of all citizens.

The matter of public administration still seems distant for some Pentecostals. They rather see it as an instrument of the state. However, public administration is oriented towards the service of citizens. The state is the steward of the people's resources, which it must administer with a view to the common good.[50] The role of those working in public administration is not to be conceived as impersonal or bureaucratic but rather as an act of generous assistance for citizens undertaken with a spirit of service.

Political Choice

In reference to the purpose of political parties, Alberto Roldán is of the opinion that they have the task of fostering widespread participation and making public responsibilities accessible to all. Hence, political parties are called to interpret the aspirations of civil society, orienting them towards the common good and offering citizens the effective possibility of contributing to the formulation of political choices. They must be democratic in their internal structure and capable of political synthesis and planning.[51]

Another instrument of political participation is the referendum,[52] whereby a form of direct access to political decisions is practiced. The institution of representation in fact does not exclude the possibility of asking citizens directly about the decisions of great importance for social life.

---

[50] Although this approach to the moral components for political participations is general and focus on the Pentecostal point of view, there are however some indications that even in the context of Honduras this area of public service has already been discussed. See for instance, Gustavo Blanco and Jaime Valdaverde, *Honduras: Iglesia y Cambio Social* (Tegucigalpa: Editorial Guaymuras, 1990), pp. 95-103. The authors argue that the State must be at the service of its citizens. The level of service committed by those who govern should validate their political participation.

[51] Alberto Roldán, 'Missão, Unidade e Identidade da Igreja', *Proceso Regional de Reflexão para Quarta Assembléia Geral do CLAI* (Quito, Ecuador: CLAI, 2000), pp. 15-17.

[52] Yoder, *The Politics of Jesus*, p. 69.

Information is among the principal instruments of democratic participation. Participation without an understanding of the situation in the political community, the facts, and the proposed solutions to problems is unthinkable. It is necessary to guarantee a real pluralism in this delicate area of social life ensuring that there are many forms and instruments of information and communications. It is likewise necessary to facilitate conditions of equality in the possession and use of these instruments by means of appropriate laws. Among the obstacles that hinder the full exercise of the right to objectivity in information, special attention must be given to the phenomenon of the news media being controlled by just a few people or groups. This has dangerous effects for the entire democratic system when closer ties between governmental activity and the financial and information establishments accompany this phenomenon.

Traditionally, Pentecostals have used the media to broadcast the gospel message of personal salvation and to teach about Christian principles, values, and doctrine. They have not used the media with the purpose of transforming culture or government intentionally. Nonetheless, Roldán argues that the media must be used to build up and sustain the human community in its different sectors: economic, political, cultural, educational, and religious. Society has a right to information based on truth, freedom, justice, and solidarity.[53] He also states that the current information system must contribute to the betterment of the human person. It must make people more mature, more aware of the dignity of their humanity, more responsible or more open to others, in particular to the neediest and the weakest.[54]

In the world of the media, the intrinsic difficulties of communications are often exacerbated by ideology, the desire for profit and political control, rivalry, and conflicts between groups and other social evils. This happens to be of concern to most Pentecostals as well. However, instead of being intimidated by that negative impact, they are now proposing that moral values and principles be applied to the media.[55] In addition, the ethical dimension should be related

---

[53] Roldán, *Missão, Unidade e Identidade da Igreja*, p. 18.

[54] Roldán, *Missão, Unidade e Identidade da Igreja*, p. 16.

[55] Concerning the positive impact of Christian media over society, Larry Webb goes further to address the matter of moral values in the dramatic changes

not only to the content of communication and the process of communication but also to fundamental structural and systemic issues, which often involve large questions of policy bearing upon the distribution of sophisticated technology and product.

In all areas of communication one fundamental moral principle must be applied: the end and measure of the use of media are the individual and the community. A second principle is complementary to the first: the good of human beings cannot be attained independently of the common interest of the community to which they belong. It is necessary that citizens participate in the decision-making process concerning media policies. This participation has to be genuinely representative and not skewed in favor of special interest groups when the media are a moneymaking venture. This appears to be one of the most significant challenges for Pentecostals with regards to the current use of media.

Civil Society

Historically, in Honduras Evangelicals and some Pentecostals have contributed to the distinction between the political community and civil society by their vision of the human person understood as an autonomous and relational being who is open to spiritual matters. Concerning this Larry Webb has said, 'this vision is challenged by political ideologies of an individualistic nature and those of a totalitarian character, which tend to absorb civil society into the sphere of the state's interest'.[56] Thus, the commitment of the community of faith on behalf of social pluralism aims at bringing about a more fitting attainment of the common good and democracy itself, according to the principles of solidarity, subsidiary, and justice.[57]

Civil society is approached here as the sum of relationships and resources, cultural and associative, that are relatively independent

---

that affect society in the 21st Century. See Larry Webb, *Healthy Church DNA: Transforming the Church for Effective Ministry* (Bloomington, IN: iUniverse, 2008), pp. 25-28. Readiness for transforming change is one element that has to be present in the life of the community of faith. That way the culture and the government will be transformed.

[56] Webb, *Healthy Church DNA*, p. 32.

[57] See for instance the value of the civil society as discussed by Bastian, *La Mutación Religiosa en América Latina*, pp. 121-38.

from the political sphere and the economic sector. The purpose of civil society is universal, since it concerns the common good to which each and every citizen has a right in due proportion. Webb adds,

> This is marked by a planning capacity that aims at fostering a freer and more just social life, in which the various groups of citizens can form associations, working to develop and express their preferences, in order to meet their fundamental needs and defend their legitimate interests.[58]

Community Development

The political community and civil society, although mutually connected and interdependent, are not equal in the hierarchy of ends. The political community is essentially at the service of civil society. It is at the service of persons and groups of which civil society is composed. Civil society, therefore, cannot be considered an extension or a changing component of the political community. Rather, it has priority because it is in civil society itself that the political community finds its justification. One Pentecostal scholar who has studied the importance of the civil society as the object of service by the Political community is Bernardo Campos.[59] Although he does not reflect directly upon the necessity of the political community at the service of the civil society, he still claims that the government's main task is to be at the service of the civil and democratic institutions; something that is by no means an accomplished fact in the Latin American reality.[60]

Campos also states,

> Civil authority must provide an adequate legal framework for social subjects to engage freely in their different activities, and it must be ready to intervene when necessary and with respect for the principle of subsidiarity, so that the interplay between free associations and democratic life may be directed to the common good.[61]

---

[58] Webb, *Healthy Church DNA,* p. 82.

[59] On the issue of the participation of Pentecostals on the civil society, see Campos, *De la Reforma Protestante a la Pentecostalidad de la Iglesia,* pp. 12-18.

[60] Campos, *De la Reforma Protestante a la Pentecostalidad de la Iglesia,* p. 16.

[61] Campos, *De la Reforma Protestante a la Pentecostalidad de la Iglesia,* p. 18.

Civil society is in fact multifaceted and irregular; it does not lack its ambiguities and contradictions. It is also the arena where different interests clash with one another with the risk that the stronger will prevail over the weaker.

Lessons from the Principle of Subsidiarity

The political community is responsible for regulating its relations with civil society according to the principle of subsidiarity. It is essential that the growth of democratic life begin within the fabric of society.[62] The activities of civil society represent the most appropriate ways to develop the social dimension of the person who finds in these activities the necessary space to express him or her fully. The progressive expansion of social initiatives beyond the state-controlled sphere creates new areas for the active presence and direct action of citizens integrating the functions of the state. This important phenomenon has often come about largely through informal means and has initiated new and positive ways of exercising personal rights, which have brought about a qualitative enrichment of democratic life.

The RCC teaching of social doctrine understands that cooperation shows itself to be one of the most effective responses to a mentality of conflict and unlimited competition that seems so prevalent today. Pentecostals could capitalize on their multiple communities by emphasizing relationships that are established in a climate of cooperation and solidarity. This approach to cooperation will serve to overcome ideological divisions prompting people to seek out what unites them rather than what divides them.[63]

Many experiences of volunteer work are examples of great value that call people to look upon civil society as a place where it is possible to rebuild a public ethic based on solidarity, concrete cooperation, and fraternal dialogue. This area in particular seems a natural fit for Pentecostals. They are well known for their volunteer service and spontaneous work among people of their communities. They are called to look with confidence at the potentialities present in

---

62 Moltmann, *God for a Secular Society*, p. 90.

63 An extensive discussion of this matter has been made available by the Pontifical Council for Justice and Peace, *Compendium of the Social Doctrine of the Church* (1995). http://www.catholicculture.org/culture/library/view.cfm?id=7218&CFID=77957190&CFTOKEN=51995189. Accessed 19 April 2011.

their service and to offer their personal efforts for the good of the community.

Religious Freedom

In order that this freedom willed by God and inscribed in human nature may be exercised, no obstacle should be placed in its way, since the truth cannot be imposed except by virtue of its own truth. The dignity of the person and the very nature of the quest for God require that all men and women should be free from every constraint in the area of religion. Society and the state must not force a person to act against his or her conscience or prevent him or her from acting in conformity with it. Religious freedom is neither a moral license to adhere to error nor an implicit right to error. Thus, there are limits to religious freedom. In the case of Pentecostals, they have resolved their conflicts appealing to three sources of understanding, which are based on their hermeneutics: (1) the authority of the Scripture, (2) the revelation of the Holy Spirit, and (3) the Counsel of the elders.[64]

Freedom of conscience and religion concerns men and women both individually and socially. The right to religious freedom must be recognized in the juridical order and sanctioned as a civil right; nonetheless, it is not of itself an unlimited right. The just limits of the exercise of religious freedom must be determined in each social situation with political prudence according to the requirements of the common benefit and ratified by the civil authority through legal norms consistent with the objective of moral order. Such norms are required by the need for effective safeguarding of the rights of all citizens and for the peaceful settlement of conflicts of rights and also by the need for an adequate care of genuine public peace, which comes about when men live together in good order and in true justice, and finally by the need for a proper guardianship of public morality.

---

[64] Classic Pentecostalism has established the Pneumatic method as the source of interpretation of the Scripture, the community of faith, and the ethics pertaining thereto. The Pneumatic method includes three agents in the interpretation: The authority of the Scripture, the revelation of the Holy Spirit, and the Counsel of the Community of faith. See Kenneth J. Archer, *A Pentecostal Hermeneutic: Spirit, Scripture, and Community* (Cleveland, TN: CPT Press, 2009).

Community of Faith

Although the church and the political community both manifest themselves in visible organizational structures, they are by nature different because of their configuration and because of the ends they pursue. Evangelicals and Pentecostals reaffirmed that in their proper spheres the political community and the church are mutually independent and self-governing. The church is organized in ways that are suitable to meet the spiritual needs of believers, while the different political communities give rise to relationships and institutions that are at the service of everything that is part of the temporal common good. The autonomy and independence of these two realities is particularly evident with regards to their ends.

The duty to respect religious freedom requires that the political community guarantee the church the space needed to carry out its mission. However, the community of faith has no particular area of competence concerning the structures of the political community. The church respects the legitimate autonomy of the democratic order and is entitled to express preferences for this or that institutional or constitutional solution.

Christians must question the merit of political programs. They have the right to express their concerns, their religious or moral implications. Christians both individually and collectively do have an obligation to join in the political debate. They have a perspective that needs to be heard. Nevertheless, they should not be granted any special privileges in debates in which all citizens have an equal right to participate.

Autonomy and Cooperation

The mutual autonomy of the church and the political community does not entail a separation that excludes cooperation. Both of them, although by different titles, serve the personal and social vocation of the same human beings. Both the community of faith and the political community express themselves in organized structures that are not ends in themselves but are intended for the service of humanity to help individuals exercise their rights fully. The community of faith and the political community can more effectively render this service for the good of all, if each works better for wholesome mutual cooperation in a way suitable to the circumstances of time and place.

Pentecostals also understand that the community of faith has the right to the legal recognition of her proper identity, precisely because its mission embraces all of human reality. The church is truly and intimately linked with humanity and its history.[65] The community of faith claims the freedom to express its moral judgment on this reality, whenever it may be required to defend the fundamental rights of the person or for the salvation of souls. The community of faith is now looking for freedom of expression, teaching, and evangelization; freedom of public worship; freedom of organization and of its own internal government; freedom of selecting, educating, naming, and transferring its ministers; freedom for constructing religious buildings; freedom to acquire and possess sufficient goods for its activities; and freedom to form associations not only for religious purposes but also for educational, cultural, health care, and missional purpose.

This study initiated a discussion that may raise questions concerning the participation of Pentecostals in social concerns and the political arena. It may as well generate further studies among them over the concept of public service and the value of democracy. This dialogue between the Pentecostal and the RCC theology of public service is intended to generate reflection over non-traditional fields that obviously affect both streams – in Latin America, both Pentecostals and Catholics coexist with different theological views and attitudes toward gospel and culture. Even in the case of contradicting arguments, it is always healthy to understand what others think about common issues that are part of the same world.

---

[65] See for instance Álvarez, *Pentecostalismo y Liberación*, p. 24.

9

COMMUNITY AND DISCIPLESHIP

One of the essential characteristics of Pentecostals is that disciple-ship is carried out in the local community.[1] Pentecostals teach that once believers become members of a local congregation, they join the ministry of the body of believers and are made participants in the life and mission of the church. As disciples they are motivated to use and implement their spiritual gifts for the benefit of people. Their identity as disciples of Christ is nourished through the teach-ings of Pentecostal faith, doctrine, and mission. They are taught that the baptism of the Holy Spirit enables believers to bear witness to Christ as Savior and Redeemer. Mario Méndez explains how this discipleship process takes place: 'believers are endowed with power to become effective in their ministry, with the aim to proclaim the good news of the gospel and to promote a new condition of life for those who believe'.[2]

As we have seen, with most Pentecostals in Latin America the immediate responsibility of believers is to proclaim the gospel with an exemplary witness of life rooted in Christ and lived in temporal realities. They embrace ministry to the family and minister to many individual issues among believers. However, they seem to struggle with mission to the secular world, particularly in the work place.

---

[1] Bravo, *El Fruto del Espíritu*, p. 44.

[2] Méndez, *La Iglesia*, p. 28. The author reviews the teachings of Classical Pentecostalism and compares it with contemporary Pentecostal movements in Latin America. Another source to understand Classical Pentecostalism is Cecil M. Robeck, *The Azusa Street Mission and Revival: The Birth of the Global Pentecostal Movement* (Nashville, TN: Thomas Nelson, 2006), pp. 81-131.

Additionally, they do not seem to have a history of consistent involvement in the world of culture. However, in recent years they have some participation in social, economic, and political responsibilities.[3] Nonetheless, historically they have missed the realities of the secular society.

The fact that Pentecostals have not been historically involved in social action, including various scenarios related to political structures and institutions, does not necessarily signify a lack of interest. As we have seen, the actual reason for missing these scenarios of mission may have to do with theological and doctrinal positions set by denominational leaders.[4] Nevertheless, it is fair to affirm that once they learn how to participate properly in these fields, they will do it with a great deal of responsibility. It is only in recent years that they have studied these realities as places where God's love is received. They need to be taught that the community of faith has to be active in the transformation of society. Their mission proposes godly solutions to anthropological and sociological needs as well as the spiritual and theological.

Lay Associations

One reference for Pentecostals that comes out of this study is to realize that social responsibility involves a wide range of matters beyond their traditional theological framework and that these ac-

---

[3] See for example, the report of Allan Anderson on the influence of Pentecostals and Charismatics at the work place. He presents it as one the contributions from Western Pentecostalism to the rest of the world. Allan H. Anderson, *El Pentecostalismo: El Cristianismo Carismático Mundial* (Madrid, España: Ediciones Akal, 2007), p. 236. Although Anderson initially wrote this book with the English title, *Introduction to Pentecostalism: Global Charismatic Christianity* (Cambridge, UK: Cambridge University Press, 2004), I preferred to use the Spanish translation for in Latin America some terms like 'secular', 'culture', and others have particular application to the local community.

[4] In the case of Pentecostal denominations originated in North America, their leaders how strong ties with conservative theology and politics. They taught the first Pentecostals to separate from the world, which was taken to extreme positions. Thus, the new converts focused on proclaiming the word, but little was done to transform the community. So most efforts toward this purpose were isolated and done by inertia. On this subject, see the work of Ademar Olivera, 'Moving Forward with the Latin American Pentecostal Movement', *International Review of Mission* 8.7 (1998), pp. 4-7.

tions are part of the formation of believers for Christian service. This endeavor is successful when lay people carry it out. They have an objective criterion of mission in the church. Lay leaders realize that groups, associations, and local church movements play a valid role in the training of believers for ministry. López states that if lay people initiate mission, they are also capable of sustaining groups of believers committed to the transformation of various sectors of the community.[5] If this mission is also present in the workplace, it will promote actions that favor the individual and the working community. Thus, mission is expressed through the action of believers who work through groups, associations, or movements. These activities should also include believers of other Christian denominations that work for the benefit of the community.

Social responsibility practiced by the community of faith is also important for the development of ecclesial associations within the larger Christian community. These kinds of associations are now being tested by some Pentecostals. Once these relationships are in place, they may represent a point of reference for working with other groups.

Social Service in the Various Sectors of Community Life

Norberto Saracco has defined service as 'the sign and expression of love, which is seen in the areas of the family, culture, work, economics, and politics according to specific aspects, which characterize the presence of Christians in the community'.[6] Thus, when looking at these demands, as stated by Saracco, on the matter of social service Pentecostals are able to express the validity of their faith principles and their love for their community where their Christian life is experienced. Such love becomes a reality when the gospel is implemented in the community through social service.[7] The credi-

---

[5] López, *Pentecostalism and Social Transformation*, p. 53.

[6] Norberto Saracco, 'Mission and Missiology from Latin America', in William D. Taylor (ed.), *Global Missiology for the 21st Century* (Grand Rapids, MI: Baker Academic, 2000), pp. 357-66. He discusses Pentecostal mission in the context of Christianity. He argues that mission is not complete until it reaches culture, economics, and social life. Then believers can identify as members of an active community of faith.

[7] Saracco, 'Mission and Missiology from Latin America', p. 359.

bility of their faith will make itself clear through the witness of social participation. Social action is the best way to validate the quality of mission of a church. Some Pentecostals are aware of this, and consequently they do not spend as much time planning so that they can be off to work with people in their communities.

Service to the Cultural Field

According to Richard Niebuhr, culture is the way of life of a group of people – the behavior, beliefs, values, and symbols that they accept generally without thinking about them and in ways that are passed on by communication and imitation from one generation to the next.[8] In the case of Pentecostals, the integration of Christian faith with these practical actions of life is arguably one of the egregious characteristics of most of their communities. They seem to be capable of operating from within their cultural reality. They have a natural network built through relationships that are included in their practice of Christian faith.[9] If one takes Richard Niebuhr's opinion into consideration, the cultural phenomena are best understood in their context and should be evaluated in the way they affect the human person in his or her integral growth and transformation.[10] That is one reason Pentecostals may have to stimulate the capacity to communicate and the ability to relate to people of other cultures and traditions. Culture is also that reality where people live and through which Christians have the opportunity to become true in fulfillment of God's purpose.

In reference to socio-cultural and political participation, Pentecostals believe that the Holy Spirit is the inspiring agent for their actions. Although they have not been historically involved in political influence, more recently some Pentecostals have begun to show

---

[8] H. Richard Niebuhr, *Christ and Culture* (New York, NY: Harper and Brothers, 1951), p. 212.

[9] Wilson, 'Guatemalan Pentecostals', p. 56. From his Guatemalan context, the author describes the kind of relationships that Pentecostals build in the community. That ability comes natural to them and it helps in the process of evangelization. He concludes that it is one of their strengths to connect with people within the local culture.

[10] Niebuhr, *Christ and Culture*, p. 210.

interest in elected positions.[11] In their early history, Pentecostals had limited participation in politics, so their involvement was restricted mostly to spiritual transformation.

They were not able to implement a change of cultural patterns and political structures. However, today's involvement requires a commitment that works on building foundations to transform culture with a new faith and morality that is intentionally planned in accordance with the principles of the gospel. Wilson also states, 'this awareness is critical for Pentecostals, otherwise they could be limited in their cultural influence and their mission could be reduced to a simple spiritual activity that focuses only on religious matters'.[12] Therefore, one of their goals is to delineate and establish comprehensive foundations for ministry, including spiritual and social values in context.

This approach should reflect both intellectual maturity and solid moral standards that represent the nature of Pentecostalism. Their mission has to be constructed in their faith in Christ Jesus.[13] This statement of mission has to inspire believers to commit their life and ministry to the principles of the gospel. It should have the vision that mobilizes believers to serve in social and political causes inspired by the principles and values of the gospel.

Leslie Newbigin states: 'The complete development of an individual and society are essential in the growth of culture'.[14] Hence, the ethical values of culture must take priority in the social activity initiated by the community of faith. In light of Newbigin's statement, if Pentecostals fail in paying attention to this dimension, they could easily fall into the pitfall of making culture an instrument that distorts God's purpose for humanity.

---

[11] One particular case is Pastor Harold Caballeros of Guatemala. Due to his commitment as a Christian he decided to run for office in his country. Another one is the case of Pastor Mario Tomás Barahona in Honduras. Although he is aligned to the most politically conservative party, he and his church are involved in the political arena of Honduras. These pastors are aligned with the Neo-Pentecostal movement in their countries and to some extent, their connection with Classic Pentecostals happens through the spiritual foundation of their life and ministry, for they are both Spirit-filled pastors.

[12] Wilson, *Guatemalan Pentecostals*, p. 62.

[13] Saracco, 'Mission and Missiology from Latin America', p. 360.

[14] Lesslie Newbigin, 'Christ and Cultures', *Scottish Journal of Theology*, 31.1 (1978), pp. 1-22.

Niebuhr also states: 'a culture can become sterile and headed for decadence when it centers in itself. If it falls into inward interest, it will only perpetuate old and obsolete ways of social life'.[15] If Pentecostals would pay attention to Newbigin and Niebuhr, they would realize that the formation of a culture capable of enriching individuals demands participation of the whole individual, whereby men and women must have the opportunity to express their creative skills and intelligence.

This formation requires persons who use their capacity to activate self-control in their actions as well as personal sacrifice, solidarity, and the capability to pursue and promote the common good of people. Further studies on Pentecostalism may explore how willing Pentecostals are to cooperate with other organizations in social work and how capable they are to integrate these traditions into their own understanding of mission.

The social service and political participation of members of the community of faith suggest studying some important areas of interest. One of them is the right that every individual has to human and civil culture, specifically a culture that operates in harmony with the dignity of every individual without distinction as to gender, race, nationality, or social status. All members of the community have the right to be part of free and open education. They should also be free to access social communication. Ideally, every person should have the freedom to debate, discuss, conduct research, and share his or her thoughts within high standards of social responsibility.

The Revelation of Truth

Another challenge for Pentecostals is related to the content and revelation of truth. According to Lamin Sanneh,

> The question of truth is essential for culture because it remains each man's duty to retain an understanding of the whole human

---

[15] Niebuhr, 'Christ and Cultures', p. 198.

person in which the values of intellect, will, conscience, and fellowship are pre-eminent.[16]

Therefore, a correct anthropology has to be the criterion for shedding light on and verifying every historical form of culture. Sanneh also said,

> The Christian commitment in the field of culture is opposed to all forms of reductionism and ideological perspectives of human life. The dynamism of openness to the truth is guaranteed above all by the fact that different cultures are basically different ways of facing the question of the meaning of personal existence.[17]

In connection with the previous remarks, if Pentecostals pay attention to those values and spiritual dimensions of the culture, they may be well equipped to continue to spread the cause of integral mission. I think at this point it would be appropriate to study what Lesslie Newbigin once wrote:

> When spirituality is eliminated, culture and the moral life of nations are corrupted. The authentic spiritual dimension is an essential part of man and allows him to open his actions to the horizon in which they find meaning and direction. Human spirituality is manifested in the forms taken on by a culture, to which it gives vitality and inspiration. The countless works of art of every period in history bear witness to this. When the spiritual dimension of the person or of a people is denied, culture itself starts to die off, sometimes disappearing completely.[18]

This is important for the quality of service and respect that Pentecostals are now attributing to the condition and dignity of life at personal and social levels.[19] Therefore, Pentecostals may understand the social value of spirituality in their approach to individual and

---

[16] Lamin O. Sanneh, *Encountering the West: Christianity and the Global Cultural Process* (Maryknoll, NY: Orbis Books, 1993), pp. 62-64.

[17] Sanneh, *Encountering the West*, p. 63.

[18] Newbigin, 'Christ and Cultures', p. 18.

[19] Macchia, *Spirituality and Social Liberation*, p. 45. The author highlights the new condition of life that the Holy Spirit generates in spirit-filled believers. The dignity of life is re-constructed and new levels of progress are experienced. Such is the life in the Spirit.

community life which also refers to the purpose of God for humanity.

Mission and the Use of Media

In the promotion of the Pentecostal culture, the community of faith has begun to pay attention to the use of mass media. Pentecostals now seem to be examining the content and purpose of the message delivered by the media and multiple choices that people have when they access the media. Most of these choices have moral implications, so they should be examined as they affect people's lives.

Pentecostals offer a long tradition of wisdom rooted in the gift of discernment and revelation of the Holy Spirit. Unfortunately, most Pentecostals have narrowed the use of media to the proclamation of the gospel. In a way, they have neglected the multiple choices offered by the contemporary media now led by the power of the Internet. Thus, Pentecostal missiology may have to be challenged to provide instruction for the proper use of media by those who have a specific calling to serve in this field.

Pentecostals may have to look at the media as instruments of mission. The media industry should be held accountable for the right use of communication and the healthy circulation and promotion of ideas, which further information, knowledge, ideas, and respect for others. There must be regulatory systems that have the authority to evaluate and discipline the violators of social principles.[20] Pentecostals will have to be involved in the creation of communication structures that set policies and regulate fairness in the distribution or opportunities in the use of technology. These decisions require objective spiritual and moral standards because they may determine who benefits from the media industry and who does not. The media could become instruments of injustice or imbalance, generating social evil, and suffering on the part of information recipients. So, Pentecostals will have to find ways to verify whether the agents who control the mass media and information

---

[20] See for instance David I. Smith and John Shortt, *The Bible and the Task of Teaching* (Nottingham, UK: Stapleford Centre, 2002), pp. 89-100.

technology are aiming to eliminate social injustice and economic imbalance.[21]

Solidarity with the Poor

Pentecostals are also affected by the complexity of emerging economic contexts in the twenty-first century. Believers are now in need of guidance for their economic decisions and financial actions. Pentecostals also realize that economic and financial principles are needed in order to operate with a godly mission and purpose in these spheres. When economics ignores Christian values, then the centrality of humanity is compromised and the quality of economic activity is corrupted.

Pentecostals are aware of the presence and actions of evil in the economic world. They strive towards compassion for the poor as a way to help resolve the problem of poverty.[22] Their participation in the sphere of economics should be geared towards discerning and recommending economic models that are beneficial to the poor and marginalized. The question of economic development cannot be reduced to an exclusively technical problem. This would deprive Christian faith of its purpose and content, since it is always concerned with the dignity of all individuals and the well-being of their society.

According to Samuel Duryea, believers must seek out economists who think about and seek to develop the economy with an urgent consideration for responding to the drama of poverty with a redemptive purpose.[23] He also states: 'economic efficiency requires a harmonized system open to social justice and healthy political participation'.[24] In effect, economic networks must make human solidarity an integral part of the core values of their activities. Here,

---

[21] Newbigin puts it this way: 'The way we understand human life depends on what conception we have of the human story'. See Lesslie Newbigin, *Gospel and a Pluralist Society* (Grand Rapids, MI: Eerdmans, 1989), pp. 16-24.

[22] Saracco, 'Mission and Missiology from Latin America', p. 360.

[23] S. Duryea and C. Pagés, 'Human Capital Policies: What They Can and Cannot Do for Productivity and Poverty-Reduction in Latin America', in S. Duryea and C. Pagés (eds.), *American Foreign Economic Relations: Policy Dilemmas and Opportunities* (Miami, FL: North–South Press, 2001), pp. 18-24.

[24] Duryea and Pagés, 'Human Capital Policies', p. 22.

Pentecostals would do well to recognize that they need to organize and support associations of believers who are capable of influencing economic decisions in ways that enhance the dignity of the individual and the community.

Although this matter has yet to be openly incorporated into Pentecostal missiology, the new generation of Pentecostals seems to be making efforts to include it in their approach to mission, especially as they continue to grow numerically.[25] The economy is obviously a complex matter, and this brief discussion cannot do justice to the issue of mission in the economy. My intention is to look at the economy through the lens of justice and compassion as a way of contributing something distinctively Pentecostal to the discussion of mission. Nevertheless, this matter of Pentecostal mission and the economy will have to be addressed properly in further studies.

Mission and Politics

Even though many Pentecostals have historically declined their right to engage in politics, the truth is that political involvement and participation is now being revisited and referred to as a worthy cause and a responsible expression of their commitment to serve people.[26] Some of the criteria that inspires believers toward political participation are established on a strong spirit of service, the urgency for implementing justice, attention to the deep conditions of poverty in society, confronting suffering at all levels, and furthering dialogues for peace and justice. Henceforth, those who are already occupying positions of service within institutions that deal with complex community difficulties are called upon to pay special attention to the observance of these values, whether in local government or in national institutions.

Accordingly, René Padilla argues that the responsibilities of those involved in social institutions and political service demand a solid commitment to Christian values that reflect the moral dimension of those who participate in social and political life.[27] Padilla

---

[25] Llano Sotelo, *Pentecostalismo y Cambio Social*, p. 66.

[26] Llano Sotelo, *Pentecostalismo y Cambio Social*, p. 60.

[27] See for instance C. René Padilla, 'Los Evangélicos: Nuevos Actores en el Escenario Político Latinoamericano', in C. René Padilla (ed.), *De la Marginación al Compromiso: Los Evangélicos y la Política en América Latina* (Buenos Aires, Argentina:

also states, 'neglecting appropriate attention to moral standards of social and political service may lead to the dehumanization of life. Thus, it is crucial to uncover the structures of evil that prevail at social and political institutions'.[28] Consequently, believers who take this stand may have to pay the price for their honest actions, but that will be their testimony of faithfulness and commitment to the gospel.

Historically, Pentecostals have placed political commitment in the context of the autonomy of church and the state. They draw a clear distinction between the political and religious spheres.[29] This sort of distinction has come about and is observed by most Pentecostal churches and is part of a heritage from contemporary Western civilization. Life is in society, and all who live in it must be accountable to one another. Here, autonomy is in regards to the attitude of individuals who have the obligation to respect and appreciate freedom as provided to human life in community. According to Mariz, this means that other Christians outside the Pentecostal stream may also teach such respect and appreciation for freedom. They also understand their role and responsibility to promote moral truths and to defend social justice and freedom.[30] Hence, in their mind, when Pentecostals defend human dignity, they think it is the responsibility and privilege of all members of the church.[31]

Pentecostals also seem to understand that the principle that identifies autonomy carries significant respect for other confessions of faith. Thus, with regards to the state this is obliged to respect religious organizations and to guarantee freedom for them to exercise their spiritual activities. For Padilla, a pluralistic society is capable of granting healthy communication between and for the various spir-

---

Fraternidad Teológica Latinoamericana, 1991), pp. 5-19. The author addresses influence of Christians in the different fields of politics. Evangelicals have begun to face political crisis with proposals based on Christian principles.

[28] Padilla, 'Los Evangélicos: Nuevos Actores en el Escenario Político Latinoamericano', p. 14.

[29] Mariz, 'Perspectivas Sociológicas Sobre el Pentecostalismo y el Neopentecostalismo', p. 23.

[30] Mariz, 'Perspectivas Sociológicas Sobre el Pentecostalismo y el Neopentecostalismo', p. 28.

[31] See for instance C. René Padilla, *Misión Integral* (Buenos Aires, Argentina: Ediciones Kairós, 1987), p. 102.

itual traditions.[32] This matter is important for the purpose of deter-ring religious intolerance, which continues to exist even in the most democratic societies.

Historically, intolerance has excluded some Christians from so-cial activities. They were separated from their right to participate in social and political decisions. In reference to this, John Stott pointed out, 'this denial, which can lead to anarchy whereby the strong pre-vail over the weak, has to be rejected and opposed in any legitimate pluralist and democratic society'.[33] Thus, the marginalization of Christianity would not bode well for the future of society or for a consensus among peoples. Instead, it would threaten the spiritual and cultural foundations of civilization.

Pentecostals are also learning to be discerning in their choice of political instruments, such us becoming members of a party or in-volving themselves in other kinds of political activity.[34] In their own ways they are choosing instruments and forms of participation that are consistent with the gospel. In any case, their choices are orient-ed by the love of God among believers and strive towards the good that is common to all members of the community. However, Pente-costals may not be able to find a party that is capable of embracing the ethical demands of the gospel. Therefore, they see their political adherence not as ideological but as critical. They could be critical in ensuring that a party's political platform ends up pursuing the common good of society and also responds to the spiritual reality of the individual.

According to Frank Macchia, the distinction between the de-mands of faith and the socio-political duties is evident in the politi-cal options available and the choices that Christians make in select-ing candidates for public service. Membership of a party is, there-fore, regarded as a personal decision.[35] Nevertheless, at some point, this individual choice of a party needs to take into consideration the views and advice of the community of faith. Macchia recommends

---

[32] Padilla, *Misión Integral*, p. 80.

[33] John Stott, *La Misión Cristiana Hoy* (Buenos Aires, Argentina: Ediciones Certeza, 1977), p. 23.

[34] See Gerber, *Missions in Creative Tension*, p. 56. The author argues that Pentecostals have some participation in political choices. They still do it with limitations, yet they are entering into debates that affect the community.

[35] Macchia, *Spirituality and Social Liberation*, p. 68.

that the matter of choice should be guided by the consensus of the community of faith in the way Pentecostals reach decisions.[36]

The New World Order

Due to human nature, even in a limited way, every individual yearns to know the meaning and purpose of his or her life and the consequences of his or her actions at the end of his or her days. Pentecostals would do well at helping to answer these questions and to offer the message of hope found in the gospel. However, the response is still individual, and so transformation of the community may only be ensured when a significant number of people join the congregation. It could also be argued that despite significant numbers of believers in some communities, people continue to suffer under the impact of evil. Violence, immorality, and other forms of evil are threatening the foundations of society. Paradoxically, large numbers of people in many Latin American communities today are members of the Pentecostal family, yet they still do not seem to be making a significant difference in their society. This particular matter will have to be addressed in further studies.

It would be difficult for Pentecostals to decide for future generations and to determine the sort of life they will live. International and interdependent relations have become increasingly complex, less ordered, peaceful, and dangerously motivated by the double standards set by a faceless so-called international community. However, human life seems to be in the hands of scientists and technocrats. People are also beginning to claim their rights but have to concede to the decisions made by their authorities, which is also a violation of their human rights.

Some Pentecostals have responded to these questions about the meaning and purpose of life. For instance, Dana Robert has elaborated on this by stating,

This gospel liberates the dignity of the human person and ensures the freedom of men and women as no human law can do. Pentecostals have an opportunity now to practice the mission of

---

[36] Macchia, *Spirituality and Social Liberation*, p. 45.

the church in their communities by helping human beings to discover in the ultimate meaning of his or her existence.[37]

Pentecostals know well that the Holy Spirit alone is capable of satisfying the deepest needs in the hearts of people. The gospel's purpose is to announce and proclaim the freedom of God's children. It rejects all bondage resulting from the actions of evil. It respects the dignity of conscience and its freedom of choice. Pentecostals also insist that the Holy Spirit encourages the exercise of human talents in the service to humanity. As a matter of fact, He commands everyone to love one another.[38]

Emphasis on a Trinitarian Faith

In the perfect community of God, Jesus Christ, and the Holy Spirit, Pentecostal faith sees the light of moral principles that are the sole and irreplaceable foundation of stability and tranquility of the world's order. According to Wonsuk Ma,

> This Trinitarian faith guarantees internal and external balance in theology, doctrine, and ministry. Such balance becomes the safeguard for a healthy world order. This theological dimension sets the foundation for life in society, which also testifies to God's plan for the world. Men and women are able to interpret and solve their needs in that divine order designed for their community.[39]

For Pentecostals, this is an area of concern. They also understand that any form of exploitation and violation of social injustice is an offence to God and humanity. Hence, there is a spiritual obligation and a human demand for dramatic change that calls for social transformation ensuring justice, peace, and love for all members of the community. Hence, Adolfo Miranda argues that in order to bring such transformation to completion, some will have to invest

---

[37] Dana L. Robert, 'From Mission to Mission to Beyond Mission', *International Bulletin of Missionary Research* 29.2 (April 2000), pp. 50-56.

[38] Saracco, 'Mission and Missiology from Latin America', p. 359.

[39] Wonsuk Ma, 'Biblical Studies in the Pentecostal Tradition: Yesterday, Today and Tomorrow', in Murray W. Dempster, Byron D. Klaus, and Douglas Petersen (eds.), *The Globalization of Pentecostalism: A Religion Made to Travel* (Oxford, UK: Regnum Books, 2000), pp. 52-69.

sacrificial efforts in the cause, especially at critical times in the history of society.[40]

At every critical moment there is a cultural, political, or socioeconomic deficiency arising from particular material interests in the world. It is in this difficult moment when Pentecostals may have to make use of their spiritual sensitivity to face moral issues that work against the benefit of humanity. Concerning the social implications, Miranda argues that believers must not be seduced to surrender their mission or to think that these challenges will be solved easily.[41] On the contrary, it is Christ and the assurance that He gives which will save them: 'I am with you, always!'[42] Therefore, it is not just a matter of learning about effective social skills or implementing attractive programs.

Pentecostals need to know that the plan already exists in the teachings of the gospel. In this plan, Christ is the center. Men and women are invited to His presence, so they will know, love, and imitate Him personally. Once they become part of His congregation of believers, they will experience the benefits of life with the Trinity. Such a Trinitarian relationship enables them to experience and fulfill God's redemptive plan for humanity.

Mission, Family, and Education

Pentecostals have already recognized that the family is the first agency at work in the formation of the dignity of men and women in society. The family is God's design in the construction of community life, whereby love constitutes the link to fellowship and healthy relationships. The family is uniquely designed to teach and nurture ethical, social, and spiritual values essential for the well-being of its members.

The family preserves and teaches social virtues and contributes to society when children learn to respect and pursue the common good. The family enables its members to appreciate freedom and to

---

[40] Adolfo Miranda Sáenz, 'Nicaragua: La Metamorfosis Política de los Evangélicos', in C. René Padilla (ed.), *De la Marginalización al Compromiso: Los Evangélicos y la Política en América Latina* (Buenos Aires, Argentina: Fraternidad Teológica Latinoamericana, 1991), p. 78.

[41] Miranda, Nicaragua: 'La Metamorfosis Política de los Evangélicos', p. 81.

[42] López, *El Nuevo Rostro del Pentecostalismo Latinoamericano*, p. 64.

grow in their social responsibilities which are elements indispensable for the functioning of the community.[43] It is through formation in the family that the fundamental values of human life are communicated and assimilated.

Pentecostals continue to emphasize that life in a family is God's design and original plan for raising children. Parental love draws forth the best in their children. Parents' love is the biblical model that inspires and guides education in society. Thus, education is enriched with the Christian principles derived from the love of God. Children learn about goodness, service, kindness, constancy, and self-sacrifice, which are highly regarded in ethical and moral relationships. Dane Smilde argues,

> Parents have the right and duty to educate their children. This responsibility is connected with the existence of human life. It is original and primary with regard to the educational role of others, on account of the uniqueness of the loving relationship between parents and children. It is irreplaceable and inalienable, and therefore incapable of being entirely delegated to others or usurped by others. Parents have the duty and right to impart Christian education and moral formation to their children, a right the State cannot annul but which it must respect and promote. This is a primary right for the family that Pentecostals must not neglect or delegate.[44]

The family is responsible for providing integral education to children. Family education aims to instill Godly principles that form children in view of God's purpose for their lives. It teaches about the good of the society where they live and develops a sense of responsibility in assuming duties that benefit the community. This environment is ensured when children are educated in love which cultivates the basis for the virtues of justice and peace.

---

[43] López, *El Nuevo Rostro del Pentecostalismo Latinoamericano*, p. 133.

[44] David A. Smilde, 'Gender Relations and Social Change in Latin American Evangelicalism', in Daniel R. Miller (ed.), *Coming of Age: Pentecostalism in Contemporary Latin America* (Lanham, MD: University Press of America, 1994), p. 40.

Mission and the Embrace of Hope

Pentecostals are good at teaching that the gospel provides individuals with the real possibility of overcoming evil and appropriating God's blessing. They strongly proclaim and teach that the Lord Jesus Christ is the only redeemer of humanity. They teach that men and women are bought with the price of the sacrifice of Christ.[45] Although they are clear that all of humanity has fallen into sin and human depravity, they believe there is hope for all who repent and confess Jesus Christ as the Savior of their lives. They also realize that there is hope for better conditions of life for those who are initiated into the 'new life' as believers who are integrated into the community of faith. Pentecostals also teach that the world is the object for the establishment of the kingdom of God.[46]

Pentecostals also know about the effects of 'the mystery of lawlessness'.[47] They are aware that in the human person there exist sufficient qualities and energies of goodness[48] because men and women are made in the image of their Creator. They form part of the redemptive plan of Jesus Christ in the Incarnation. This is confirmed by the ministry of the Holy Spirit who fills the earth with the love of the Father through the sacrifice of the Son.[49]

Pentecostals teach that the Christian hope develops great energy towards a commitment beyond the spiritual needs. It is capable of transcending different social fields, generating confidence with the purpose of promoting a better humanity. Pentecostals encourage believers to model themselves after the character of Christ in their social and family relationships. To do so means practicing a faith that offers hope to those who suffer under all kinds of oppressive and social evils[50] and with confidence await the glory that is to come.[51]

This statement finds a biblical basis in the words of the Apostle Paul, 'For our struggle is not against flesh and blood, but against

---

[45] Saracco, 'Mission and Missiology from Latin America', p. 362.

[46] See Russell P. Spittler, 'Suggested Areas for Further Research in Pentecostalism', *Pneuma: The Journal of the Society for Pentecostal Studies* 5.1 (1983), p. 39.

[47] Miranda, 'Nicaragua', p. 80.

[48] Padilla, *Misión Integral*, p. 79.

[49] Saracco, 'Mission and Missiology from Latin America', p. 359.

[50] Miranda, 'Nicaragua', p. 81.

[51] Padilla, *Misión Integral*, p. 71.

the rulers, against the authorities, against the powers of this dark world and against the spiritual forces of evil in the heavenly realms'.[52] All members of the community of faith are expected to observe such a commitment, although these convictions are also found in members of other groups, which may represent a point of encounter and of reference between believers and other individuals of good will.

The Spirit and the New Civilization

Pentecostal missiology will have to incorporate those principles that sustain society. One important principle is human solidarity, which stimulates that action of love that arises above all other gifts granted to the community of believers.[53] Love is the foundation for the Christian attitude that motivates social activity but also affects human relationships in the political arena.

Community life is shared on the principle of the primacy of love, one of the distinguishing marks of Pentecostalism.[54] Jesus taught that love is the foundation of human relations, so this commandment of love provides the basis for the transformation of society.[55] In the same way, love is the basis for healthy moral behavior and the foundation of the emerging social order[56] that leads to personal and social transformation.

Through the practice of ministry, Pentecostals also emphasize that love is present in the community and is capable of permeating social relations. This teaching is important for those who work for the good of the community. Believers are instruments of inspiration by virtue of the message of love that they announce. True Christian love fulfills the purpose of the gospel. Pentecostals will have to express this love socially and politically as well and must embrace the entire community.

---

[52] Bonilla, 'La Misión de la Iglesia según el Libro de los Hechos', pp. 14-16.

[53] See for instance C. René Padilla, 'Hacia una Evaluación Teológica del Ministerio Integral', in Tetsunao Yamamori, Greg Rake, and C. René Padilla (eds), *Servir con los Pobres en América Latina: Modelos de Ministerio Integral* (Buenos Aires, Argentina: Ediciones Kairós, 1997), pp. 29-52.

[54] Dussel, *The Church in Latin America*, p. 65.

[55] Fumero, *La Iglesia Enfrentando el Nuevo Milenio*, p. 20.

[56] Costas, *Missional Incarnation*, p. 16.

René Padilla suggests that the social expression of love opposes egoism and individualism. The goal of love is the development of individuals who mutually influence one another to grow together in the binding of God's love.[57] Contrarily, individualism leads to the distortion of order in society. History exposes the selfish attitude as well as the altruist motivation of people. Believers are enabled by the Spirit of God to take a stand in favor of justice and peace because this is part of the fulfillment of the gospel.

Pentecostals also affirm the statement of Scripture that love is the greatest commandment in favor of society. Loving believers respect others and their right to be different. Love requires commitment to justice and makes men and women capable of practicing its principles. The love of God inspires people to live a life of self-sacrifice: 'Whoever seeks to gain his life will lose it, but whoever loses his life will preserve it'.[58] Love will find its full expression in the capacity of individuals to establish healthy relations with one another. True love takes its place in humanity when people commit their lives to Christ Jesus.

As stated earlier, the discussion in this chapter is theological in purpose. Due to the nature of the research, I avoided those matters that are commonly known and discussed among Pentecostal missiologists.[59] Therefore, instead of focusing on the virtues and strengths of Pentecostalism, which are obvious, I decided to explore issues that may seem extraneous to those who study Pentecostalism such as political involvement, ethics, culture, and democratic participation that have not been studied or documented before.

Throughout this chapter, we have come to the conclusion that Pentecostals, particularly in Latin America, are now learning that evangelization also includes and legitimizes social action and re-

---

[57] Padilla, 'Hacia una Evaluación Teológica del Ministerio Integral', p. 46.

[58] Costas, *Missional Incarnation*, p. 16.

[59] There are, however, some Pentecostal scholars who have initiated discussions on socio-economic issues, political participation, and human transformation. Among those include Norberto Saracco, 'Argentine Pentecostalism: Its History and Theology' (PhD, University of Birmingham, 1989); Darío López, *El Nuevo Rostro del Pentecostalismo Latinoamericano* (Lima, Perú: Ediciones Puma, 2002); and Bernardo Campos, *De la Reforma Protestante a la Pentecostalidad de la Iglesia: Debate Sobre el Pentecostalismo en América Latina* (Quito, Ecuador: Ediciones CLAI, 1997). These scholars have opened new ways of presenting integral mission to Pentecostals for their consideration.

sponsibility which ultimately lead believers to promote human growth and transformation in their local communities. To accomplish this purpose, Pentecostal mission may have to move forward to face current social trends with a great deal of responsibility. They may also add new areas of service, which are now extended beyond the spiritual experience of redemption. One positive thing is that they are now willing to confront social evils and to promote transformation for political structures when possible.

For the implementation of this model of mission, this study suggests that Pentecostals initiate and maintain significant dialogues with fellow mission agencies and other sources of mission and knowledge that work for the good of the community. Such interdisciplinary activity would enable Pentecostals to offer relevant teachings about social action and community development. Through these teachings, they may enhance knowledge and action to promote reconciliation, justice, and social transformation.

We also found that *Missio Dei* has not always been easy for Pentecostals in Latin America. As we have seen, Pentecostals come from the socio-economic margins of society. Most of them were born and still live within those levels. Hence, the message that they preach and the gospel that they announce are destined to reach out to people of the margins. Henceforth, Pentecostals did not plan to go to the margins to reach out to the poor, for they were already there. Most of them were also marginalized, along with people who are the subjects of evangelization.

Therefore, we are referring here to a significantly different context of mission, which involves most Pentecostals throughout Latin America. Incidentally, Pentecostals do not see their context of ministry from the point of view of foreign missionaries who have left their homeland in order to reach out to people of other contexts. On the contrary, most Pentecostals see themselves as members of the community, and as such, they become agents of transformation to their own people. This fact in itself is a major breakthrough in the practice of integral mission. What they need now is solid teaching and training on the matter.

This section also makes reference to the theological implications of the new context of Pentecostal mission. As stated earlier, such a theological approach contains a significant message of hope for the poor and the marginalized, which is presented in a two-fold way:

first, the sinner is redeemed from his or her old fallen life and placed into a new relationship with a Trinitarian God. The Holy Spirit, who guides the new convert to learn about the character of Christ, leads such a relationship to a personal encounter with the Father. The key to success is to apply this Trinitarian relationship of love into the reality of the new life, both personal and in the community. Second, through a process of discipleship, the believer is led into a better condition of life. He or she is naturally lifted to experience redemption in their socio-economic condition as well. Those who become born again into the Pentecostal family commonly know this experience as a blessing. Thus, society is naturally transformed when more people are added to the family.

Pentecostals are capable of promoting a civilization of love. Their Trinitarian faith enables them to understand and manage their relationship with God. This spiritual dimension becomes true as they practice the principles of the gospel, which could also be seen through the implementation of family values provided by Christian education. Such a new reality provides them with hope for the future and enables believers to work for a society that shows the love of God and where its members are also capable of considering and treating one another as brothers and sisters in Christ.

10

MISSION OF PENTECOSTAL SPIRITUALITY IN LATIN AMERICA

In this chapter I am approaching current issues related to Pentecostal spirituality in Latin America. I describe the observation of the themes and my methodology is largely related to personal observation, although in the second half of the study I do a bibliographical revision of themes related to general Pentecostal spirituality. Such revision also includes some authors from other geographical areas,[1] but their works also move deeper into this topic.

In the beginning of the chapter I describe my personal assessment of the general situation of Pentecostal spirituality in Latin America. I approach the matter from a classical Pentecostal point of view, so the language, the description, and the discussion of current situations are expressed with this background in mind.

---

[1] Some Latin American scholars did extensive studies on Protestant, Evangelical, and Pentecostalism during the second half of the 20th Century. Some of those works are now considered classics. See Willems, *Followers of the New Faith*, and Christian Lalive D'Espinay, *Haven of the Masses: A Study of the Pentecostal Movement in Chile* (London, UK: Lutterworth, 1969). An Evangelical perspective comes from the writings of the late Orlando Costas, *The Church and Its Mission: A Shattering Critique* (Wheaton, IL: Tyndale House, 1974); and *idem*, *Theology of the Crossroads in Latin America* (Amsterdam, Netherlands: Editions Rodopoi, 1976). For information on Brazil, see William R. Read and Frank A. Ineson, *Brazil 1980: The Protestant Handbook* (Monrovia: CA: MARC, 1973).

Pentecostal Spirituality in Latin America

What do we understand about Pentecostal spirituality in the Latin American context? In the case of Latin America, this Christian discipline can be thought of as that experience that is lived by believers, whose spiritual framework includes beliefs, practices, and sensibilities, which put the believer in an ongoing relationship with the Holy Spirit[2] making such experience useful to the community of faith. Steven Land once stated that in order to understand the major qualities of Pentecostal spirituality one has to proceed in two ways. First is the unique *ritual symbols* used by Christians in a congregation as primary factors that affect spirituality in the local context. Those factors could be observed and practiced in the community and symbolize a cluster of sensibilities, qualities, beliefs, and practices connected to spiritual life. Second is a general outline of descriptive symbols that Pentecostals use to explain their *experience with God*.[3] The verification of these factors occurs in the lifestyle, behavior, and commitment of believers to the principles learned in a process of discipleship. In Latin America, Pentecostals also include in their spirituality the manifestations of miracles, healings, signs, wonders, and other gifts of the Spirit in actual church life. Their commitment to Christian mission is tied to these spiritual beliefs and operations, typically known as charismas.

Latin American Pentecostals describe their spirituality using human emotions and feelings attributed to the action of the Holy Spirit in their lives, particularly during the time of praise and worship. They implement diverse forms of human activity in order to affirm their experience with the Holy Spirit.[4] At some point the levels of education of the believer could also measure the nature and quality of the emotions that are linked to spiritual activity.

---

[2] Land, *Pentecostal Spirituality*, p. 72. Although Land writes from an American context, his approach to Pentecostal spirituality is closer to what most denominational Pentecostals are practicing in Latin America. However, the general approach to spirituality by Latin American Pentecostals is very close to the spiritual dynamics of the Roman Catholic Church, at least on the liturgical side of it.

[3] Land, *Pentecostal Spirituality*, p. 86.

[4] Daniel Chiquete, *Haciendo Camino al Andar. Siete,* p. 125. The author writes from his Mexican context and offers fresh ideas regarding the approach of Pentecostals to worship and the practice of the spiritual gifts in mission to the Community.

Moreover, the action of the Holy Spirit affects behavior, attitudes, and emotions, which are ways to connect humanity with the divine. In this regard Esdras Betancourt furthered the notion that there are sociological, psychological, and spiritual benefits in the exercise of charisms.[5] The Holy Spirit does a holistic tune up in the individual, thus making every believer a solid witness of the gospel that changes culture and re-directs society toward better conditions of life.[6]

So Pentecostal spirituality is more than just a simple spiritual manifestation, it involves the whole person and affects his or her world holistically. The Holy Spirit enables believers to transform their community using every resource available to develop human life that is healthy and faithful to Christ. So in order to describe how Pentecostal spirituality works I suggest the following indicators, which may be considered as some of the most visible spiritual trends observed in the region.

Spiritual Background of Latin American Pentecostalism

The Roman Catholic Church (RCC) arrived in Latin America in 1492, with the first colonizers. It was that kind of Catholicism that had not been affected yet by the Reformation. Hence for nearly 520 years after that arrival, the RCC became the main religious tradition that shaped the culture, society, economics, politics, and spiritual life of Latin America. This is the historical heritage of a society that now models family principles and values, cultural traditions, and the religious behavior of the entire Continent. It is clear then that most Latin American Pentecostals have their theological and spiritual background founded on the RCC religious model. Based upon this fact, it is fair to affirm that Latin American Pentecostals are Catholic people converted to Pentecostalism.

Alternatively, Pentecostalism has about a century of history in the continent. In general, the first Pentecostals of Latin America have their origin in two streams, which are largely accepted by most Pentecostal historians. One was brought by Pentecostal missionaries from North America who had a strong evangelical background and

---

[5] Esdras Betancourt, 'Los Beneficios del Bautismo con el Espíritu Santo', *El Evangelio* (April 1976), pp. 8-9.

[6] Betancourt, 'Los Beneficios del Bautismo con el Espíritu Santo', p. 8.

a second stream of Pentecostalism which initiated among local free evangelical congregations in the region. One example is the 1909 Pentecostal movement that began in Chile and later on in Brazil in 1914. These free Pentecostal movements took place after the teachings and practices of holiness by some Methodist congregations that settled in Latin America before the Pentecostal awakening in the region. In any case all of these Pentecostal movements were established among Catholic societies and cultures of the area.

The dialectic relationship between the historical RCC and the new Pentecostal streams initiated a third stream of spirituality. On the one hand, there was the Pentecostal faith, which was established among Catholic masses of poor and marginalized people who embraced a new way of Christianity with a new and strong spiritual commitment to the gospel. On the other hand was the Pentecostal faith, which was established among middle class Catholics that was known later on as the Catholic Charismatic Renewal movement. Charismatics in Latin America had their Pentecostal experience but decided to stay in the Catholic Church, contrary to what happened with the lower class, where Catholics left their church and became denominational Pentecostals. They joined either the historical Pentecostal denominations of the 20th Century or the free Pentecostal organizations available in their communities.

The clash between Pentecostals and the historical RCC also initiated new and creative ways of Pentecostal and charismatic expressions. At some point Catholics have been Pentecostalized and also Pentecostals have been catholicized, thus generating a new spirituality that reflects both streams in the practice of ministry and the sacraments.[7] These new streams could be observed among Neo-Pentecostal congregations that have incorporated new leadership

---

[7] Although from another geographical area, one example of this phenomenon is the El Shaddai movement in the Philippines. Pastor Mike Velarde is a Catholic lay Pastor who ministers in the Pentecostal and Charismatic style. Catholics are not suspicious of his affiliation for he claims to be Catholic, yet they receive the benefits of a Pentecostal and Charismatic practice of ministry. This phenomenon is particularly useful in a RCC society like in the Philippines. El Shaddai has grown extensively, particularly among the Filipino people who refuse to leave their Catholic tradition. See Mariano 'Mike' Z. Velarde, *El Shaddai's Miracle Assurance Police against Sickness, Famine, and Bankruptcy* (Makati, Philippines: El Shaddai, DWXI-PPFI, 1933), pp. 31-36.

models, such as the Apostolic and Prophetic movement as understood and operated by Latin Americans.

Classic Pentecostalism is different in Latin America than in North America. The two regions show different historical backgrounds that must be acknowledged. In North America most Pentecostals come from the evangelical tradition, whereas in Latin America they inherited a strong RCC background.

North American Pentecostals seem to be increasingly challenged by the same social issues plaguing the broader society. Yet the insufficient solutions they often posit are based on less than adequate understandings of the complexity of the spiritual issues that affect their current cultural context. Their responses often degenerate into one of two inappropriate approaches. The first produces literal propositions that fail to engage the contemporary context fully, while also negating the Holy Spirit's ongoing work in equipping the church for contemporary ministry. The second reduces the authority of Scripture to a minimal role in determining the basis for fundamental Christian actions and attitudes.

In North America, brokenness, economic disparity, poverty, health care, undocumented immigration, family and social concerns continue to challenge an authentic Christian witness from the church and its leaders. Moreover, many of these leaders hold a lingering distrust for theological education and they are unprepared for the academic challenges that an educated society requires. This is only to mention some issues related to North American Pentecostalism, which reflect a different reality compared to Latin American Pentecostalism. However, much deeper research will have to be done in order to explain properly these affirmations.

In the case of Latin America, the growing disenchantment with the RCC and the search for other spiritual alternatives has moved Pentecostals to identify new ways to experience their spiritual life while Catholicism is also seen as a fallen religious system. Most of them resent the fact that the Catholic Church kept them, for centuries, alienated from the new experience they have now discovered. The Catholic Church also represents, in their mind, an agent of alienation, oppression, and compromise with the demonic powers of the world.[8] The spirit of Pentecost is the 'new wine' that must be

---

[8] See Howard, 'Great Things to Come', pp. 38-39.

preserved in 'new wineskins' in order to keep it sound and effec-tive.[9] For Pentecostals in Latin America to witness is to unveil the truth to those who have remained deceived or neglected by an ob-solete religious system.[10] Conversion then occurs when the individ-ual understands the gospel as revealed by the scripture and the Holy Spirit, and joins the Pentecostal family followed by the new para-digm of the life in the Spirit experienced by believers at the com-munity of faith.

Here it is also important to highlight the dialectical relationship that occurs between Pentecostals from North American back-ground and those from the RCC background. Although they may enjoy the same Pentecostal experience, their traditions push them into different wings of reality. This clash also generates a new Pen-tecostal way of expressing faith, theology, and spirituality. In some cases, this encounter may generate frustration, but intentional un-derstanding may lead believers into exercising comprehension of the historical differences observed on both sides. Thus a new Pen-tecostality[11] emerges in the new community of the Spirit in Latin America.

In light of the above it is reasonable to conclude that there are significant differences between Latin and North American Pente-costalims. So it is also fair to present the case for a unique Latin American Pentecostal Spirituality.

Current Trends in Latin American Pentecostalism

It is well known that Pentecostalism in Latin America has grown significantly in recent years. This growth can be observed mainly through high numbers in attendance, which is currently seen in a significant number of congregations recently established in the area. Also these new churches and ministries have impacted local com-munities in a number of fields for the benefit of humanity. These are some indicators that Pentecostalism is by now one of the most influential spiritual movements in the region.[12] For instance, the

---

[9] See Mt. 9.17.

[10] Tapia, 'Why is Latin America Turning Protestant?', pp. 28-29.

[11] See Campos, *De la Reforma Protestante a la Pentecostalidad de la Iglesia*, pp. 65-76.

[12] Bill Sundstrom, 'Growing Confidence Spurs Latin American Out-reach', *Christianity Today* 3 (February 1997), p. 87.

Church of God (Cleveland, TN) is now reporting more than eight thousand congregations and expects more that fifteen thousand by the year 2020. Like this, other Pentecostal movements are also reporting a high number of members.[13]

Why is this happening? There may be many reasons that explain it, but I would like to focus on one that I think is crucial for Pentecostals to continue to grow, that is, Pentecostal spirituality.[14] A lot has been said about the response of Pentecostalism towards disaster, poverty, and social unrest in the world. Historically, Latin Americans have responded positively to the Pentecostal offer of hope to people in times of crisis.[15] However, Pentecostalism would have not been received with such positive attitude if not for the spiritual impact of devoted believers serving in the communities. Such devotion is facilitated by prayer, fasting, and other spiritual methods used by the congregations to inspire devotion and commitment to the great commission.

Like in other places of the world Latin American Pentecostals have learned to depend on prayer and fasting for most of their actions.[16] They believe these disciplines are necessary in order to sharpen their focus on mission. At the local congregations they are taught that holiness is the standard of life for God's people. They also realized how important it is to have experienced sanctification and the baptism of the Holy Spirit in order to be effective and well prepared to express God's love to people and serve them in their local communities. Most Pentecostals have concluded that if every believer uses his or her priestly call from God then each one is capable of carrying out his or her ministry in a healthy spiritual condition. This notion leads them into a prayerful life as the main source of spiritual enrichment and this discipline seems to remain active at

---

[13] Exact figures on Pentecostal churches for all countries of Latin America do not exist yet. This data comes from different sources, see William R. Read, Víctor M. Monterroso, and Harmon A. Johnson (eds.), *Latin American Church Growth* (Grand Rapids, MI: Eerdmans, 1969), pp. 313-25; also, Patrick Johnston, *Operation World* (Carlisle, PA: OM Publishing, 1993), p. 65; and Emilio A. Núñez and William D. Taylor, *Crisis and Hope in Latin America*, p. 112.

[14] Harvey Cox, *Fire from Heaven*, p. 82. Cox's work confirms the impact of Pentecostalism in the last 100 years.

[15] Tapia, 'Growing Pains', pp. 12-13.

[16] On this matter, see Álvarez, 'The South and the Latin American Paradigm of the Pentecostal Movement', pp. 135-53.

all levels of Christian service.[17] Pastors and local church leaders pound on the importance of prayer and fasting for the purpose of strengthening believers in order to edify their personal spirituality and to serve effectively in ministry.

Respect from Outside the Community of Faith

So it is clear that personal conversion, commitment to Christ, sanctification, and the baptism of the Holy Spirit are events that enable believers to be effective in the action of reaching out to the needy, the poor, and the marginalized. Once people respond to the preaching of the gospel, those who accept Christ are consolidated into the congregation through a systematic program, which leads new believers into solid programs of discipleship. These actions create a culture of evangelism and church growth, which is intentionally planned and executed as citywide efforts that involve local people in ministry. Many believers are part of small groups where they experience much of their Christian life. Pentecostals consider all of these events as part of their faith and spiritual and human transformation. As a result, congregations grow numerically and are now capable, in some places, to influence local authorities in the communities. Thus, local governments are now paying attention to the voices and opinions of these congregations.[18] So believers seem to be taking part in the decisions and plans of local authorities on behalf of their people.

The Spiritual Battle for the Region

It is clear that this kind of spiritual influence eventually causes positive effects in society. In order to make this point clear, I must say here, that Latin America is now facing one of the most dramatic situations in its spiritual realm. There are two extremes that can be clearly identified: on one side there is the transforming power of

---

[17] See López, *Pentecostalimo y Transformación Social*, 29; also López, *Los Evangélicos y Los Derechos Humanos*, pp. 65-75. López's work is important for he writes from the context of the poor in the marginalized areas of Lima, Peru. He is one of the first scholars to address the issue of transformation from the margins of society.

[18] Wells-Davies, 'La Naturaleza de la Conversión Pentecostal en la Argentina', p. 161.

the gospel and on the other there is also the destructive sources of evil that still remain strong in the continent.[19]

The church is growing strongly and continues to transform people's lives and communities, but the power of evil also continues to increase its destructive power over those who remain marginalized from the gospel. There is a spiritual conflict that is currently battling for the control of Latin America. While evil increases violence, death, destruction, and immorality through economic, social, and political structures, the church intensifies prayers and Christian action for the sake of those who are the direct victims of the schemes of evil. Because of this spiritual conflict Latin America is now going through a historical battle that affects the entire human and spiritual reality.[20] Christians know and understand this well so they are intentionally intensifying prayer. There is no doubt the Holy Spirit is at work in the continent.

Agents of Evil Enthroned in Political Structures

Political authorities – even those who enter into power democratically – are in a position to manipulate their constitutions in order to remain in control of their nations without term limits. The situation worsens with the support of the international community, which also practices double standards toward governments and countries, depending on the interests of those who control politics in the world. Thus, corruption is found at all levels and seems to have permeated most political structures of today's world.

This phenomenon is clearly observed in several Latin American governments. Such political structures and personalities deform the culture of economics, social relationships, and people's moral behavior. This reality has given birth to new forms of evil such as the drug traffic, gangs, and diverse forms of violence. Civility has been

---

[19] Wolfgang Bünne, *Explosión Carismática* (Terrassa, España: Editorial CLIE, 1994), p. 141. The original title was: *Dritte Welle ... Gesunder Aufruch?* (Bielfeld: CLV, 1991). The author does a critical analysis of the doctrines and practices of so-called 'Three Waves' of the Holy Spirit. He studied the most current trends of the Charismatic and neo-Pentecostal leaders and churches.

[20] An extensive survey on Latin American Pentecostalism was done by Soneira, 'Los Estudios Sociológicos sobre el Pentecostalismo en América Latina', pp. 29-47.

severely affected by the negative power of corruption at all levels. As I write, some Central American countries are undergoing one of the darkest times in history under the attack of these evils. For instance, Honduras was recently labeled as one of the most violent countries of the world, but the other Central American nations and Mexico are also facing similar circumstances. Evil is affecting all citizens and demands that individuals make a choice to accept or reject participating in evil 'business'.

Spiritual Influence from Pentecostal Congregations

Latin American Pentecostals have understood the serious responsibility that they have assumed under the given circumstances of this time. For them there is no turning back in their commitment to the truth of the gospel.[21] In the midst of corruption, poverty, and violence, they are aware of their important role in the redemption of their nations – the opportunity is now.

Pentecostals are headed to evangelize the poor, the weak and the marginalized. They focus their efforts to spread hope and a new condition of life as the main source to counter attack the destructive forces of evil. They realize victory is possible if they observe and practice their faith by showing solidarity with those who are hurting but are willing to accept the message of hope delivered by fellow Christians.

Pentecostals are also practicing an intelligent reading and interpretation of the Scripture as well as commitment to the great commission even if this means sacrifice or suffering. Their personal relationship with the Holy Spirit keeps them focused on their mission and strong in the battle against evil. The altar is still open and occupied by the poor, the weak, the sick, and the marginalized. Pentecostal congregations continue to witness and win people for Christ. They seem to be relevant and very active in their ministry '*a-la-Pentecostal*'.

---

[21] Cleary, 'Latin American Pentecostalism', pp. 127-45 (133).

Growing Numerically but Social Evils Persist

In countries like Guatemala, for instance, Pentecostals have been criticized for claiming large numbers of adherents yet the country remains one of the most violent and corrupted of the hemisphere. Such criticism does not seem to be accurate for it does not report what actually happens with the two extremes that struggle for the control of Guatemala. Pentecostals are using every way possible to counter attack the forces of evil. Prayer has intensified and social work has increased dramatically and intentionally in most communities.[22] Assistance to the poor and marginalized has intensified. Believers are making every effort possible to advance the transformational power of the gospel in politics and socio-economic terrains.

Poverty and insecurity about the future lead to a search for ultimate answers. Pentecostals in Latin America come from the most marginalized segments of their society. The movement was born in the midst of the poor masses and it represents their voice in articulating the revelation and hope that the Holy Spirit has given to those who had no other voice. In some circles Latin American Pentecostalism has been referred to as 'a revolution of the poor'. For them there cannot be a dichotomizing between theory and praxis in a world of poverty and insecurity. Here theory arises from the praxis to further praxis that eventually leads to change and to the building of a different society. It is the community of faith that determines the destiny and ultimate answers that both edify the believers and send a prophetic message to the world to find the answers in the incarnated Pentecostal Jesus.

My argument is that Pentecostals have made a significant impact in the process of the evangelization of Latin America. I also recognize that there are irreconcilable variables in understanding and approaching mission in the continent. However, for the purpose of this study I am staying consistent with the notion of mission as known by Pentecostals in Latin America. They understand that mission moves them to the proclaim the gospel of Jesus Christ as the fulfilment of the great commission. Such proclamation reaches out

---

[22] Campos, 'In the Power of the Spirit', pp. 41-50 (50). From a Pentecostal and sociological perspective, Campos' main interest is to examine the role of Pentecostalism in context, particularly in the context of marginalization, which is the typical social and economic condition of Pentecostals in Latin America.

to every man and woman who is in need of spiritual salvation, which, once accepted, adds transformation to the individual and their world.[23]

For most Pentecostals is Latin America, the first responsibility of a believer is to look for the salvation of others, especially those who are close such as relatives and friends. This thrust generates new conversions, which continues to grow in numbers.[24] Once a community is reached by the gospel, transformation starts at home, at the barrio, and in the community. Believers no longer participate in worldly activities and scenarios of evil. These events are multiplied from one community to another, congregations continue to grow and spiritual revival is seen mostly through a devoted prayer life and the subsequent outpourings of the Holy Spirit that take place with the manifestation of spiritual gifts in the life and ministry of believers.

Such growth also brings about social transformation. New converts leave behind old paradigms of life and now look for new options and possibilities. This Pentecostal growth has reached higher levels of influence. Entire communities have changed by the influence of Pentecostal life and spirituality. The results are obvious and can be seen in the family, school, and in social relationships. Once the inner circle of relationships is won for Christ the next step is to reach out to other families and communities so the cycle keeps multiplying on and on.

Having presented this picture, then the anti-thesis comes in. Pentecostal growth also awakens the forces of evil. The enemy of God and all of his fellow demons has had control of the people of Latin America for centuries. They are not willing to let that possession go to other hands. An obvious battle for the possession of territories, people, and political structures arises.[25] God's people on the move

---

[23] On the matter of Pentecostalism and evangelism in Latin America, see Yara Monteiro, 'Congregación Cristina en Brasil, de la Fundación Centenario: La Trayectoria de una Iglesia Brasileña', pp. 77-140 (90).

[24] Rodolfo Girón, 'The Latin-American Missionary Movement: A New Paradigm in Missions', *AD 2000* (2000). http://www.ad2000.org/celebrate/giron.htm. Accessed 19 November 2011.

[25] World Evangelical Alliance, *The Grand Rapids Report on Evangelism and Social Responsibility: An Evangelical Commitment* (Exeter, UK: Paternoster, 1982), pp. 43-44.

conquering territory formerly possessed by the enemy are now challenging the forces of evil and they are not going to relinquish what has been theirs for a long time. Two spiritual realities are combating for the control of Latin America and the manifestation of both forces can be seen in the fields of socio-economics, political structures, and spiritual and moral behavior.

Inherited Patterns from Outside

Not all things are looking good among Latin American Pentecostals. Some seem to be prone to absorb the bad habits or the junk teachings of Charismatics and Neo-Pentecostals from North America. The prosperity gospel has permeated the middle and upper class of the region. Televangelism influenced by the new apostolic and prophetic movement has incorporated the teachings of the gospel of faith and prosperity to promote new forms of ministry,[26] which challenges the teaching and practices of traditional Pentecostals. These movements own the Christian mass media and are in control of the promotion of a 'new-gospel' message, while most Pentecostals continue to serve their communities in the traditional way.[27] Hence, most of the human and financial resources available to Christians also join these movements thus leaving Pentecostals only depending on their local efforts, mostly supported by the masses that remain working in the slums and poor areas.[28]

Fortunately, the middle and upper classes are not large enough yet to represent a threat to the missional congregations established

---

[26] Rigoberto Gálvez, *Prácticas Dudosas en el Ejercicio de Nuestra Fe: Un Estudio de la Religiosidad Popular Evangélica, Una Autocrítica* (Ciudad Guatemala: Guatemala: Editorial Fortaleza, 2009), p. 151.

[27] See Garrard-Burnett and David Stoll, *Rethinking Protestantism in Latin America*, p. 118; Also, Robeck, Jr., 'Selected Bibliography on Latin American Pentecostalism', pp. 193-97. See also Russell P. Spittler, 'Are Pentecostals and Charismatics Fundamentalists? A Review of American Uses of These Categories', in Karla Poewe (ed.), *Charismatic Christianity as a Global Culture* (Columbia, SC: University of South Carolina Press, 1994), pp. 103-16.

[28] See Jim Henderson and Matt Casper, *Jim & Casper Go to Church: Frank Conversation About Faith, Churches, and Well-Meaning Christians* (Ventura, CA: Barna Books, 2007). See also Diana Eck, '*A New Religious America: How a "Christian Country" Has Become the World's Most Religiously Diverse Nation*' (San Francisco, CA: Harper & Row, 2001).

among the poor and marginalized across the region. Nevertheless this contradiction creates unrest, disorder, and concern within Pentecostal circles for they do not have enough resources to face such an avalanche.[29] In the meantime Pentecostal leaders are in the waiting mode to observe when and how will this latest fad evolve. Yet, they continue to train their leaders so they can respond appropriately to the current demands and to continue expanding and plating new churches.

Besides this spiritual condition, Pentecostals in Latin America also observe some of the following characteristics.

Best Mission is Community Orientated

In the context of Pentecostal spirituality, community service is born out of solidarity with God who frees the body of believers from competitiveness and disciplinary self-absorption to learn how to live and practice the spiritual virtues that encourage one another to mission. Pentecostals are now able to share caring and mentoring relationships with one another in their own context of service. They are no longer controlled by their busyness and heavy workloads. Instead believers make time to celebrate, enjoy, and worship in true bounds of love and community. Lois McKinney observes that when Christians experience community life, institutional and societal norms no longer control them. They have recognized their negative values, and have begun, instead, a journey toward community. She also observes that this is still a long and difficult journey of hope, but people can be changed, and even structures can be transformed.[30]

Emphasis on the 'Priesthood of All Believers'

In the Pentecostal communities the goal of ministry is that of corporate work and development for effective service. The local congregation and its ministry are both the object and context for mission in the community. For most Pentecostals to serve in the world is more than the expression of those wanting to express their par-

---

[29] Gálvez. *Prácticas Dudosas en el Ejercicio de Nuestra Fe*, p. 154.

[30] See Lois McKinney, 'From Loneliness Toward Solitude and Community', in Duane Elmer and Lois McKinney (eds.), *With an Eye on the Future* (Monrovia, CA: MARC, 1996), pp. 87-92; Also, Hugo Slim and Paul Thompson, *Listening for a Change: Oral Testimony and Community Development* (Philadelphia, PA: New Society, 1995), p. 78.

ticular abilities, vocations, or gifts. The gospel has shaped believer's speech, action, and lifestyle. So congregations are now exercising a lifestyle, thinking, and spiritual labor that is guided by the assurance that ministry is found in the spiritual experience of Christ who works through the Holy Spirit in the heart of believers.[31] Pentecostals accept that believers work with Christ by using the spiritual gifts given to them by the Holy Spirit.

In Pentecostal spirituality a deeper understanding of mission is not enough. There must be an intentional spiritual discipline observed in their lives that equips them for mission even if it means adopting new strategies, new ideas, or new strategies for service. Pentecostal service is dynamic and aims to implement the spiritual meaning of the New Testament's doctrine of the priesthood of all believers. For this principle to be successful it must be executed thoroughly and this is the spiritual breath of all believers as they move forward to witnessing for Christ. Under this category, all believers are ministers, and they serve their communities under the endowment of the Holy Spirit.[32] The Holy Spirit has gifted them with special abilities for effective service.[33] The Apostle explicitly states that each believer is a unique creation in Christ Jesus with specific, before-hand-ordained ministry, to accomplish the mission of God in every people group.[34]

In his understanding of the corporate ministry practiced by Pentecostals, Peter Hocken has suggested that for Pentecostal spirituality it is central to participate in ministry, whereby as a movement, all participants have an equal dignity and participation.[35] He also affirmed that the Holy Spirit was poured out on 'all flesh', not just upon ordained clerical flesh, not just educated degreed flesh, not just aristocratic propertied flesh.[36] In regards to Pentecostal spirituality Hocken also suggests that the least educated, the least affluent and those with no social status, the Holy Spirit could equally equip these people for ministry. They all could be recipients of the spir-

---

[31] Campos, *De La Reforma Protestante a la Pentecostalidad de la Iglesia*, pp. 90-106.

[32] 1 Peter 2.9, 10.

[33] 1 Corinthians 12.11.

[34] Ephesians 2.10.

[35] Peter Hocken, 'Cecil H. Polhill – Pentecostal Layman', *Pneuma: The Journal of the Society for Pentecostal Studies* 10.2 (Fall 1988), pp. 129-37.

[36] Hocken, 'Cecil H. Polhill', p. 138.

itual gifts; all could become instruments of the Lord in word and act.[37] This is a significant recognition of a truth amply demonstrated since early Pentecostal history.

The Natural Development and Exercise of the Charismata

Pentecostals operate under the hermeneutic that all the elements of the New Testament's ministry and experience may be hoped for, sought, and expected today since none of them permanently ceased when the apostolic age ended. Those elements now available for the believer are (a) post-conversion Spirit-baptism, as seen in the book of Acts.[38] Another element is (b) *glossolalia* (not understood as *xenolalia*) given primarily for private devotional use; (c) interpretation of tongues, when the gift is manifested as part of the charismatic 'liturgy';[39] (d) prophecy, understood as a spontaneous utterance in one's own language which expresses the heart of God to the gathered community of the Spirit for the purposes of edification, exhortation, and comfort.[40]

Other charismatic elements available are (e) gifts of healing through prayer and the laying on of hands; (f) deliverance from demonic influences in the authority of the name of Jesus; and (g) words of knowledge, understood as supernatural exposure of information to nurture individuals and the body of believers.[41] In Latin America, Pentecostals also understand the spiritual gifts to have a missiological purpose. The missiological purpose of the Pentecostal experience is clearly observed in the context of the New Testament.[42]

Therefore, the issue of spirituality in Pentecostal ministry must be seen and interpreted missiologically. Thus Pentecostal spirituality is not simply a matter of inwardness. There is also the outward dimension of spirituality, experienced in Christian service. There is no place for a dichotomy between heart and mind or between mind

---

[37] Hocken, 'Cecil H. Polhill', p. 130.

[38] Acts 2.1-4; 8.14-17; 10.44-46; 11.15-17; 19.1-6.

[39] 1 Corinthians 14.26-28.

[40] 1 Corinthians 14.3.

[41] For more information on this subject, see Ingrid J. Parker, 'Pentecostalism 'Reinvented': The Charismatic Renewal', in Harold Smith (ed.), *Pentecostals from the Inside Out* (Wheaton, IL: Victor Books, 1990), pp. 146-48.

[42] Acts 1.8.

and service. In Latin America, Pentecostals are now practicing a committed life that David Bosch called a 'spirituality of the road'.[43]

Indicators of Success in the Pentecostal Community

The following set of indicators may help to understand and measure success within the Pentecostal community. They are seen as the natural outcome of the primary Pentecostal reality of being baptized in the Holy Spirit and a dedicated and committed life to Christ. These indicators can be identified as: (a) obvious numerical results in ministry (quantifiable results), (b) clear evidence of church growth and ministerial growth, (c) a living exercise of charismata, (d) dynamic preaching, (e) overall prosperity, (f) a passionate Christian lifestyle following after the principles of the Word of God, and (g) a strong missionary orientation.

One special indicator is a powerful Pentecostal preaching or witnessing which is spiritually anointed and passionate. It is expressed as a divinely driven communication based on the truths of the Scripture. Pentecostal preaching comes from the heart of the preacher straight to the heart of the listener. It provides wholesome spiritual nourishment for God's people and conviction to the unbeliever.

A second noteworthy characteristic is militant evangelism. Pentecostal spirituality provides believers a paradigm for the blending of the community of faith under the ultimate goal of winning the lost, with all the other ministry activities. Hence, in counseling, preaching, organizing, promoting, visiting the sick, or any other ministries, Pentecostal spirituality focuses on seeking and searching for the lost as central in ministry.

Christian Character and Pentecostal Spirituality

There are four elements that characterize Pentecostal spirituality. First, Pentecostal spirituality is expressed through compassion and love. True Pentecostalism reflects Christ's character in its personal lifestyle. Moreover, it shows the fruit of the Spirit with the evidences of love, joy, peace, patience, kindness, goodness, and faithfulness among those who follow the Lord.

---

[43] David J. Bosch, *A Spirituality of the Road* (Scottsdale, PA: Herald Press, 1979), p. 100. See also, Bosch, *Transforming Mission*, p. 496.

Second, Pentecostal spirituality is Christ-like in forgiveness. The goal of Pentecostal life is to model Christ's character before the community; it shows how believers resolve conflict and demonstrate mercy. It also shows them how to forgive.

Third, Pentecostal spirituality models commitment to build people. Pentecostals are people who see with eyes of discernment and call forth the best from within a person. They are people who look beyond the idiosyncrasies of the present and see with eyes of faith what they *can be*, not just what *is*.

Fourth, Pentecostals are peacemakers. If the role of the Holy Spirit is to witness to Christ and help God's people to become more Christ-like, and since Christ was the Prince of Peace, then it seems logical that a Pentecostal becomes a peacemaker in his or her community. Nothing is more inconsistent with who the believers are, than turmoil, dissention, and strife. Hence, peace is something Pentecostals make. This is not something they should expect to be handed to them.

Reflection in Pentecostal Spirituality

Reflection in the Pentecostal context must address more than simple meditation on biblical truths. It also has to do with *praxis*.[44] Pentecostal reflection has the function of forming persons who can serve after the model of Jesus.[45] It appeals to the life outlook; the clarification and strengthening of convictions and beliefs that provide personal identity and order and penetrate professional activities and Christian service. In light of this need for reflection in the process of spiritual growth, Hough and Cobb proposed a new leadership paradigm to lead the church. This leadership functions as 'practical theologians'.[46] These individuals are engaged in 'critical

---

[44] On the issue of *praxis* as a model of education and social transformation, see Jackie D. Johns, 'Yielding to the Spirit: The Dynamics of a Pentecostal Model of Praxis', in Murray W. Dempster, Byron D. Klaus, and Douglas Petersen (eds.), *The Globalization of Pentecostalism: A Religion Made to Travel* (Oxford, UK: Regnum Books International, 1999), pp. 70-84.

[45] See Ted W. Ward, 'Servants, Leaders, and Tyrants', in Harvey M. Conn and Samuel F. Rowen (eds.), *Missions and Theological Education* (Farmington, MI: Associates of Urbanus, 1984), pp. 19-40.

[46] Schubert M. Ogden, 'Christian Theology and Theological Education', in Don S. Browning, David Polk, and Ian E. Evison (eds.), *The Education of the Practical Theologian: Responses to Joseph Hough and John Cobb's Christian Identity and Theological Education* (Atlanta, GA: Scholar Press, 1989), pp. 21-26.

reflection of the church's practice'.[47] Without such reflective leadership the church will lose its identity.

Pentecostal spirituality could also be understood in the context of its historical development. After a Century of uninterrupted growth; the Pentecostal community, in the 21st Century has become more extensively networked. Thus it is imperative that a far greater attentiveness must be given to the needs and expectations of its constituency. The Pentecostal community must be served through multiple models of ongoing contact and interaction between local leaders and the community of faith.[48] Believers are called to forge healthy working relationships with pastors and lay leaders in local congregations, social agencies, and other Christian entities so that the people may have access to the life of the community beyond formal church activities.

This model of reflection emphasizes the importance of an environment where there is a continual interaction between society and the community of faith. Therefore, a broad spiritual network fosters healthy relationships within the larger perimeter of the Christian community.

Lastly, Pentecostal spirituality offers remarkable resources to further spiritual formation.[49] This enhancement has enabled Pentecostals to enter into the third millennium and meet the multiple responsibilities of a post-modern society. Pentecostals are now able to reach the urban poor, the upper class, the university world, and the marginalized.[50] A good number of those converts are also committed to cross-cultural service.

Summary

It is clear that Pentecostals are making a significant impact in the spiritual life of Latin America. They continue to grow in numbers mainly in the midst of the poor and marginalized – the gospel is

---

[47] Ogden, 'Christian Theology and Theological Education', p. 25.

[48] See Robert W. Ferris, *Renewal in Theological Education: Strategies for Change* (Wheaton, IL: Billy Graham Center, 1990), p. 127.

[49] Frank D. Macchia, *Spirituality and Social Liberation: The Message of the Blumhardts in the Light of Wuerttemberg Pietism* (Metuchen, NJ: Scarecrow, 1993), pp. 25-34.

[50] Lois McKinney, 'New Directions in Missionary Education', pp. 241-50.

announced to most people and the spiritual benefits are imparted to those who believe in Christ Jesus as Lord and Savior.[51] Moreover, believers are also impacting the political and socio-economic structures of important communities. Pentecostals are aware of their role in the spiritual warfare for the control of Latin America and they have engaged the enemy with the power of the Holy Spirit.[52] Once taking all of these facts into consideration it is fair to conclude that Pentecostalism is making a difference and the transformation of Latin America depends on their spiritual efficiency.

Pentecostals are becoming involved in socioeconomic and political concerns in the continent, however they are still limited in their participation.[53] This reality also affects their spiritual life, for they are still finding their way through the new conditions of life in their local communities. The Roman Catholic Church is still in control of the culture, which influences family values, social structures and behavior, education, and even politics. Pentecostals are learning to practice their spirituality in the midst of this reality. One thing that helps them is the high numbers of conversions. By natural growth they are changing lives and therefore changing society. Incidentally, the Roman Catholic Church is now inserting some Pentecostal liturgy into their Catholic liturgy. For instance, Catholics are using praise and worship styles that they have copied from Pentecostal churches.

Pentecostals also have some limitations that need significant attention. For instance, their involvement in ecumenical dialogue is limited. There are some attitudes toward other members of the body of Christ that need to be corrected. Pentecostals are also prone to split from main denominations when disagreement becomes hard to overcome. Thus training to dialogue with other

---

[51] See the work of Luis Orellana, 'El Futuro del Pentecostalismo en América Latina', pp. 141-51.

[52] See for instance Pablo Deiros, *La Acción del Espíritu Santo en la Historia: Las Lluvias Tempranas* (Miami, FL: Editorial Caribe, 1998), p. 92; See also Juan Sepúlveda, *De Peregrinos a Ciudadanos. Breve Historia del Cristianismo Evangélico en Chile* (Santiago, Chile: Comunidad Teológica de Chile, 1999), p. 91.

[53] A large discussion on this matter is presented by Heinrich Schäfer, 'La Generación del Sentido Religioso: Observaciones Acerca de la Diversidad Pentecostal en América Latina', in Daniel Chiquete and Luis Orellana (eds.), *Voces del Pentecostalismo Latinoamericano* (Concepción, Chile: RELEP, 2009), III, pp. 45-65 (50).

members of the body who differ in opinion is necessary. Obviously there are other limitations that could be considered as part of some Pentecostal limitations, which could be done in further studies. However, for the purpose of this presentation I would rather mention the above issues. If they succeed in an intentional effort to overcome them, their expansive growth may develop stronger ministries across the area.

A century of Pentecostalism in Latin America has caused that new opportunities and possibilities emerge for the good of the region. Latino worship continues to grow strong even in other geographical regions. That is one of the reasons why Pentecostal spirituality is becoming significant in Latin America. Pentecostals are everywhere and witnessing to everybody, using creative ways of praise, worship, teaching, and preaching.[54] Lay people have made their way through the religious systems to participate actively in ministry. Owing to Pentecostal spirituality, Latin American seems to have entered into a time of spiritual awakening, and Pentecostals contributed to this development.

---

[54] With regards to extensive growth of Pentecostalism in Latin America, see the remarks of Álvarez, *Alborada de Tiempos Fecundos*, pp. 30-31.

11

HISTORICAL AND FUTURE SCENARIOS

In this section we will examine the historical connections of Pentecostal missiology with other Christian traditions both in Latin America and worldwide. We will look at the emerging contexts of contemporary church mission and how that connection has contributed to the development of recent missiology in Latin America.[1] This information is also significant to Pentecostals for they have served the poor and marginalized in a unique fashion. They still may need to elaborate on a thorough theology of integral mission that may incorporate some principles discussed in this work.

---

[1] These are some Pentecostal scholars who have contributed to mission theology in recent years: Mario R. López, *Historia y Misión del Protestantismo Hondureño* (San José, Costa Rica: Editorial Visión Mundial Internacional, 1993); Gilberto Alvarado López, *El Poder Desde el Espíritu. La Visión Política del Pentecostalismo en el México Contemporáneo* (Buenos Aires, Argentina: Publicaciones Científicas para el Estudio de las Religiones, 2006); Darío López, *Pentecostalismo y Misión Integral: Teología del Espíritu, Teología de la Vida* (Lima, Perú: Ediciones Puma, 2008); Mario G. Méndez, 'La Iglesia: Fuerza del Espíritu, Su Unidad y Diversidad', in Carmelo Álvarez (ed.), *Pentecostalismo y Liberación: Una Experiencia Latinoamericana* (San José, Costa Rica: Departamento Ecuménico de Investigaciones, 1992); Elizabeth Salazar Sanzana, *Todas Seríamos Rainhas: Historia do Pentecostalismo Chileno da Perspectiva da Mulher* (ThM, Instituto Metodista da Ensino Superior: Brasil, 1995); Norberto Saracco, 'Mission and Missiology from Latin America', in William D. Taylor (ed.), *Global Missiology for the 21st Century* (Grand Rapids, MI: Baker Academic, 2000); Norberto Saracco, 'Reflections on the Pentecostal Contribution to the Mission of the Church in Latin America', *Journal of Pentecostal Theology* 1.1 (1992); Bravo, *El Fruto del Espíritu*. Other scholars are cited in the following chapters.

The discussion is based on contemporary texts written by missiologists and documents that have come out of major consultations where mission was discussed. It is also limited mostly to evangelical scholarship, which began to expand after the Lausanne Congress on World Evangelization in 1972. Lausanne is recognized by most missiologists as representing a watershed[2] for current evangelical mission theology.

Those international events had repercussions in Latin America as well. The evangelical conferences and the World Council of Churches (WCC) assemblies debated missiological trends that took place during the time they met. Moreover, they invited representatives from evangelical and protestant churches from Latin America to participate in their meetings. Therefore, it is fair to state that most evangelical and protestant denominations followed the missiological models that emerged at those gatherings.

It was during this time that Pentecostal churches began to grow significantly. The ministry context incidentally pointed to integral mission. Meanwhile, in the evangelical world, the Fraternidad Teológica Latinoamericana or FTL (Latin American Theological Fellowship) organized the Congreso Latinoamericano de Evangelización or CLADE (Latin American Congress of Evangelism) five times and also published the Boletín Teológico Latinoamericano (Latin American Theological Bulletin), which became the main source of information on evangelical theology and mission in the region.

This was also a context of social-economic unrest and political revolution in Latin America. It was the time of Liberation Theology, proposed by some RCC priests, with lay activists in solidarity alongside the poor of the region.

The above context seems to be the natural connection of Latin American Pentecostalism with Evangelicals, Protestants, and Catholics. In this chapter, I discuss the Lausanne movement and the WCC connection with Pentecostal mission. The discussion is also sensitive to the social, economic, and political contexts where Pentecos-

---

[2] On the importance of the Lausanne and Rome, cf. Jacques Matthey, 'Mission et Évangélisation dans L'Optique de Lausanne, Rome et Genève', *Perspectives Missionnaires* 1.10 (1985), pp. 36-50.

tals practiced their faith and mission in the communities.[3] They were effective in such contexts of poverty and oppression in most local communities of Latin America.

Mission in the Historical Movements

Pentecostal missiology was born and grew out of its own experience and beliefs[4] through the influence of the evangelical and conciliar movements. In Latin America, a number of Pentecostal churches reflect the confluence of these two major streams that participated in its formation and approach to Christian service. Historically, both the evangelical and the conciliar streams have exercised a strong influence on the Pentecostal approach to integral mission.[5] However, I will limit the research to the second half of the twentieth century, when most contemporary missiological issues began to emerge.

Before the 1970s, Pentecostalism was not recognized officially as a Christian movement by most evangelical organizations and the conciliar movement.[6] Although they had evolved from the evangeli-

---

[3] Wilma Wells-Davis, *Embattled but Empowered Community: Comparing Understanding of Spiritual Power in Argentine Popular and Pentecostal Cosmologies* (London, UK: Brill, 2010), p. 107. In her research about Pentecostalism in Argentina, Wells-Davis states, 'Pentecostalism cannot be explained adequately without considering the cultural substrata in which it took root'. Incidentally, this seems to be the reality for most Pentecostals across Latin America.

[4] On the subject of Pentecostal mission that emerged from its own experience and beliefs, see the work of Deysy J. García, *El Movimiento Pentecostal en México* (Coyoacán, México: La Editorial Manda, 2010), pp. 110-20. She states, 'the expressions of the Pentecostal message cause a social impact', that is evident in the transformation of the community. See also Roberto Domínguez, *Pioneros de Pentecostés en el Mundo de Habla Hispana: México y Centro América* (Barcelona, España: Editorial Clie, 1990), pp. 68-74; and José A. Watanabe, 'Pensamiento Pentecostal: Un Acercamiento a la Cosmovisión Pentecostal', in Daniel Chiquete and Luis Orellana (eds.), *Voces del Pentecostalismo Latinoamericano* (Concepción, Chile: RELEP, 2009), III, pp. 143-56.

[5] Some ideas about the influence of the conciliar and evangelical streams on the Pentecostal movement, at a global scope, could be found in the account of Harold D. Hunter of the Brighton conference in 1991. See Harold D. Hunter 'Celebrating 100 Years of Prayer for Christian Unity. Full Communion: A Pentecostal Prayer', *Ecumenical Trends* 37.1 (January 2008). http://www.iphc.org/sites/default/files/Hunter_FullCommunion.pdf. Accessed 12 January 2013.

[6] Ofelia Ortega, 'Mission as An Invitation for Life', *International Review of Mission* 88.348-349 (2009), pp. 88-96.

cal stream, Pentecostal churches were still considered as heretical,[7] and therefore, not worthy of consideration as a legitimate Christian constituency.

Evangelicals themselves did not start developing serious missiological thought until the international congresses that took place during the 1960s and 1970s. Another element that affected Pentecostal missiology was their acceptance to participate as members of the conciliar movement.[8] Several independent Pentecostal networks of Latin America, especially of Chile and Argentina, became affiliated with the WCC, although some have argued that this may have been simply a way to obtain formal recognition. Yet, for decades they had struggled against denominational rejection, particularly from some influential segments within the evangelical stream. Pentecostals have also been affected by the influence of the RCC, which has been present in Latin America for over 500 years. Catholic theology and traditions have shaped Latin American societies in their approach to life, religion, and culture.[9] Most members of the Pentecostal community left the RCC by way of conversion.[10] They have joined the Pentecostal faith, but they still carry their catholic traditions, customs, and social patterns of behavior. Pentecostal missiologists will definitely have to evaluate the historical influence of the RCC on their members when it comes to participation in social concerns.

A Review of Evangelical Mission

The 1960s was characterized by the increase of social and economic injustice in the developing world. This opened the eyes of protest-

---

[7] Robert R. Owens, *The Azusa Street Revival its Roots and its Message* (Lanham, MD: University Press of America, 1988), p. 89. The author deals with the margination of Pentecostalism in America in the early stages of development, which had historical implications for the future relations between Pentecostals and the mainstream denominations. See also Andrew Kirk, *What is Mission?* (London, UK: Fortress Press, 2000), pp. 38-55.

[8] See Anderson, *An Introduction to Pentecostalism*, pp. 19-38.

[9] See for instance Benjamin Keen and Keith Haynes, *A History of Latin America* (Boston, MA: Houghton Mifflin Harcourt, 2009), pp. 178-90. The authors discuss the influence of the Roman Catholic Church on the cultures of Latin America.

[10] Enrique E. Dussel, 'Un Análisis Contextual de la Iglesia Católica en America Latina', *Pastoralia* 9.1 (1979), p. 72.

ers in the West and other geographical areas. Social activists hoped that those oppressive powers and unbreakable structures could be substituted for better ones. At this point, this was considered as mission thinking and involvement in transformation. Hence, a growing influence of liberation theology on the poor and oppressed in the Two-Thirds World raised multiple questions that demanded answers from evangelical leaders. Evangelical leaders understood the need to convene in large assemblies to discuss the most urgent issues affecting the world at that time. They realized it was important to bring the newly emerging issues to the table in order to offer objective solutions and respond to the demands of their constituencies.

In December 1960, the Evangelicals called a congress in Chicago that focused on the promotion of worldwide evangelism. Although the main purpose of the organizers was to promote evangelization in the traditional way, some of the speakers expressed their concern about the revolutionary spirit that had been permeating the minds of many people in the church and around the world. This was the first time they acknowledged the emerging strength of liberation theology in Latin America. Thus, they looked at this occasion as an opportunity to dialogue about the social responsibility of the church to respond to social concerns. Speaking to the student world about the unfinished task, Erick S. Fife, missionary secretary of Inter-Varsity, declared:

> We have to understand that there have been sweeping changes that have taken place in the world's mind since the last World War, and these students are up against all the time and are living in an intellectually stimulating environment. They are looking for mission boards, which they feel are facing the challenge of this day and generation. They are looking for a freedom from prejudice, racial and denominational. They are looking for a mind open to the Lord and His work.[11]

Christian Weiss, who once was the mission director of the Back to the Bible Broadcast, became interested in underscoring 'the obli-

---

[11] Eric S. Fife, 'The Student World and the Unfinished Task', in John O. Percy (ed.), *Facing the Unfinished Task* (Grand Rapids, MI: Zondervan, 1961), p. 123.

gation of Christians to train at the highest academic level national leaders who would be able to give direction to the course of their governments'.[12] Another speaker from Latin America, Emilio Antonio Núñez said in his plenary message:

> The spirit of the compassionate Christ is one of the main characteristics of genuine Christianity. It is necessary to keep the balance in the emphasis that is given to the challenge of the peoples' needs. There is a possibility of giving the impression that the message of salvation is only for the sick and the poor people of the world. The other extreme is to be so afraid of the social gospel that the opportunity for medical missionary work and all humanitarian actions are neglected.[13]

It should be noted that the speech of the Congress on World Missions in Chicago did not go beyond social assistance as a demonstration of Christian social responsibility. In those days, evangelical leaders were not yet discussing whether political or social action was a duty of the Christian. Issues related to social justice and the prophetic role of the church were not yet included on the agenda. At this time, they were more interested in church planting and growth among natives of other lands, which was another colonial way of referring to mission outreach or world missions. This model of mission was also learned and practiced by the Pentecostal denominations based in North America.

However, in the declaration of the 1966 Evangelical Congress at Wheaton, Illinois, the evangelicals went beyond social assistance in their conclusion. They stated that action was recommended against social evils, such as racial discrimination, and against all forms of social injustice. Some observers concluded that this new emphasis on social action was related to the presence of a good number of participants from the Majority World.[14] In contrast to the Mission Congress of Chicago five years before, a large number of Latin American leaders were present at Wheaton. Although most of them

---

[12] G.C. Weiss, 'An Inquiry into the Obligation of Christians', in John O. Percy (ed.), *Facing the Unfinished Task* (Grand Rapids, MI: Zondervan, 1961), p. 262.

[13] Emilio A. Núñez, 'The Ideal Missionary', in John O. Percy (ed.), *Facing the Unfinished Task* (Grand Rapids, MI: Zondervan, 1961), pp. 173-74.

[14] Padilla, 'Evangelism and Social Responsibility', p. 5.

seemed to be more interested in anti-ecumenism than in social responsibility, they did not oppose the final declaration on social concern.

Another significant congress on evangelism took place in Berlin, Germany in 1966. This was sponsored by *Christianity Today* magazine in celebration of its tenth anniversary. The theme of the congress was: 'One race, one gospel, and one task'. There were more than a thousand participants from over one hundred countries,[15] and according to Athol Gill, the issue of evangelism and social concern was raised in-group discussions, but it was not adequately debated. To be sure, the congress statement did include a lengthy section condemning racism, but it did so in purely personal terms, and in describing the 'one task' of the church it spoke only of evangelism. Among all papers presented at the congress only one dealt with evangelism and social concern, and it was devoted almost entirely to racism as a barrier to evangelization.[16]

It is obvious that during the 1960s, the understanding of the social responsibility of God's people in regards to justice and social concerns was still in the process of formation. It took several years for them to realize how important it was for the church to assume its prophetic role in a very critical time of human history. Incidentally, there were other parallel events that made Evangelicals think and re-examine their mission as it relates to social responsibility. One movement that shook their social and mission theology was the World Council of Churches.

At this point in time, Pentecostals took no part in the evangelical debates. Not only were Evangelicals uneasy with the reports of Pentecostal growth, but also Pentecostals were still sore from their rejection by Evangelicals. Nevertheless, the origins of Pentecostal missiology can be traced to these days when Evangelicals began to meet in these historical congresses. These were the venues where social concerns began to be discussed by the evangelical movement.

---

[15] Stanley Mooneyham, 'Facing a New Day in Evangelism', in C.F.H. Henry and Stanley Mooneyham (eds.), *One Race, One Gospel, One Task* (Minneapolis, MN: Worldwide Publications, 1967), pp. 12-14.

[16] Gill, 'Christian Social Responsibility', p. 90.

The Conciliar Approach to Mission

The next assembly of the WCC convened in Uppsala, Sweden in 1968. The thrust for social transformation had become so strong that some radical theologians presented in a thesis that the priority of mission was to tackle social and political corruption. This had to be accomplished through the humanization of power structures worldwide, following God's purpose as entrusted to his missionaries, which was already at work within the movements that sought social and political transformation.[17] There were two WCC programs that seemed controversial at the time: the program to end racism and the one to enter into dialogue with other confessions of faith.

The WCC conference of Bangkok started in December 1972 and concluded in January 1973. It began with the theme of salvation today but turned to focus on other heated issues emerging at that time, particularly in Latin America. This was the time when Christian groups and revolutionary movements began to exert pressure on the governments of Latin America on issues of poverty and political freedom. Due to the delicate reflection on salvation and mission, the conference concluded addressing three major debates:

1. Salvation was understood by the delegates as spiritual but included other aspects of humanity, which had to do with the well-being of individuals and their society. The salvation granted by God through his Son Jesus Christ included four elements clearly stated: (1) salvation of the poor from human exploitation and economic injustice, (2) salvation of human dignity from political oppression and human suffering, (3) salvation for the individual and his or her world against spiritual and socio-economic forces that alienate him or her from the rest of the world, and (4) salvation that brings forth hope against spiritual and social evils that cause anxiety and defeat.

---

[17] Usually the Hebrew word 'shalom' is translated 'peace'; however, its meaning is much wider. Shalom also refers to 'justice in human relationships', it also denotes 'reconciliation', and even further it means 'well-being' for the purpose of complete development of the person and his or her world. See for instance the explanation on this word by Walter Brueggermann, *Living Toward a Vision: Biblical Reflections on Shalom* (New York, NY: United Church Press, 1982), p. 100.

It was clear that salvation means provision from God that embraces the whole person and his or her world.[18] However, each one of these components involves different priorities according to the context and the reality of each particular society. Hence, at that moment in human history, salvation meant peace for the people of Vietnam, freedom for Angola, reconciliation and justice for the people of Northern Ireland or simply personal salvation for any given society without faith in hope. In Bangkok, the delegates agreed that justice had to be reflected in the conversion of the sinner and in the social and economic system that surrounds him or her. When people are able to involve themselves in this dynamic mission, churches become free from rigid religious structures and become recipients of healing and restoration that takes all four aspects of salvation into account.[19]

2. At the WCC conference in Bangkok, for the first time delegates representing the Majority World appeared on the platform delivering strong criticisms of structures imposed by Western societies. Before Bangkok, people at these types of convocations tended to speak with one voice. This time, leaders from the developing nations took the right to speak and challenged organized religion. They condemned the alienation of mission by a domineering Western mentality of colonial conversion of souls. This voice was particularly strong among the Asians, Africans, and some Latin Americans who made it to the conference.

The freedom experienced by the delegates in their speeches was significant. Their words traveled quickly to the Christian world. 'Christ came to redeem real men, not pale reflections of other men' and 'Christ came to answer questions that I ask and not those which others think I ought to ask'.[20] Most conveners exercised their right to identify as Christians. They concluded that each congregation should have a right to formulate theology and the freedom to develop its own structure, liturgy, and doctrine. Models should not be imposed or imported from North America and there should be

---

[18] World Council of Churches, *Bangkok Assembly: Minutes and Report of the Assembly of the Commission on World Mission and Evangelism* (Geneva: Switzerland: WCC, 1973), p. 72.

[19] World Council of Churches, *Bangkok Assembly*, p. 72.

[20] World Council of Churches, *Bangkok Assembly*, p. 78.

room for an open dialogue with other confessions of faith. 'There is no one universal theology, but a variety of theologies, which respect the various social and political contexts in which they have come into being.'[21]

At the Bangkok conference they demanded contextual theology, which sought to end the Western domination of mission theology and practice. Furthermore, the delegates were eager to recognize the creative skills and talents of non-Western Christians. Thus by strengthening contextual theology, Christianity would have the multiple expressions of mission in the world.

3. The delegates looked for responsible solutions to the differences between the churches in the West and those of the developing nations. At this point, the delegates agreed that the churches in other contexts should have independence and that their own decisions and vision for ministry should be respected. The WCC conference of Bangkok became famous for a unique document that was presented to the floor, the so-called 'moratorium'.[22] The document demanded that missionaries and cross-cultural staff workers should withdraw from missionary service so as to enable the national churches and movements to assume their mission responsibility without outside interference.

The moratorium demanded an end to outside financial support. It would drive the nationals to establish their own identity and agenda. The repatriation of missionaries would enable them to take action in their own industrialized societies, thus bringing change to

---

[21] James L. Mays, 'Justice, Perspectives from a Prophetic Tradition', *Biblical Interpretation* 37.1 (1972), pp. 5-17. In those days, theologians were developing the notion of 'contextual theology'. They were trying to include social, economic, and political concerns to witness to Christ. They thought to include contextual theology in the field of systematic theology and not simply adapt the term as one more item of discussion. This was perhaps one of the most significant theological additions to mission at the conference of Bangkok.

[22] It is not quite clear when or how the proposal for the 'moratorium' was presented to the floor. Some historians think that the term was initially used in 1971 during the East Asia Christian Conference. There the delegates began to harbor the idea of sending the missionaries home in order to allow the local churches to develop their own ministries without the external interference of Western missionaries, whom at this historical moment were thought of doing cross-cultural work with a colonial mentality. See Emerito P. Nacpil, *Jesus' Strategy for Social Transformation* (Grand Rapids, MI: Abingdon Press, 1978), p. 32.

the denominational structures in order to foster peace and justice in the world. The purpose here was to renew the already damaged relations between Christian organizations. The moratorium would help build respect and cooperation between Christians from different traditions across the world. Nonetheless, the critical spirit reflected in the document had a remarkable impact on the delegates because it initiated a heated debate on the floor over the real purpose of missionary work, especially in the way they were perceived in the so-called mission field.[23] At this time, missionaries were sent mostly from the West to under-developed nations, which were economically and socio-politically disadvantaged.

The conference in Bangkok also saw that the Paris Society of Evangelical Missions had now become the French Evangelical Department for Apostolic Action. The French had created an international system, which would enable cooperation between churches. Their aim was to serve as a fellowship of Christian organizations that worked together with mutual resources in the proclamation of the gospel. Some Bangkok delegates offered this model as an alternative to the moratorium.[24] It was clear that the conference in Bangkok was confronted by inequality and double standards in church relations. This was perhaps one of the reasons for the high level of confrontation that took place in the gathering.

Mission in the Congress of Lausanne
During the decade of the 1970s, many beliefs and expectations were revisited in the Christian world. However, for the purpose of this survey, I will touch briefly on these topics, mentioning only those generally considered as the most relevant. The first report of the Club of Rome[25] in 1971 articulated some important concerns,

---

[23] See Gerald H. Anderson, 'A Moratorium on Missionaries?', *Christian Century* (January 16, 1974), pp. 42-56. In his article, the author evaluates the impact of the document upon the Christian movement at that time.

[24] Anderson, 'A Moratorium on Missionaries?' p. 52.

[25] The Club of Rome, founded in 1968, has acted since the beginning as a think tank. It members are involved in political issues and are concerned for the future of the world and its inhabitants. By nature, the club is not interested in the church, but rather, it is concerned about unlimited economic growth, and the fact that the world will have to realize the limits of the economy. More information about the Club of Rome is available at http://www.cluboffrome.org/. Accessed 12 December 2011.

such as the growth of the church being subject to limitations, the world being finite, and the church having to realize that financial resources are limited as well.

Evangelicals also acknowledged the failures of capitalist models in the famines of Africa and other economic, social, and political tragedies in the world. Since this was also the time when the world experienced the first oil crisis, Western societies became more aware of the weaknesses of their economic systems and that their response to the crisis was insufficient. From then on, Christian leaders realized that mission understanding and practice had to be updated all the time. New approaches to mission were adopted, which began to focus on training and equipping nationals for ministry. It was these kinds of conclusions that paved the way for the Lausanne movement that gathered three years later.

In 1974 the International Congress on World Evangelization took place in Lausanne, Switzerland. It was organized and sponsored by mostly western evangelical churches. The Pentecostal representation, which had no voice, was minimal and those who attended were at the congress representing themselves.[26] The Billy Graham Evangelistic Association convened the event. Although this is not openly acknowledged, one of the purposes of the Lausanne Congress was to respond to the ambiguities of the ecumenical movement and its theological approach to unity, cooperation, and social responsibility. Lausanne demanded that mission had to focus on the purpose and essentials of the gospel.

The Lausanne Congress became a landmark for the new emerging evangelical models of ministry now trending worldwide. As an obvious reaction to the WCC ecumenical thrust of Bangkok, the Lausanne Covenant clearly disassociated evangelicals from any association with ecumenism. The Lausanne Covenant made clear that

---

[26] Among the few Pentecostal leaders from Latin America who attended the Lausanne conference was José G. Minay. He is a Chilean Pentecostal associated with the Church of God (Cleveland, TN). It was after that conference that Minay began to speak about the importance of social service among Pentecostal churches. His discourse included the poor and the marginalized in Guatemala. See Richard Waldrop, 'The Social Consciousness and Involvement of the Full Gospel Church of God of Guatemala', *Cyber Journal of Pentecostal-Charismatic Research* (2004). http://www.pctii.org/cyberj/cyberj2/waldrop.html. Accessed 10 October 2009.

the priority of mission is 'to evangelize those who have not yet heard of Christ, the Savior and Lord of the world. Thus all efforts in any Christian organization must contribute to strengthening the mission to witness to all unreached people groups'[27] of the world. The intention of the Lausanne Congress was to expose the threats of ecumenism and revitalize those areas that the WCC was clearly neglecting.[28]

In order to distance the evangelical bodies from the statements of Bangkok, the Lausanne Covenant[29] separated the work of salvation from any relationship with political liberation. It stated that that the proclamation of the gospel does not seem to be typically involved with political participation. It affirmed that salvation is individual; the person has to accept Christ as his or her Savior and Lord.[30] Nevertheless, in response to the social concerns of the Two-Thirds World delegates, Lausanne had to re-think the concept of social responsibility as practiced by Christians. Consequently, they included a small declaration that affirmed social action with the condition that social responsibility was freed from any idea of 'messianic' purposes.[31]

---

[27] See Donald McGavran, *Effective Evangelism: A Theological Mandate* (Phillipsburg, NJ: Presbyterian and Reformed Publishing Company, 1988).

[28] See the work of John Stott, 'The Lausanne Covenant: An Exposition and Commentary', *The Lausanne Movement* (2001). http://www.lausanne.org/en/documents/lops/69-lop-3.html. Accessed 10 October 2011.

[29] The Lausanne Covenant is a document written as declaration from the delegates who participated in the conference. The Covenant has been consulted and taken as a reference by all of the evangelical constituencies. Certain organizations even require those wishing to become members of certain groups or societies to sign the Lausanne Covenant personally. See Lausanne Movement, *The Lausanne Covenant* (2001). http://www.feb.org/lausanne_covenant.htm. Accessed 04 September 2006.

[30] John Stott, *Lausanne Movement* (2000). https://www.lausanne.org/content/john-stott-and-the-lausanne-movement. Accessed 7 December 2015.

[31] The word 'messianic' serves to identify theological terms. The tendency of those who adhere to this trend is to sacramentalize social and political causes as direct manifestations of the kingdom of God. There are those who tend to over emphasize social action and could be at risk for lacking balance with spiritual disciplines. See Charles Gailey and Howard Culbertson, *Discovering Mission* (Kansas City, MO: Beacon Hill Press, 2007), p. 222.

The Lausanne Covenant is also cautious about dialoguing with believers from other confessions of faith. Their only hope of salvation would be to follow the evangelical proclamation of the gospel. Once they confess Christ, then they are welcome into the fellowship of believers.

The Lausanne Covenant became the main source of guidance for most evangelicals worldwide. The Lausanne Committee became the 'spokesperson' for various evangelical bodies.

In the case of Pentecostals, Lausanne welcomed them as long as they remained evangelical in their approach to theology and mission. However, there were some indigenous, non-Western Pentecostals who decided to join the WCC instead. Independent Pentecostals wanted to keep their distance from denominational Pentecostalism, and one way to demonstrate their freedom was to apply for membership with the WCC.

Some independent bodies from Chile, Argentina, Brazil, and other Latin American countries were accepted as members of the WCC assembly. This situation generated internal difficulties among Pentecostals. The world now saw those Pentecostals who aligned to the evangelical movement via the Lausanne movement versus those who were members of the WCC. However, the Lausanne Covenant marked the difference between 'evangelicals' and 'ecumenical', and this division has existed between the WCC and LCWE ever since 1974.[32]

The mid-1970s is considered a period when the notion of mission shifted. This paradigm was so interesting that even the Vatican published a document in 1975 addressing the matter of mission in a contemporary manner. The publication came in the form of an apostolic exhortation, *Evangelization in the Modern World*[33] and introduced a general understanding of mission from the RCC point of view. Also, in 1975 the Nairobi, Kenya Assembly of the WCC presented an integral approach to mission, bringing together the two poles of witnessing and solidarity. In those times, there was a redis-

---

[32] Extensive information with regards to Evangelical involvement in ecumenism can be found in Harold Edward Pruitt, *Ecumenism and Theological Convergence: A Comparative Analysis Between Edinburg 1910 and the Lausanne Movement*, (DTh, University of South Africa, 2009), p. 116.

[33] Paul VI, *Evangelization in the Modern World* (London, UK: Catholic Truth Society, 1976), p. 123. It is also known as *Evangelii Nuntiandi*.

covery of the specifics of the gospel within the global mission of God.

Hopes of Convergence for Evangelicals and Ecumenicals

It is clear that, during the 1970s, there were two strands present in the world conferences on mission and evangelism. However, at the very beginning of the next decade in Melbourne, Australia in 1980, the study on the church and the poor by the WCC's Commission on the Churches' Participation in Development and the experience of the Urban Rural Mission movement linked with the Commission on World Mission and Evangelism to define the assumptions and priorities of the kingdom.[34] It was at Melbourne that these two traditions came together under the auspices of the WCC. The debate of Melbourne was 'Your Kingdom Come'. This conference analyzed the assumptions and the preconceived priorities of integral mission. The manifestation of the kingdom of God[35] became the most important theme of discussion.

The participants understood that a fundamental change of values and structures in the practice of mission was necessary.[36] This was very important for independent Pentecostals, for they saw this approach to integral mission as an opportunity to show that the spiritual gifts are evident signs of the Kingdom of God here and now. This turn of events put them in the position of advantage with regards to those Pentecostals governed by Evangelicals in the Lausanne movement.

The Base Communities

Clearly the Brazilian experience of the Base Communities became very influential in the debate initiated by the Latin American delegates. The conference was led to conclude and affirm that 'the poor' are the subjects of the gospel, and therefore they should be

---

[34] Pruitt, *Ecumenism and Theological Convergence*, p. 22.

[35] The Kingdom of God is a prominent theme in the New Testament. However, the Kingdom of God is mostly revealed in the declarations of Jesus Christ himself. See for instance Saracco, 'Las Opiniones Liberadoras de Jesús', pp. 3-9.

[36] See World Council of Churches, *Your Kingdom Come: Mission Perspectives* (Geneva, Switzerland: WCC, 1980).

prioritized in mission. The WCC described *Missio Dei* as the action of God for and through the poor who are the victims of social injustice. They have been marginalized and excluded from God's shalom – a term that also defines the final purpose of God for humanity. To redeem the poor to the state of shalom, the work of mission should be one of liberation, involving a change in the relation between the rich and the poor, the weak, and the powerful. Thus, the poor and their redemption became the yardstick that measured Christian mission. Therefore, mission goes beyond personal salvation because it is also responsible for carrying good news to those oppressed by social, political, and economic evils. Mission is therefore valued by the level of involvement in spiritual and social responsibilities on behalf of those who suffer alienation.

Priorities of Latin America

The shifting in the priorities of mission was perceived as a movement that operates in two directions: one from the center to the periphery and the other from the periphery to the center.[37] It was also clear in the debate that Christ himself initiated this movement. Jesus, the King, was neither born in a palace nor in a hospital. He was born in a manger. At the time of His trial, He was not executed inside the city, but instead He was marginalized and crucified outside the city on a mount called 'the skull'. He gave a clear indication that the good news of the gospel moves dynamically from the periphery to the periphery. The Kingdom of God is not found in the centers of political, economic, and religious power. Instead, it is found outside the city walls among the marginalized and the poor. Thus, God's message of redemption and judgment is in the periphery with the sick, the wretched, and the weak. The location of *Mis-*

---

[37] It was during the debate about development that the terms 'center-periphery' were introduced. These terms helped to reinterpret and correct the traditional concepts of growth and transformation. They contributed to break the rigid classification of 'developed' and 'under-developed' nations. It was clear that in every country there are contexts of unemployment, limited infrastructure, and poverty in extremes. See Jacques Matthey, 'Milestones in Protestant Ecumenical Missionary Thinking from the 1970s to the 1990s', *Ecumenical Mission Study in the WCC* (1999). http://www.sedos.org/english/matthey.htm. Accessed 04 September 2006.

sio Dei is with and among the poor, and it moves forward form the periphery to the centers of power in the world.

Criticism on the Use of Political Power

The conference of Melbourne in 1980 was strongly against the abuse of power. The attitude of Christ on the cross raises questions about the use of power in mission. On the cross, Christ renounced the use of power in order to present the Kingdom of God through the life of a servant. The vulnerability of the Savior of the world is to be reflected in the life and ministry of those who serve in mission. According to one of the highlights of the Melbourne conference, Christians are to renounce and refuse to use any form of imposition as instrument for conversion. This was perhaps one of the most significant conclusions that emerged from this conference. The institutional church could become counter-witness to the message of the cross over those who force the system upon the needs of people.

The Lausanne Movement and Mission Priorities

In that same year of 1980, the Lausanne movement seemed to be interested in other issues related to church mission. During the conference that took place in Pattaya, Thailand, delegates were eager to find ideas that would be methodologically congruent and organizationally compatible with the conclusions reached in the Lausanne Covenant, especially those highlighted as mission priorities. The most important issue was the proclamation of the gospel to those who have yet to hear of Christ. The most significant question on the floor of the conference was 'How will they hear (the gospel)?' In the various workshops, cross-cultural workers advocated an agenda which would enable missionaries to reach out to those populations that do not have churches in their midst.

The Pattaya delegates focused on finding feasible ways to cooperate in cross-cultural service. Although individuals cannot be considered isolated units, it was equally important to further mission to every people group and not just to political 'nations' since there could be many 'nations' in one particular country. Pattaya made it clear that the role of the church in a particular country is to reach the 'unreached people groups'.[38] Therefore, a more refined analysis needed to be made which is what Pattaya attempted to do. The conference reported that some seventeen thousand people groups in the world had not heard the gospel at that time.

Several workshops were conducted to organize and analyze data that could then provide scope for strategic planning in world evangelization. However, the Pattaya conference had a different approach to evangelism. Evangelicals began to talk about evangelizing unreached people groups while the WCC was inclined to social work among the poor. The difference in itself opened a door to incipient dialogue between Evangelicals and the WWC. It was clear that for both movements the poor and the marginalized had become the focal point of mission.

Mission and Evangelism

In 1992 a new document was introduced by WCC: 'Mission and evangelism: An ecumenical affirmation',[39] which brought into focus some key developments that had taken place in the mission debate since the 1960s. This work encapsulated the results of mission conferences and also involved participation by the Orthodox churches, the orders of Roman Catholic mission, as well as congregations and dialogues with various evangelical groups. As a result, a comprehensive view of mission was identified.[40]

---

[38] The term, 'unreached people' was coined at the Pattaya conference to describe those populations of the world that do not have adequate Christian witness. Mission statisticians suggest that twenty percent is the minimal percentage required for a people group to be considered 'reached' with the gospel. See for instance Edward R. Dayton, *That Everyone May Hear: Reaching the Unreached* (Monrovia, CA: MARC, 1979), pp. 19-28.

[39] On this affirmation, see the official report of the World Council of Churches, '1980 – Three Mayor Conferences', *Reformed Reflections* (1980). http://www.reformedreflections.ca/missions/1980-three-major-conference.html. Accessed 12 November 2011.

[40] The use of the word '(w)holistic' has deep missiological implications. Although most ecumenical bodies have used it in their writings, the truth is that it can be applied to several meanings and by multiple disciplines. In mission circles the term could become controversial for it appeals to a certain specialized area of mission. However, the word '(w)holistic' adds a dimension of completeness in mission. It includes proclamation and social responsibility. In Latin America, scholarship has replaced the word '(w)holistic mission' with 'integral mission', thus adding a consensus of totality in the final approach to mission. See World

The combination of the 1974 Lausanne Covenant with the 1975 *Evangeli Nuntiandi* (Evangelisation in the Modern World) made a significant contribution to the readings on mission essentials.[41] For the purpose of this study, our survey examines some of the most significant contributions to mission. An in-depth study would be necessary to analyze in detail the impact and contribution of each conference. For our purposes, I will only discuss some of the conclusions that serve to illustrate the progress of mission thinking and practice among the church.

The heart of the gospel is the proclamation of the Kingdom of God. Jesus Himself inaugurated this message of salvation. He is the crucified Lord, and He is calling the world to Himself. The church has been called to witness to Christ as the only hope for salvation to the world. The mission priority of the church is to call people to repentance. Once they become born again they will receive the forgiveness of sins and will be able to live a new life.

The church in its mission manifests the love of God for the world. Such love is identified with the suffering and the poor as their only source of hope and redemption. However, the church is not only just an instrument to witness, but also carries Christ's mission as mediator between God and creation.[42] There cannot be any imbalance between proclamation and social responsibility; otherwise, the holistic power of the gospel will be annulled, and believers will be prevented from witnessing efficiently.

The WCC stated that the call to repentance is also addressed to nations, families, and people groups. It also said that personal conversion and a decision for Christ are necessary for the individual to receive the salvation of Christ. Without this personal conversion

---

Council of Churches, *Mission and Evangelism: An Ecumenical Affirmation* (Geneva, Switzerland: WCC, 1982), p. 34.

[41] This matter of affirmation and the relations of the WCC with Rome and Lausanne are also reported by Matthey, 'Mission et Évangélisation Dans L'Optique de Lausanne', pp. 36-50.

[42] See, Jacques Matthey, 'Serving God's Mission Together in Christ's Way: Reflections on the Way to Edinburgh 2010', *International Review of Mission* 99.1 (2010), pp. 21-38. The author argues that God who reaches to the world initiates mission and the church is an instrument that carries such mission. On the same matter see, Bosch, *Transforming Mission*, pp. 389-90.

there can be no true commitment to follow Him in a life that is of service.

Interpersonal relations are the main sources of evangelism. The Holy Spirit compels individuals to respond to the gospel with faith when sound relations are established.

Most people who have never heard the gospel are also the weakest and the poorest of the world. Coincidently, they are the victims of an evil economic system and unjust social class relations. Thus, to test the credibility of evangelism, the delegates proposed the following argument, 'a proclamation that does not hold forth the promises of justice to the poor of the earth is a caricature of the gospel'.[43] However, 'Christian participation in the struggles for justice which does not point towards the promises of the Kingdom of God also makes a caricature of a Christian understanding of justice'.[44]

It was clear that the participants in the 1982 missiological debate intentionally avoided defending their own positions. Such an attitude showed a genuine willingness to converge in a document that represented high standards of courtesy and respect. All the groups involved in the dialogue with the WCC understood this attitude and cooperated in the success of the event. Years later in 1987, another joint statement was issued in Stuttgart, Germany with regards to partnering in evangelism. This declaration also involved the same level of respect and courtesy.[45] The document identified points of agreement rather than magnifying problems. The delegates at Stuttgart then appealed for the establishment of an evangelistic program that would serve to strengthen the relations among Christians working for a common purpose.

Emerging Contexts of Evangelism

This WCC conference held in 1989 did not attract the same attention from the media as other conferences. This may have been due

---

[43] World Council of Churches, Mission and Evangelism, p. 42.

[44] World Council of Churches, *Mission and Evangelism*, p. 34.

[45] The conclusions of the Stuttgart conference can be found in the World Council of Churches, *Monthly Letter on Evangelism* (Geneva, Switzerland: WCC, 1987), pp. 1-2.

to the simultaneous gatherings taking place in Basel, Switzerland in the same year. In 1989 the European Ecumenical Assembly on Peace and Justice met in Basel and may have affected the next assembly at San Antonio, Texas. However, San Antonio helped highlight advances in mission thinking amongst the different Christian bodies.

Later on that year, the evangelical delegates formally reported to the San Antonio leadership that the Lausanne Congress was going to convene in Manila. During the San Antonio conference, the delegates reviewed the progress made in the dialogue on theological and missiological issues. The idea of bringing the two international movements together for a joint meeting was put forward by the evangelical and Pentecostal delegates in San Antonio. They had accepted the invitation to participate as observers at this assembly of the WCC. Unfortunately, the proposal did not come to fruition, and such a meeting has never taken place.[46] Below are some of the points which arose from the San Antonio assembly that are helpful to this study.

The WCC's dialogue with people of other faiths has generated different reactions. Evangelicals do not hide their discomfort with this purpose and tend to oppose the idea. The theological debate on mission does not seem to have been accepted, and therefore relations with the WCC cannot be fully established. The mission sector could not integrate Christians opposed to dialogue with non-Christian religions. Evangelicals were convinced that by entertaining this idea, the WCC had gone too far in its approach to ecumenism, and therefore the nature of mission was placed in jeopardy.[47]

The definition and description of the nature of this dialogue was not clearly established in the conference of 1982 though San Antonio brought more details and explanations to the issue. In the first place, the delegates re-affirmed that Christians could not offer a different plan of salvation other than the salvation in Jesus Christ.

The San Antonio delegates also insisted that Christians could not set limits on God and His saving grace. Nevertheless, they acknowl-

---

[46] J. Matthey, 'Milestones in Protestant Ecumenical Missionary Thinking from the 1970s to the 1990s', *International Review of Mission* 88.1 (July 1999), pp. 291-303.

[47] Matthey also discussed this topic in his paper presented at Edinburg, 2010. See Matthey, 'Serving God's Mission Together in Christ's Way', pp. 25-27.

edged the tension generated by these statements, and they were honest in declaring that they were not able to resolve it. Perhaps, the main contribution was to put the matter forward openly for discussion, helping the ecumenical movement to clarify its position regarding mission and dialogue. They were also eager to affirm the need for the proclamation of the gospel to all people groups with special emphasis on those who have yet to hear it. This declaration was perhaps the main reason why some evangelical churches decided to join the WCC in the following years.

The conference of San Antonio was a more positive step towards church participation on behalf of peace and justice. Although this appeal had been present in every WCC conference, in San Antonio the conditions were favorable for a more decisive statement.[48] The delegates spoke about the creative and redemptive power of the sovereign God. Significantly, they spoke about power: the power of the resurrection of Christ and how this extended to movements that protest against injustice and oppression.

Even though the San Antonio delegates tried to steer away from socio-political arguments, they could not refrain from making critical pronouncements on political issues. A huge contribution of San Antonio was the expansion of the universe of mission with the inclusion of the field of creation, which essentially called forth responsibility for the environment. There was also a demand of land for the poor, the peasants, the marginalized, and the minorities. This was premised on the understanding that God was the creator of the world and is therefore the true owner of land. Thus, mission came to be perceived as a movement towards justice and peace, along with the integrity of creation, as previously launched by the WCC in the conference of Vancouver, Canada in 1983.

The assembly of Vancouver was significant because of the ways in which the delegates debated openly about the issues of peace and justice on behalf of the poor and the marginalized of the world.[49] The delegates also pressured Christianity in the developed nations

---

[48] Matthey, 'Serving God's Mission Together in Christ Way', p. 26.

[49] Paulo Suess has written an article that identifies current trends in the Ecumenical community concerning the service of the church to the poor. See Paulo Suess, 'Missio Dei and the Project of Jesus: The Poor and the "Other" as Mediators of the Kingdom of God and Protagonists of the Churches', *International Review of Mission* 92.4 (2003), pp. 550-59.

to pay attention to creation. It was clear to them that the developed countries were committing serious abuses against nature for the sake of the economy. To this date, the debate continues in different forums worldwide.

The WCC conference in San Antonio upheld popular religiosity and folk festivities observed by non-Western communities. It valued positively the symbolic religious language as well as themes that referred to earthly fertility and sexuality. Naturally, the most conservative Evangelicals and Pentecostals, who see these popular expressions of religion as pagan and contrary to the teachings of the Scripture, rejected these conclusions.

The conference of San Antonio recognized and appreciated cross-cultural ministries in the world. This was important at this time since the WCC had publicly kept silent on the matter since the 1982 Bangkok conference. Moreover, San Antonio reaffirmed the need to repair broken relations between Christians of the prosperous North and those of the developing South. This could only happen through an honest and sincere dialogue.[50]

Lausanne II (Manila 1989)

The Lausanne II Congress on World Evangelization also convened in Manila, Philippines in 1989. There were over 3,000 delegates and 170 countries represented on the floor. The conference took place in September 1989 just a few months after the WCC's Congress of San Antonio. The participants in the LCWE were not selected by any ecclesial authority or sent by their churches. Denominational friends invited them, and they attended using their own resources. Thus, the Congress did not have official recognition from most evangelical denominations. However, the Congress was established with a very large agenda.

At Lausanne II, the discussions of the evangelical world centered around themes such as gospel and culture, evangelism and social responsibility, Christian lifestyle, conversion, and discipleship in contemporary trends. The Manila Manifesto remained consistent with the Lausanne Covenant, which became the mission manual for

---

[50] John Stott (ed.), *Making Christ Known: Historic Documents from the Lausanne Movement 1974–1989* (Grand Rapids, MI: Eerdmans, 1997), p. 29.

most Evangelicals. However, there were some new topics presented in Manila that should be considered within the framework of this study.[51]

Humans are created in the image of God. They are sinful and in need of redemption. They are lost without Jesus Christ. Lausanne sees this reality as a pre-condition for the proclamation of the gospel. Since there is no hope for salvation outside of Jesus Christ, the work of evangelism and discipleship must take place at every church. Hence, the message of the gospel is to be carried by all who believe in Christ.[52]

There was emphasis on the historical Jesus Christ. Christians are commissioned to announce Jesus of Nazareth who died on the cross and was also resurrected according to the Scripture. Contrary to Lausanne I, the delegates were open to opinions that favored dialogue with people of other faiths but refused to move from the position that there is no salvation without Christ.[53] Lausanne II rejected false doctrines and repudiated half-true gospels.

The role of apologetics recovered its place in the church. In Manila, Evangelicals emphasized the importance of the proclamation of the gospel without hesitation and fear. The theme was 'the whole gospel to the whole world by the whole church'.[54] Moreover,

---

[51] The 21 affirmations of the Manila manifesto can be found in B.A. Robinson, 'The Manila Manifesto: An Elaboration of the Lausanne Covenant 15 Years Later', *Lausanne Committee for World Evangelisation* (2003). http://www.religioustolerance.org/evan_cove2.htm. Accessed 10 February 2007. See also LCWE, *The Manila Manifesto: An Elaboration of the Lausanne Covenant 15 Years Later* (Ontario, CA: LCWE, 1989), pp. 12-16.

[52] The Lausanne movement keeps the ideas of John Stott afresh. His teachings on evangelism and discipleship continue to influence the Evangelical churches and beyond. His ideas about evangelism and discipleship can be found in his book on Romans. See John Stott, *The Message of Romans, The Bible Speaks Today* (Leicester, UK: Leicester and Downers Grove, 1994), pp. 53-55.

[53] Evangelicals have arguably softened their position with regards to interreligious dialogue. Arthur Glasser sees no problem in talking to people of other confessions of faith, as long as they do not question the lordship of Jesus. See Arthur Glasser, 'A Paradigm Shift: Evangelicals and Interreligious Dialogue', *Missiology* 9.4 (1981), pp. 392-408. See also T.C. Muck, 'Evangelicals and Interreligious Dialogue', *JETS* 36.4 (1993), pp. 517-29.

[54] See for instance Christopher J.H. Wright, 'Whole Gospel, Whole Church, Whole World', *Christianity Today* (2009). http://www.christianitytoday.com/ct/2009/october/index.html. Accessed 12 January 2011. Building his position upon

Christians were enabled to defend it. Thus apologetics became an essential responsibility in the preaching and other duties assigned by the church.[55] In addition, Manila concluded that evangelism is the first priority in the mission of all Christians. This includes a sound balance between faith and good works.

Manila concluded that the gospel is good news to the poor. The delegates understood that the message of Christ contains prophetic denunciations against any kind of injustice and oppression.[56] Christians were to remain humble before God and eager to protect the poor and the weak because Christ's favor is with them for salvation, redemption, and the solution to their most basic needs.

Manila emphasized the presence of the Holy Spirit in mission, and the Holy Spirit is the most important source of power for mission.[57] This was perhaps the most visible recognition of Lausanne to the Pentecostal teaching of spirituality, particularly of spiritual warfare.[58] The delegates also insisted that God wants to be understood as the main evangelist in this world.

Manila reaffirmed the priority of the local congregation in the work of mission. It also emphasized the importance of cooperation

---

the Lausanne II manifesto, Chris Wright makes reference to the positive attitude of the Christian witness in times of proclaiming, defending, or serving the gospel.

[55] Alistair McGrath wrote an article that defines contemporary Evangelical apologetics. He builds his argument based on the Lausanne manifesto in Manila of 1989. See Alistair E. McGrath, 'Evangelical Apologetics', *Bibliotheca Sacra* (1988) http://www.theologicalstudies.org.uk/article_apol_mcgrath.html. Accessed 24 July 2011.

[56] Timothy Keller, 'The Gospel to the Poor', *Redeemer City to City* 33.2 (2008), pp. 6-7. The author takes a stand against the colonial mentality of benevolence. Instead he calls for a mission that brings the gospel to the poor with a holistic approach. It is more than giving; it requires a complete relationship, just as Jesus related to them.

[57] Matthey, *Serving God's Mission Together in Christ's Way*, p. 27.

[58] At that moment in history it was obvious that the Pentecostal and Charismatic movement had permeated Evangelical mission. Evangelicals began to study about spiritual warfare, particularly with regards to evangelism. These are some works published on or after the Lausanne II conference, Murray W. Dempster, Byron D. Klaus, and Douglas Petersen, *Called and Empowered: Global Mission in Pentecostal Perspective* (Peabody, MA: Hendrickson, 1990); and Chuck Kraft, *Christianity with Power: Your Worldview and your Experience of the Supernatural* (Oxford, UK: Blackwell, 1991). He also wrote on spiritual warfare, see Kraft, *Deep Wounds Deep Healing: Discovering the Vital Link Between Spiritual Warfare and Inner Healing* (Pasadena, CA: Regal Books 1992).

in evangelism. This cooperation is now seen in the partnerships between churches and para-church bodies.[59] At some point, there was discussion concerning the relationship that some of the delegates have with the WCC. This matter was left to their own decision. Lausanne was not going to tell them with whom should they relate as partners in ministry.

The challenges of the new millennium were discussed. Manila focused on the urgency of the call to proclaim the gospel among the unreached people groups of the world.[60] The coming of the new millennium represented a step closer to the coming of the Lord, and the church had to be aware of it. The new emphasis of Lausanne was: 'the whole gospel to the whole world by the whole church'.[61]

The urgency of evangelism was presented as a reaction to the newly created and militant movement known as 'AD 2000 and Beyond'. This movement aimed at reaching out with the gospel to the 'unreached people groups' located at an imaginary geographical window from West Africa to East Asia, 10 degrees to 40 degrees north of the Equator. It has been called since then the 10/40 Window. 'Those people, many of who were present at Manila, insisted on the urge to evangelize all unreached peoples living within that 10/40 Window'.[62]

The participation of Pentecostal delegates together with other charismatic leaders who willingly opened themselves up to participate with other evangelical leaders in the planning for the future of

---

[59] On the matter of local and para-church partnership in mission, see the article of John S Hammett, 'How Church and Para-Church Should Relate: Arguments for a Servant-Partnership Model', *Missiology* 28.2 (2002), p. 201.

[60] See for instance the report of The Lausanne Movement, 'Unreached People Groups', *Lausanne Global Conversation* (2010).
http://conversation.lausanne.org/en/home/unreached-people-groups. Accessed 23 August 2011.

[61] The theme of the whole gospel to the whole world by the whole church is discussed by Os Guinness and David Wells (eds.), 'Global Gospel, Global Era: Christian Discipleship and Mission in the Age of Globalization', *Lausanne Global Conversation* (2010). http://conversation.lausanne.org/en/home/unreached-people-groups. Viewed 23 August 2011.

[62] Thomas Wang (ed.), 'Countdown to AD 2000', in *The Official Compendium of the Global Consultation on World Evangelization by AD 2000 and Beyond* (Pasadena, CA: William Carey Library, 1989), p. 236.

mission was noticeable. For these leaders to accomplish unity and cooperation at this level, they had to step outside their traditional ecclesiastical circles and show themselves vulnerable for the sake of God's work.[63] This could be seen as a new attitude of cooperation and recognition among Christians. This process of evolution in church relations furthered networking in the task of mission.

Global Consultation of World Evangelization (GCOWE)

In January 1989, about three hundred evangelical and mission agency leaders met in Singapore to consider what the Holy Spirit was saying to the church in regards to world evangelization. They were convened by the AD 2000 and Beyond movement, created by some members of the Lausanne Movement.[64] Representatives from Asia, Africa, North America, Europe, and Latin America pledged to cooperate in order to fulfill the Great Commission by the year 2000.

Luis Bush emerged as leader of the Global Consultation on World Evangelization by the year 2000 and Beyond (GCOWE). Despite the diverse Christian and national backgrounds represented among the 300 participants, there was a unanimous expression of commitment with regard to the Consultation Manifesto. It stated the following: 'We believe that it is possible to bring the gospel to all people groups by the year 2000'.[65] In reference to this Thomas Wang, head of the Lausanne movement, affirmed that the spirit of GCOWE led the leaders to 'Get ready, stop playing games, stop divisiveness and turn complacency to enthusiasm'.[66]

The focus of GCOWE was to facilitate efforts towards world evangelization using national and international networks. There were some debates concerning inter-denominational dialogue and cooperation. Some leaders insisted on ecumenical relations particularly with the Roman Catholic Church in order to complete the task. Those efforts were strongly opposed by most Latin American rep-

---

[63] See Jan van Butselaar, 'San Antonio et Manille: Deux Cultures Missionnaires', *Perspectives Missionnaires* 1.20 (1990), pp. 19-22.

[64] AD 2000 Movement, *Countdown to AD 2000*, p. vii.

[65] AD 2000 Movement, *Countdown to AD 2000*, p. viii.

[66] AD 2000 Movement, *The Official Compendium*, p. ix.

resentatives who even threatened to abandon the consultation if that theme continued to be discussed.[67]

Conversely, very little discussion was presented concerning the poor and the transformations of the societies where the church is located. Much of the emphasis was on the 10/40 Window, where most of the unreached people groups existed. GCOWE was dominated by an eschatological fundamentalism that was more concerned about the end of the millennium than for the transformation of the world with the gospel.[68]

The Fall of the Berlin Wall

In 1989 when the WCC held its conference in San Antonio and Lausanne II in Manila, those delegates were the last to be present in worldwide Christian conferences because of the politically and economically divided East and West. It was in the autumn of 1989 that the Berlin Wall fell.[69] This reality introduced a new world order with new challenges and opportunities for the church.[70] Mission was now rephrased and reorganized within a new culture of globalization.[71] All of a sudden, Christian leaders saw rapid change and new and

---

[67] AD 2000 Movement, *The Official Compendium*, p. 16.

[68] The Global Consultation on World Evangelization gave birth to the AD 2000 Movement and Beyond. The aim was a church for every people and the gospel for every person by AD 2000. The leaders claim that God has used the AD 2000 and Beyond Movement to mobilize the Church and to focus on the unreached people groups. See John D. Robb, *Focus! The Power of People Group Thinking* (Monrovia, CA: MARC, 1989), pp. 32-34.

[69] Francis Fukuyama, among many authors, makes reference to the fall of the Berlin Wall as the beginning of current new world order, which affects human life entirely. See Francis Fukuyama, *State-Building: Governance and World Order in the 21st Century* (New York, NY: Cornell University Press, 2014), p. 102.

[70] See Robert L. Rothstein, *Global Bargaining: UNCTAD and the Quest for a New International Economic Order* (Princeton, NJ: Princeton University Press 1979). The author traces contemporary trends in the formation of the United Nations Conference on Trade Development (UNCTAD) and its role in the New International Economic Order (NIEO). On the same topic, see Gwynne Dyer, *Future Tense: The Coming World Order* (Toronto, Canada: McClelland & Stewart, 2006), pp. 24-26.

[71] A significant contribution to the new culture of globalization was made by, Roland Robertson, 'Mapping the Global Condition. Globalization as the Central Concept', in Mike Featherstone (ed.), *Global Culture: Nationalism, Globalization and Modernity* (London, UK: Sage Publications, 1990), pp. 15-29.

powerful advances in technology that affected communication[72] and the ways in which the gospel message was delivered.

The realities of the new world order opened new opportunities for mission in a globalized world. The next decade was full of surprises and great challenges for the church. In the next historical revision, I will highlight some of those elements that are meaningful for mission and for the purpose of this study.

Mission After the Cold War

With the beginning of the new world order announced by the President of the United States after the first Gulf War, Christianity had to adjust to the new reality. Moreover, 'with the demise of Marxism and Communism there is no global ideology, which places the poor at the center of its vision for a better human future'.[73] This statement reflects a strict concern for the poor and not for the Marxist ideology as practiced by the former Soviet Union. It acknowledges the fact that the cause for them, having been abandoned by all socio-political systems, became a concern for the church. Therefore, the arrival of the 1990s represented a new challenge for the poor and the marginalized.

It was in 1996 that the WCC organized the next Conference on World Mission and Evangelism – the last gathering of this nature held in the twentieth century. The meeting took place in Salvador, Bahía, Brazil, with the theme 'Called to One Hope: the Gospel in Diverse Cultures'. All of the preparations for this conference were decentralized through studies carried out in different locations and times. Some of the conclusions of this gathering are important for the emerging new contexts of mission.[74]

During the 1990s, the ecumenical world realized that the gospel was not available worldwide and that Christianity should be placed

---

[72] See Carolyn A. Lin, 'Communication, Technology and Global Change', in Carolyn A. Lin and David J. Atkin (eds.), *Communication, Technology and Social Change: Theory and Implications* (Mahwah, NJ: Routledge, 2007), pp. 17-35.

[73] Bryant L. Myers, *The New Context of World Mission* (Monrovia, CA: MARC, 1996), p. 17.

[74] See Christopher Duraisingh, 'Called to One Hope: The Gospel in Diverse Cultures', *Conference on World Mission and Evangelism Salvador, Bahia, Brazil* (24 November-3 December, 1996).

into a number of people groups in the world that did not have a Christian church. They realized the richness in a variety of cultures and their respective expressions of the will of their Creator. No denomination or people group can claim to have the exclusive right for the dissemination of the gospel. Missiologically, all cultures are to be considered equal and have the same value before God. Not only does God want to reach out to all cultures, but He also wants people from all cultures to become evangelists and missionaries. Obviously, all churches in all places would have to carry the gospel message to other cultures as well.

The proclamation of the gospel is cross-cultural, and so are the subjects, the evangelists, and the missionaries. God wants to complete the mission of evangelism in every culture and people group. He wants all cultures to have a share in the proclamation of the gospel, and then, I presume, the mission would have been accomplished. 'Therefore the gospel should be able to come into being and develop in each culture according to its own genius'.[75] Every Christian context should be creative in the way they live and present the gospel.

The WCC conference of Salvador, Bahia, also brought other insights. Along with the natural gifts and talents of every culture, there are also sinful elements of destruction, violence, exclusion, and contempt. This paradox is real: every culture shows elements of reconciliation, solidarity, and peace, but the ways of evil are also present, particularly among those who do not know Christ. There are two elements that could help in understanding this cultural sin.

Christianity continues to struggle against the discrimination and oppression of women.[76] This is a common sin of most cultures dominated by men. Those who work in solidarity with women report that some local cultures do not afford them dignity and oppressively deny them their human rights. Women are not encour-

---

[75] World Council of Churches, 'Mission and Evangelism', p. 46. The WCC assembly of Salvador, Bahia, recorded this statement in order to affirm the local creativity of Christians. It emphasized the use of local resources in the context of the church.

[76] On the matter of oppression of women and their struggle for self-determination, see Sharon Smith, *Women and Socialism: Essays on Women's Liberation* (Chicago, IL: Haymarket Books, 2005), pp. 35-36.

aged to develop their natural talents and potential capabilities.[77] This kind of discrimination or oppression was not caused by international structures of power but by local culture. There are social structures, customs, traditions, and beliefs that subject women to oppression.[78]

Religion is part of the culture, but culture cannot use religion to preserve customs, ethnic identity, and traditions. This issue is particularly difficult in Latin America since some countries or societies often use religion to preserve culture, society, traditions, and even political hegemony.[79] For obvious reasons, I could not elaborate more on this matter, but the theme could be a subject of investigation in further studies.

Salvador made it clear that culture cannot be used to obscure the principles of the gospel. Mission needs to identify the trends that lead a society to create or facilitate oppressive systems, exploitation, and violence against the poor and marginalized. Such negative trends could be seen in the United States with discrimination, violence, and intimidation directed towards foreigners, especially undocumented Hispanic immigrants who have recently arrived in the country. Political leaders have used the war against terrorism to persecute the Latino community. To some extent, Hispanics have become scapegoats in the war against terror. However, what is more detestable is that Christians have either justified those actions or simply remained silent. Prophets and pastors were blinded by their political views and their fundamentalist theology of legality.

At the WCC conference of Melbourne, the delegates concluded that the identification of cultures could not be imposed in top-down fashion by ecclesiastical centers such as Rome or Geneva, for instance. This had to be achieved through ecumenical dialogues, taking into consideration all the specific realities of cultures and communities.[80] Christians who live in those cultures should be the

---

[77] Smith, *Women and Socialism*, p. 42.

[78] Smith, *Women and Socialism*, p. 36.

[79] On the influence of religion over culture in Latin America, see David Lehmann, *Struggle for the Spirit: Religious Transformation and Popular Culture in Brazil and Latin America* (Oxford, UK. Wiley, 1996), pp. 68-75.

[80] Religious dialogues have taken place in recent years between different confessions of faith. That seems to be a pattern, which may lead religious groups to share space in the same communities. See for instance John B. Cobb,

ones to identify the forces or elements contrary to the practice of *Missio Dei*. The international ecclesiastical community thus realized that the most significant data was acquired in cooperation with the local churches and communities. However, this was problematic for the protestant family since it did not have a common center like the Orthodox and the Catholic Church. Nevertheless, Protestants could make good use of their non-directive structures to be creative and offer new alternatives to the traditional structures of the Orthodox and Catholic Church.

This is an area where either the Lausanne movement or the WCC could prove their usefulness. These are platforms where Christians can develop what might be called an intercultural hermeneutic – an essential element in maintaining unity among the various churches rooted in their respective cultures.

The debate on gospel and culture is far from closed by the Salvador, Bahía Conference.[81] It has continued and been particularly enriched by the wide definition of culture used at Salvador, which also included religion. As a result, the debate on enculturation can no longer avoid the question of syncretism – a delicate question if ever there was one.[82]

The 1991 WCC Assembly in Canberra, Australia was deeply divided by the very controversial presentation by Chung Hyun Kyung, in which she used symbols from a traditional Korean religion in her exposition of Christian theology.[83] The evangelical delegates, as well as those from the Orthodox churches, vehemently distanced themselves from that approach. The difficult discussions that may take place between the Orthodox churches and other members of the WCC came up with new definitions for the diversi-

---

Postmodernism and Public Policy: Reframing Religion, Culture, Education, Sexuality, Class, Race, Politics and the Economy (Albany, NY: State University of New York Press, 2002), pp. 15-19.

[81] An update on the debate of gospel and culture could be found at Ed Matthews, 'Relationship Between the Gospel and Culture: The Continuing Debate', *Journal of Applied Missiology* 1.2 (2003), pp. 2-4.

[82] On the subject of enculturation in the context of Latin America, see Johannes Wilbert, *Enculturation in Latin America: An Anthology* (Los Angeles, CA: UCLA Latin American Center Publications, 2008), pp. 8, 9, 237.

[83] The integration of traditional Korean religion with Christian theology is broadly described by Sung-Bum Yoon, *Korean Confucianism and Korean Theology* (Seoul, Korea: Kamsin Publications, 1998), pp. 15-45.

ty, freedom, and limits that are present in the discussion of the en-culturation of the gospel. This issue was also present in the ecu-menical dialogue between the WCC and Pentecostals, particularly in the presentation of the gospel to local groups in the developing world.

This matter continues to be an area of conflict for Protestants who show strong reservations in their approach to popular or folk religion.[84] Protestants think historical churches have over-borrowed popular religious and folk culture, and this has become a hindrance in the dialogue between Christians concerning mission. San Anto-nio may have opened the door for these discussions of religious experiences, but at the Salvador conference delegates went even further when they tried to distinguish between the syncretism that is faithful to God and His purpose for the world and the syncretism that is contrary to the purpose of the gospel. Members of the protestant family did not accept the distinction that there is such a thing as syncretism that is faithful to God's purpose.

In the area of common witness and the total rejection of any form of proselytizing, the 1996 conference re-confirmed state-ments by previous WCC assemblies. For the WCC delegates, it was crucial to reiterate non-proselytizing, particularly in the context of Eastern Europe, where there was a reopening to forms of Christi-anity after the Cold War.

The orthodox churches that felt invaded by the protestant churches reinforced the issue. Among those new Christian groups, Pentecostals seem to have had no respect for the religion of the local people or churches.[85] The attitude of the orthodox churches may have also been a response to the arrival of other Christian tra-ditions into their traditional spheres of influence.

Finally, the attention given to the language and demands of the poor was significant in Salvador, Bahía, where representatives from indigenous people groups demanded respect for their culture and

---

[84] See Paul G. Hiebert and R. Daniel Shaw, *Understanding Folk Religion: A Christian Response to Popular Beliefs and Practices* (Grand Rapids, MI: Baker Books, 2000).

[85] World Council of Churches, *Towards Common Witness: A Call to Adopt Responsible Relationships in Mission and to Renounce Proselytism* (Geneva: WCC Publications, 1997), pp. 4-5.

expressions of identity.[86] They requested true partnership with the historical churches in their approach to mission. If this partnership could be established, then the missionary concern for the poor decided upon at Melbourne would help revitalize the Christian message for the developing world. In the twenty-first century, these indigenous groups are becoming more forceful and proud bearers of their culture, religion, and traditions.

After this encounter with indigenous people groups, missiologists have been compelled to integrate two trends that have been inserted into the mission agenda of the church: one was the catholic adoption of the preferential option for the poor and the other was the attitude of Christians toward other religions.[87] This has led to some new reasoning, for instance, that God has been at work amongst these people before the missionaries arrived with the gospel message. This shift became very clear; these peoples could no longer be seen as poor or pagans and neither simple objects of economic development nor just objects of mission. Instead, they were claiming their status as partners in mission.[88] This was a powerful conclusion, for it launched a new approach to evangelism. Before missionaries get to the un-evangelized people, already God has been working with them. The arrival of missionaries is just the connection needed for them to come to the full knowledge and purpose of the gospel.[89] In other words, God gets to them first in their own culture and knowledge, and then He sends missionaries in for the final connection.

New Context of World Mission

This WCC conference about mission and evangelism took place in Athens, Greece in 2005. The aim of this gathering was to explore and detect the common grounds for dialogue between mission bodies and tension observed in the field of mission as evangelism is

---

[86] The recognition of the plurality of mission was addressed seriously, during the WCC conference at Salvador, Bahia, Brazil. See the report in Viggo Mortensen and Nielsen Andreas (eds.), *Walk Humbly with the Lord: Church and Mission Engaging Plurality* (Grand Rapids, MI: Eerdmans, 2010), p. 257.

[87] Mortensen and Andreas, *Walk Humbly with the Lord*, pp. 300-307.

[88] Mortensen and Andreas, *Walk Humbly with the Lord*, p. 152.

[89] Mortensen and Andreas, *Walk Humbly with the Lord*, pp. 152-53.

carried and exercised around the world, especially in most countries of the Southern hemisphere. Athens also called for the Holy Spirit to heal and reconcile as Christians have been called in Christ to build reconciling and healing communities.[90]

In Athens there was a need to appreciate the mission efforts and gifts, which have been practiced in different contexts of the world. It was clear that the Holy Spirit had used different models of Evangelization depending on the context.[91] Therefore, the Athens delegates felt compelled to appreciate these efforts as God guided them in His purpose among the peoples of the world. Wonsuk Ma, a Pentecostal scholar from Korea, presented a keynote address with regards to the role of pneumatology in mission among the poor.[92] It was clear that Christians and mission agencies needed to hear from each other in order to learn how to enhance their missiological task.

The following section explores some of the most relevant issues debated in Athens concerning mission in the twenty-first century.[93]

Aim of the Gospel

In Athens the delegates realized that the Holy Spirit continues to work in the hearts, lives, and history of all people groups, in order to overcome evil structures of power and liberate people to serve God's purpose on earth. They also admitted that Christians have also been 'implicated in colonialism, racism, and sexism but the

---

[90] A full report of this event is found in Jacques Matthey, 'Come Holy Spirit, Heal and Reconcile', in Jacques Matthey (ed.), *Report of the WCC Conference on World Mission and Evangelism, Athens, Greece* (Geneva, Switzerland: WCC Publications, 2005), pp. 12-16.

[91] Matthey, 'Come Holy Spirit, Heal and Reconcile', p. 15.

[92] Wonsuk Ma, 'When the Poor are Fired Up: The Role of Pneumatology in Pentecostal-Charismatic Mission', *Transformation* 24.1 (January 2007), pp. 28-34. The author states, 'Pentecostalism is a religion of the poor, not for the poor'. Even though the historical churches marginalized them, these people who come from the lower social and economic level have now potential to become the main players in mission. Ma argues that this role is evident by the fact that the Holy Spirit chose to use them through significant activities such as healings, baptism in the Spirit, prophecy, and miracles, as well as drastic conversion experiences.

[93] For extensive information, see World Council of Churches, 'Preparatory Paper', *Report of the WCC Conference on World Mission and Evangelism, Athens, Greece* (Geneva, Switzerland: WCC Publications, 2005), pp. 4-10.

gospel encourages the church to make a great effort for liberation and self-criticism'.[94]

International Approach to Mission

Delegates also concluded that Christians must speak of the *Missio Dei*. This calls for justice for all individuals and the holistic healing for creation. In this mission, the whole church has been called to participate. There should be no exceptions for peoples regardless of their culture, religion, and race.[95]

In order to accomplish this mission, all Christians are called upon to participate. Their approach to mission must be holistic, for it seeks to overcome the dualism between Christians and non-Christians as well as the spiritualization of the gospel.[96] Mission is the incarnation of the good news of Christ to witness and liberate. It also involves education, the proclamation of the Word, and healing for those who are hurt.

They also concluded that participation in God's mission includes the healing of our own communities through solidarity with the needs of other people and an intentional willingness to recognize their own failures in the mission process.[97]

The delegates were convinced that the Kingdom of God manifests in the context of the people and that the goal of the church is the proclamation of the holistic message of salvation in Christ.

Contemporary Mission Trends

Although the emphasis of the congress in Athens was more on reconciliation and healing, there were several other issues debated. Among those, I have selected the following.

---

[94] Matthey, 'Come Holy Spirit, Heal and Reconcile', p. 14.

[95] This information is available at Sebastian C.H.K. Kim, Pauline Kollontai, and Greg Hoyland (eds.), *Peace and Reconciliation: In Search of Shared Identity* (Burlington, VT: Ashgate Publishing Company, 2008), p. 39.

[96] Kim, Kollontai, and Hoyland, *Peace and Reconciliation*, p. 39.

[97] On the matter of salvation for all people, see Veli-Matti Kärkkäinen, *Holy Spirit and Salvation: The Sources of Christian Theology* (Louisville, KY: Westminster John Knox Press, 2010), p. 346.

Mission and Development

Mission and development was the main focus of the Athens Conference. The general approach was that Christians needed to overcome the dualism not just maintain the tension.[98] Delegates insisted that the church's duty and responsibility is to share the entire gospel. To do this, Christians need to be witnesses of Christ in word and in deed. The church must serve communities by instilling better conditions for those who still live in poverty and experience fear. The gospel could not be complete unless it engages with these tangible and urgent needs of the world.

Healing and Reconciliation

Healing and reconciliation had a prominent place at Athens. Christians are called in Christ to be healing and reconciling communities.[99] Athens debated these terms defining the kind of community God desires His people to become: a community that bears witness to the Gospel in word and deed, that is alive in worship and learning, that proclaims the Gospel of Jesus Christ to all, that offers young people leadership roles, that opens its doors to strangers and welcomes the marginalized within its own body, that engages with those who suffer and with those who struggle for justice and peace, that provides services to all who are in need, that recognizes its own vulnerability and need for healing and that is faithful in its commitment to the wider creation.[100]

Gospel and Culture

This dialectic had been central to the Salvador, Bahia conference. This had called upon Christians to become counter-cultural in raising their voices responsibly and making their presence influential in the midst of pagan societies.[101] In Athens Christians were urged to be active in their home settings and work places to ensure free and fair elections and to promote healthy education for their local communities.

---

[98] See for instance the article of Ernst M. Conradie, 'Mission as Evangelism and as Development? Some Perspectives from the Lord's Prayer', *International Review of Mission* 94.375 (2005), pp. 557-75.

[99] Kärkkäinen, *Holy Spirit and Salvation*, p. 346.

[100] Matthey, 'Come Holy Spirit, Heal and Reconcile', p. 16.

[101] See Alvin J. Schmidt, *How Christianity changed the world* (Grand Rapids, MI, Zondervan, 2009).

Dialogue and Witness

In Athens, the debate on interfaith relations was held in the midst of tension. Presenters from Europe, North America, and Asia were convinced that God speaks only through their faith. They were eager to object to any source of pagan religion in their understanding of the revelation of God. They were willing to admit that God could speak thorough various cultures but that caution should be observed when other religions claim to have received such revelations.

Human Solidarity and Cultural Diversity

The delegates at Athens recognized that there is a need for global partnerships in mission but that Christians should be careful in not promoting a single theology or culture.[102] Athens debated the need for a liberating interdependence or a dialogical sharing among all the diverse experiences and expressions of the love of God in Christ. This could be seen as alternatives to some undesirable movements of globalization. If the Western churches supported the need for globalization in mission, one good cause could be the need to combat the problem of AIDS in Africa.

The dialogue became more difficult when some speakers also included the issue of human rights in their presentations. They spoke about the rights of homosexuals in the agenda for the implementation of justice in North America.[103] This discussion opened a theme that could not be answered at that time, and the delegates were dismissed with questions that have yet to be answered in this area.

Christian Unity and Mission

In Athens many speakers came from churches organized by confessional unions or traditions rooted in Western cultures. This caused controversy among the delegates because a large number of them

---

[102] Conradie, 'Mission as Evangelism and as Development?', p. 4.

[103] The Athens conference ended with the conviction that Christianity will have to prepare theologically to respond to the emerging gay agenda in the world. One author that faces the issue extensively is Ronnie W. Floyd. He argues that Christians are being challenged from several fronts regarding this matter and they need to prepare well to face it in the right way. See Ronnie W. Floyd, *The Gay Agenda: It's Dividing the Family, the Church, and a Nation* (Green Forest, AR: New Lift Publications, 2004), pp. 17-19.

came from independent groups that have gathered together in denominational organizations around the world.

Some delegates from the South introduced the matter of equality in the sharing of responsibilities related to Christian mission. It was clear that some models of Christianity from North America have become sources of splits and fragmentation instead of agents of unity. Delegates initiated a dialogue that would propose a solution to this difficulty. For most of them, mission could only be carried out in true unity reflected through effective partnerships.[104]

Mission as Contextual and Universal

The Athens delegates were eager to dialogue about the importance of a theology that is contextual and emphasizes mission. Although the conference aimed to reinforce the significance of the contextualization of mission, the theme reached higher levels of discussion. The organizers invited presenters from different locations of the world to address the mission situation in their own particular settings. Nevertheless, most of them presented papers with strong demands for justice, reconciliation, healing, and unity. This was the case of some South African representatives in particular, who quoted the late David Bosch's work as he called for 'bold humility – bold in our witness to God's truth made known in Christ, humble in our recognition that our perceptions of that truth are necessarily limited by history and culture'.[105]

---

[104] At the CWME of the WCC in Athens, the theme of healthy partnerships was presented and later published by Ola Yjorhom, *Apostolicity and Unity: Essays on the Porvoo Common Statement* (Geneva, Switzerland: WCC Publications, 2003), pp. 24-32. In his presentation he values partnership as an effective model for evangelism in the current world.

[105] Bosch, *Transforming Mission*, p. 590.

CONCLUSION

In order to present a convincing case, we had to establish a historical foundation about recent mission history so as to understand and build an adequate framework related to current trends in the understanding and practice of mission by scholars and practitioners. To accomplish this purpose, we surveyed several texts written by missiologists and some documents that have come out of major Christian consultations that referred to mission.[1]

These sources were helpful in creating a framework of reference for understanding some historical developments of mission on the global and local levels. Therefore, when we had to approach authors and documents produced at consultations in Latin America, we had adequate references to understand mission and its practice in particular countries. Thus, as we bring this discussion to a conclusion, here are some points highlighted as conclusive.

The following remarks are written to Pentecostals, Charismatics, and Neo-Pentecostals. The reader will notice that one of the purposes of this work is to raise mission awareness about integral mission among the renewal movements in Latin America.

Missio Dei in Latin America

Pentecostals are now studying other models of mission in the region. Some of the findings of this research show that other Christian organizations have invested lots of energy and resources in mission particularly among the poor. There are specific cases and scenarios that could be studied. One example is the case of natural

---

[1] Campos, *Experiencia del Espíritu*, pp. 53-68.

disasters like Hurricane Mitch in Honduras. Individuals, churches, and non-governmental organizations joined efforts to rebuild the country. Several lessons could be learned from those efforts.

Although this study engaged the debate of Pentecostal mission in Latin America specifically, we could not ignore the historical influence of the RCC on the lives and mindsets of most Latin Americans. For instance, there are countless numbers of religious practices and traditions initiated in the RCC that are observed culturally and religiously even on the part of those who have decided to leave the RCC because of conversion to Pentecostalism. A great number of former Catholics have now become members of the Pentecostal family, but culturally speaking they still carry values and principles rooted in historical Catholicism.

Anthropologists and missiologists recognize that Catholic liturgy and popular festivities are still part of Latin America even when they adhere to another Christian tradition.[2] This variable is particularly meaningful in the development of theology, for it touches the heart of the people with their understanding and practice of religion. These findings helped us build the case for gospel and culture as experienced in Latin America, especially in the context of Honduras.

Dialogue with the Roman Catholic Church.

As stated above, a significant number of Pentecostals may have formally bequeathed their religious adherence to the RCC. However, in their culture, history, and tradition they still adhere to their Catholic background when it comes to religious behavior and practice of faith, especially in liturgy.[3] Therefore, it will not be easy for the new streams of Christianity in Latin America to erase the RCC heritage and influence on the understanding and practice of mission. This relationship still exists, and further studies are needed to explain Christian mission in Latin America in terms of its mixture

---

[2] See Vaccaro, *Identidad Pentecostal*, pp. 23-31; and Bryan Wilson, *Sociología de las Sectas Religiosas* (Madrid, España: Guadarrama, 1970), pp. 74-82; also Ernst Troeltsch, *El Protestantismo y el Mundo Moderno* (México, DF: FCE, 1983), pp. 108-14.

[3] Vaccaro, *Identidad Pentecostal*, p. 28.

of catholic and Pentecostal traditions in terms of the approach to integral mission.

Due to the influence of the RCC in the religious life and culture of Latin America, we were curious to see if there was a concept of integral mission in RCC teachings. Although the term is not used by catholic missiologists, it could be found in their practical approach to Christian mission, particularly in the so-called option for the poor teaching.[4]

This dialogue between Catholics and Pentecostals suggested some ideas and insights into the debate about integral mission in Latin America. We explored the Pentecostal notion of the development of the human person in God's plan of love. We also studied the Pentecostal thinking about salvation for the individual, the community, and the whole person in their development of Christian mission. Moreover, since Pentecostals appear to be mostly community-oriented in their understanding and practice of mission, we also looked at the Pentecostal motivation toward common areas related to mission, such as education and cultural formation. Some of our findings may seem controversial to both Catholics and Pentecostals, but the study suggests new possibilities and opportunities for a more complete understanding and practice of mission on the continent.

We also looked into the historical relationship between RCC theology and the development of Pentecostal mission in Latin America. There are themes commonly known as part of the catholic theology, which we considered significant in the formulation of

---

[4] I also found that integral mission is still a new theological term being used among Pentecostals in Latin America. In the evangelical world, René Padilla has used the term integral mission in most of his publications. See for instance C. René Padilla, 'Integral Mission and its Historical Development', in Tim Chester (ed.), *Justice, Mercy & Humility: Integral Mission and the Poor* (Carlisle, UK: Paternoster, 2002), pp. 42-58; and Padilla, 'Hacia una Evaluación Teológica del Ministerio Integral', in Tetsunao Yamamori, Gregorio Rake, and C. René Padilla (eds.), *Servir con los Pobres en América Latina: Modelos de Ministerio Integral* (Buenos Aires, Argentina: Ediciones Kairós, 2005), pp. 29-52. Other scholars such as Orlando Costas and Samuel Escobar incorporated integral mission into their mission studies. See Orlando Costas, *Orlando, Christ Outside the Gate: Mission Beyond Christendom* (Maryknoll, NY: Orbis Books, 1982), pp. 78-81; and Samuel Escobar, Samuel, 'Christian Reflections from the Latino South', *Journal of Latin American Theology* 1.2 (2006), pp. 6-14.

Pentecostal mission in Latin America today. Such teachings as social responsibility, public participation, human solidarity, common good, subsidiarity, and morality have been historically taught by the RCC but have been recently incorporated as fields of study by some pastors who adhere to the new apostolic and prophetic movement. We are not legitimizing this movement and its practices, but such exercise reviewing and incorporating historical teachings of the RCC into their practice of ministry may broaden the study of mission at a certain number of Pentecostal communities in Latin America. Therefore, further research and dialogue between Pentecostal and the RCC mission seems to be necessary.

As a result of the study, we discovered some common ground that Pentecostals and RCC missiologists may want to consider for future debates. For some fellow Pentecostals, we may have gone too far in our approach to catholic theology, and this study may cause controversy. Nevertheless, we presume there will be some scholars who will be willing to participate with maturity in this debate, and so contribute to building mutual respect. This dialogue could also lead to the identification of common grounds of mutual understanding in the development of a theology of mission for Latin America. Learning through a responsible dialogue could reduce the distance between Catholics and Pentecostals in their understanding and practice of mission.[5] Though we only introduce the matter here as one of the findings of the research, we do recommend that the theme continue to be considered for further investigation. We would hope it would be investigated particularly by Pentecostal scholars who are now writing on mission history and theology in the context of Latin America.

---

[5] A dialogue between Pentecostals and Roman Catholics has been ongoing since 1972. Some representatives of the Pentecostal churches met with representatives of the Vatican with the purpose to dialogue over issues of interest on both sides. Pentecostals also have on-going dialogues with the World Council of Churches and with the Lutherans, Anglicans, Reformed, and other Christian traditions. At most of these dialogues, representatives from Latin America have been invited to participate. Some of those documents could be seen at Angelo Maffeis, *Ecumenical Dialogue* (Collegeville, MN: Liturgical Press, 2000), pp. 98-107.

Mission Among the Poor

Another key research theme was the attitude of Pentecostals toward the poor and marginalized. Historically, Pentecostals come from the poor and the marginalized.[6] They are born into the Pentecostal faith in poverty, socio-economically speaking. Therefore, when they take upon themselves the mandate of witnessing to the poor, they do not have to go to the poor because they are part of the poor themselves. Mission action here is understood from the poor to other poor.[7] Unlike other mission-sending agencies, Pentecostals did not have to invest large sums and time to train and send missionaries to reach the poor. On the contrary, the Pentecostal approach to evangelism leads the way to numerous conversions and has been able to reach multitudes quicker than traditional mission agencies. This phenomenon is recent, and it continues to grow significantly. Further research may be required to explain current trends in Pentecostal mission today.

For Pentecostals, integral mission occurs through the teaching and discipleship of new believers. The community of faith embraces new converts by example rather than indoctrination. Thus, a believer is ready to witness to Christ and the community at large about the power of transformation that occurs when persons and communities surrender their lives to Jesus Christ. The transformation of humanity is complete when individuals are sanctified and baptized by the Holy Spirit. This is the Pentecostal experience that enables the believer to witness by the power of the Holy Spirit. Their ministry is followed by signs and wonders which help people to convert to Christ convincingly and efficiently.

---

[6] See for instance the book of Schäfer, *Protestantismo y Crisis Social en América Central*, pp. 58-61. Although Schäfer wrote on Protestantism in general, at some point he acknowledged the strength of Pentecostalism as a movement of the poor and among the marginalized. Another source was written by Juan Sepúlveda, 'Pentecostalismo y Religiosidad Popular', *Pastoral Popular* 32.1 (1981), pp. 178-87.

[7] Wonsuk Ma, 'When the Poor are Fired Up: The Role of Pneumatology in Pentecostal-Charismatic Mission', *Transformation* 1.24 (2007), pp. 28-34. In his article, Ma makes the case for Pentecostals taking over evangelization even in their condition as the poor, which makes them relevant in the evangelization of the world today.

The rapid growth and multiplication of Pentecostal believers has brought new hope and opportunities to a significant number of communities in Latin America. Moreover, this phenomenon has similar occurrences in other parts of the world, which leads one to think that Pentecostal mission has earned a definite right to be taken seriously by those who study the current trends of mission in the area.

Controversial Statements

At some point in the study, we used the data collected from different Christian traditions in Latin America to introduce a discussion that may not be familiar to some Pentecostals because it addresses some RCC theological teachings related to public service, the value of democracy, common good, morality, and political participation as part of the mission of believers. We gave significant attention to these matters, for Pentecostals are now becoming more involved with matters that point to the good of the community. These issues provide common grounds for discussion among Christians.[8]

Believers are now challenged to respond to the needs that are common to society at large. Poverty has no color, age, gender, or religion. It has to be faced by all people who are part of the community, and Pentecostals are aware of this fact. Therefore, to be objective in the approach to poverty and mission, we decided to include a discussion of these matters, which would enable Pentecostals to draw valuable information in their understanding and practice of mission.

Again, the discussion focused on issues that are not traditionally addressed by Pentecostal scholars and practitioners. Due to the nature of the research, we decided to avoid those matters that are commonly known among Pentecostal missiologists. Instead, as we referred earlier, we looked into matters that may seem extraneous to those who study Pentecostalism. Issues such as political involvement, ethics, culture, and democratic participation have not been reviewed and documented as in this study.[9]

---

[8] Sepúlveda, 'Pentecostalismo y Religiosidad Popular', p. 182.

[9] On the matter of political involvement, see the classic work of Yoder, *The Politics of Jesus*, pp. 23-35. Although this is not a Pentecostal source on politics, it

This research also contains a constructive and creative attempt to produce a model of integral mission for the Pentecostal churches. We have tried to build the case for a broader perspective, referring to the Pentecostal community in general and not just Honduras or Latin America. In the end, the study is intended to become an academic reference for the understanding of integral mission in general. Pentecostals of other contexts may use it as reference for further studies.

This model calls on Pentecostals to engage the world holistically. It is a model that reaches beyond preaching the gospel and feeding the poor. It integrates God's message of hope with all social, economic, cultural, political, and spiritual needs, especially in favor of the poor and the marginalized.

Concluding Remarks

This study of integral mission is presented following two objectives: (1) it looked at the need to identify the nature of integral mission in the particular context of Pentecostal churches, and (2) the Pentecostal churches are in need of developing a solid teaching and practice of mission theology, which should be integral in its scope. This information was gathered from all sources investigated, and a conclusion was reached that gave birth to a proposal for a Pentecostal theology of mission.

Although Pentecostal churches in Latin America are currently paying significant attention to the church growth phenomenon, the numbers shown suggests that their growth is generating a certain ability to affect the community. In some scenarios, they seem to be transforming old paradigms into new life standards that will complete the fullness of God's purpose for humanity in their communities. To meet such demands, Pentecostals may have to refocus their attention on other areas of service such as community development and assistance to the poor, which are social responsibilities now being intentionally included in most Pentecostal ministries.[10]

___

offers useful insights, which some Pentecostals are looking at for their political participation in society.

[10] A significant report on the impact of Pentecostal growth and ministry in Latin America could be found at Lillian Kwon, 'Pentecostal Impact Growing in Latin America', *Christian Post Reporter* (November 9, 2006). http://www.christian

This study offers new constructive possibilities, a result that should be expected, given the creativity that has been evident Pentecostalism throughout its history.[11] Naturally, the interpretation of research has been as objective as possible in order to meet academic standards. Only time will demonstrate its validity.

This research offers an ample spectrum of mission thinking and practice. It reaches out beyond the traditional borders of Pentecostalism. It engages in dialogue with other Christian traditions and opens the opportunity for networking, cooperation, and collaboration.[12] This is part of the new mentality of the emerging generation of Pentecostals. The study offers new possibilities for the Pentecostal churches to engage in integral mission from the grass-roots level. Pentecostals are creative, and from their community they can participate actively in the common interests of society. They could serve in the democratic processes and be active participants in social concerns.[13]

Finally, Pentecostals are able to integrate new insights and ideas. They are willing to learn. They know about education and recognize the need for formal training. Excellence is now driving them to reach higher levels of efficiency and effectiveness in their service. It is with all of these ideas in perspective that this study proposes adjustments to the traditional understanding and practice of mission in the Pentecostal churches. This is one the most distinctive contributions of this research to a Pentecostal theology of mission.

Further Study

This work brings forward creative proposals, which may serve Pentecostals as they continue to study their practice and conceive new

---

post.com/article/20061109/pentecostal-impact-growing-in-latin-america/. Accessed 14 November 2009.

[11] Douglas Petersen, *Not by Might nor by Power* (Oxford, UK: Regnum Books International, 1996), pp. 186-226.

[12] On the matter of collaboration and cooperation for mission, see Lucien LeGrand, *Unity and Plurality: Mission in the Bible* (Maryknoll, NY: Orbis, 1990), pp. 8-27; see also D. Senior and C. Stuhlmueller, *The Biblical Foundations for Mission: Part I* (Maryknoll, NY: Orbis Books, 1983), pp. 9-13.

[13] Sepúlveda, 'Pentecostalismo y Religiosidad Popular', p. 24.

ideas and insights that arise from some of the matters discussed in it.

During the course of the discussion, we also made reference to other emerging issues found in the study, which will require further research and reflection. However, those pointed out here were the ones useful for the purpose of this study. In this research, we did not investigate matters such as mission to the environment, gender issues, cross-cultural evangelization, and other topics that could enlarge this study. However, we are confident there will be other occasions and opportunities for further discussion and research. These topics may come back time and again to the table of discussion, and Pentecostals will have to be prepared to respond adequately when questions arise.

Pentecostals believe that the community of faith has a role to play in the fulfillment of God's mission. Both movements began to understand and practice mission in various ways through each local member according to the gifts of each person's calling. Mario Méndez thinks Evangelicals and Pentecostals are now responding to the responsibility to proclaim and bear witness to the gospel, with the understanding that every mission effort involves all who believe and are willing to obey the call of the Holy Spirit to service.[14]

Also in relation to social responsibility Samuel Escobar argues that Christian mission is biased to the poor. It is clear that in the story of Jesus God becomes vulnerable with the poor and marginalized.[15] In the person of Jesus, God assumes a mission to transform the world by way of Christian mission. Incidentally most church members are not found among the wealthy and powerful but rather among the poor and vulnerable. What does mission mean when its representatives come from contexts of poverty and exclusion?

This ministry in the community context involves the service of devoted believers who are capable of using their spiritual gifts and natural talents.

Their faithful witness and service is needed particularly in times of intense conditions of poverty. Situations like these open sig-

---

[14] Méndez, *La Iglesia: Fuerza del Espíritu*, pp. 24-26.

[15] Tito Paredes, 'Holistic Mission in Latin America', in Brian Woolnough and Wonsuk Ma (eds.), *Holistic Mission: God's Plan for God's People* (Oxford, UK: Regnum Books International, 2010), pp. 102-16.

nificant opportunities to serve people and reminds believers about their principles of holiness and sincere love to the poor and marginalized.[16]

Here we realize that either Evangelicals or Pentecostals could be easily found at the service of the incarnated Christ. It is this Christ whose love for people is shown through Christians who propose new opportunities to humanity. They are believers from the community who carry this mission to other communities.

On Pentecostal Mission

Pentecostalism is a movement rather than a denomination. Instead of a centralized, bureaucratic organization, Pentecostals form a network linked by personal ties and similar beliefs. Pentecostal mission travels along pre-existing daily social relationships such as family, friends, or work companions. Thus, this kind of missionary activity is another source of growth in a new reformation of Christianity. This 'Reformation' is commonly understood as a 'change from worse to better', but a secondary meaning of reformation is 'the act of forming anew'. In the latter sense, Pentecostalism may indeed represent Christianity's 'next Reformation'. With its exponential growth in developing nations and its unique understanding of Christian experience, Pentecostalism could form a new Christianity in the 21st century.[17]

Pentecostals have also linked their mission service to the outpouring of gifts of the Holy Spirit. There is a common understanding among Pentecostals that the fulfillment of God's program for humanity is about to be completed. Judgments against evil and eternal blessings for the faithful ones are about to happen. Appropriation of this understanding has given Pentecostals a sense of urgency in their missionary activity.[18] Time is running out, and Pentecostals are taking over their communities spurred by a sense of

---

[16] López, *Pentecostalismo y Transformación Social*, p. 38.
[17] Paloma, *The Spirit Bade Me to Go*, p. 78.
[18] Smidt, 'The Spirit-Filled Movements and American Politics', pp. 219-39.

biblical mandate and a personal sense of calling and an empowering experience of the Holy Spirit.[19]

With all of the facts collected in this study, Pentecostals are *en route* to a strong witness to Christ in the present generation. Hence, they are now entering into the field of mission with a clear picture of their destiny and purpose. This will enable their members to serve their communities in a complete way.[20] Evidently, what is needed now is to provide adequate training for their members, so they can go out to reap the world's harvest efficiently. This project could be done intentionally through strategic planning via cooperation and collaboration with Pentecostals and non-Pentecostal bodies. This outward urge will in turn depend on the Pentecostals' ability to imbibe the lessons spelt out in this study, particularly in engaging more positively with the outside word.

---

[19] Frank D. Macchia, 'The Struggle for Global Witness: Shifting Paradigms in Pentecostal Theology', in Murray W. Dempster, Byron D. Klaus, and Douglas Petersen (eds.), *The Globalization of Pentecostalism: A Religion Made to Travel* (Oxford, UK: Regnum Books International, 1999), pp. 8-29.

[20] Harvey Cox, 'Pentecostalism and Global Market Culture: A Response to Issues Facing Pentecostalism in a Postmodern World', in Murray W. Dempster, Byron D. Klaus, and Douglas Petersen (eds.), *The Globalization of Pentecostalism: A Religion Made to Travel* (Oxford, UK: Regnum Books International, 1999), pp. 386-95.

SELECT BIBLIOGRAPHY

Alonzo, Ignacio and Iris Barrientos, *Fe y Política* (Tegucigalpa, Honduras: Editorial SETEHO, 2006).

Alvarado, Gilberto, *El Poder Desde el Espíritu: La Visión Política del Pentecostalismo en el México Contemporáneo* (Buenos Aires, Argentina: Publicaciones Científicas para el Estudio de las Religiones, 2006).

Álvarez, Carmelo E., *People of Hope: The Protestant Movement in Central America* (New York, NY: Friendship Press, 1990).

–*Pentecostalismo y Liberación: Una Experiencia Latinoamericana* (San José, Costa Rica: DEI 1992).

–*Alborada en Tiempos Fecundos: Una Teología Ecuménica y Pentecostal* (Quito, Ecuador: Consejo Latinoamericano de Iglesias, 2007).

Álvarez, Miguel, 'The South and the Latin American Paradigm of the Pentecostal Movement', *Asian Journal of Pentecostal Studies* 5.1 (2002), pp. 135-53.

–'Hacia una Hermenéutica Esperanzadora', in Raúl Zaldívar, Miguel Álvarez, and David E. Ramírez, *El Rostro Hispano de Jesús* (Barcelona, España: CLIE, 2013), pp. 114-17.

Alves, Rubem, *A Theology of Human Hope* (Washington, DC: Corpus Books 1985).

Amaya, Jorge Alberto, *Los Árabes y Palestinos en Honduras, 1900–1950* (Tegucigalpa, Honduras: Editoriales Guaymuras, 1997).

Anderson, Thomas, *Politics in Central America: Guatemala, El Salvador, Honduras and Nicaragua* (Westport, CT: Greenwood Publishing Group, 2003).

Archer, Kenneth J., *A Pentecostal Hermeneutic: Spirit, Scripture, and Community* (Cleveland, TN: CPT Press, 2009).

Argueta, Mario, *La Gran Huelga Bananera: Los 69 Días que Estremecieron a Honduras* (Tegucigalpa, Honduras: Editorial Universitaria 1995).

Avila, Mariano, *Toward a Latin American Contextual Hermeneutics: A Critical Examination of the Contextual Hermeneutics of the Fraternidad Teológica Latinoamericana* (PhD, Westminster Theological Seminary, 1996).

Assmann, Hugo, *Opresión-Liberación: Desafío de los Cristianos* (Montevideo, Uruguay: Tierra Nueva, 1991).

Azevedo, M. de C., 'Opción por los Pobres y Cultura Secular en América Latina', *Razón y Fe* 10.2 (1983), pp. 147-61.

Balda, Wesley D., *Heirs of the Same Promise* (Monrovia, CA: MARC, 1984).

Baker, Marcos, *¡Basta de Religión! Cómo Construir Comunidades de Gracia y Libertad* (Buenos Aires, Argentina: Ediciones Kairós, 2005).

Barring, Maruja (ed.), *De Vecinas a Ciudadanas: La Mujer en el Desarrollo Urbano* (Lima, Perú: SUMBI, 1988).

Bastian, Jean Pierre, *La Mutación Religiosa de América Latina: Para una Sociología del Cambio Social en la Modernidad Periférica* (México, DF: Fondo de Cultura Económica, 1997).

Bautista, Esperanza, *La Mujer en la Iglesia Primitiva* (Estela, Navarra: Editorial Verbo Divino, 1993).

Beals, Paul A., *A People for His Name: A Church-Based Mission Strategy* (Pasadena, CA: William Carey University, 1999).

Benjamin, Medea, *Don't Be Afraid, Gringo: A Honduran Woman Speaks from the Heart, The Story of Elvia Alvarado* (New York, NY: Harper & Row, 1989).

Bernal, Sergio, *La Iglesia del Brasil y el Compromiso Social: El Paso de la Iglesia de la Cristiandad a la Iglesia de los Pobres* (Rome: Pont University Gregoriana, 1986).

Berryman, Phillip, *Liberation Theology: Essential Facts about the Revolutionary Movement in Latin America and Beyond* (New York, NY: Pantheon Books, 1987).

Black, Greg, *The Triumph of the People: The Sandinista Revolution in Nicaragua* (London, UK: Zed Press, 1981).

Blanco, Gustavo and Jaime Valverde, *Honduras: Iglesia y cambio social* (San José, Costa Rica: Departamento Ecuménico de Investigaciones, 1990).

Blondet, Cecilia, 'Lecciones de la Participación Política de las Mujeres', *JACS-IEP* 9.1 (2001), pp. 189-201.

Boff, Leonardo, *When Theology Listens to the Poor* (San Francisco, CA: Harper & Row, 1984).

—*Jesucristo y la Liberación del Hombre* (Madrid, España: Ediciones Cristiandad, 1995).

Bomann, Rebecca Pierce, *Faith in the Barrios: The Pentecostal Poor in Bogotá* (Boulder, CO: Lynne Rienner 1999).

Bonilla, Plutarco, 'La Misión de la Iglesia Según el Libro de los Hechos', *La Biblia en las Américas* 5.53 (1998), pp. 12-16.

Bonino, José Miguez, 'El Nuevo Catolicismo', in C. René Padilla (ed.), *Fe Cristiana y Latinoamérica Hoy* (Buenos Aires, Argentina: Ediciones Certeza, 1994), pp. 88-99.

—*Poder del Evangelio y el Poder Político* (Buenos Aires, Argentina: Editorial Independiente Rúcula Libros, 2001).

Bravo, Benjamín, *El Fruto del Espíritu* (Lima, Peru: Ediciones Puma, 1997).

Brett, Edwuard T. and Donna. W. Brett, 'Facing the Challenge: The Catholic Church and Social Change in Honduras', in Woodward, R.L. (ed.), *Central America: Historical Perspectives on the Contemporary Crises* (New York, NY: Greenwood, 1988), pp. 41-54.

Brusco, Elizabeth, 'The Reformation of Machismo: Ascetism and Masculinity Among Colombian Evangelicals', in Virginia Garrard-Burnett and David Stoll (eds.), *Rethinking Protestantism in Latin America* (Philadelphia, PA: Temple University Press, 2011), pp. 193-97.

Bueno, David, 'The Struggle for Social Space: How Salvadoran Pentecostals Build Communities in the Rural Sector', *Transformation* 18.3 (2001), pp. 171-91.

Butler, Anthea, 'Facets of Pentecostal Spirituality and Justice', in Hubert van Beek (ed.), *Consultation with Pentecostals in the Americas* (San José, Costa Rica: World Council of Churches, 1996), pp. 28-44.

Campos, Bernardo, 'Pentecostalism: A Latin American View', in Hubert van Beek (ed.), *Consultation with Pentecostals in the Americas* (San José, Costa Rica: World Council of Churches, 1996), pp. 4-12.

–*Pentecostalismo y Cultura: La Espiritualidad Pentecostal en el Perú* (Quito, Ecuador: CLAI, 1999).

Castellanos, Julieta, Leticia Salomón, and Mirna Flores, *Ciudadanía y Participación en Honduras* (Tegucigalpa: Honduras: CEDOH, 1996).

Castillo, Cecilia, 'Imágenes y Espiritualidad de las Mujeres en el Pentecostalismo Chileno', in Daniel Chiquete and Luis Orellana (eds.), Voces del Pentecostalismo Latinoamericano III (Concepción, Chile: RELEP, 2009), pp 183-98.

Chiquete, Daniel, 'Healing, Salvation and Mission: The Ministry of Healing in Latin American Pentecostalism', *International Review of Mission* 9.3 (2004), pp. 474-85.

Cleary, Edward. L., *Crisis and Change: The Church in Latin America Today* (Maryknoll, NY: Orbis Books, 1985).

–*Mobilizing for Human Rights in Latin America* (Bloomfield, CT: Kumarian Press, 2007).

Cleary, Edward. L. and H.W. Stewart-Gambino, *Power, Politics, and Pentecostals in Latin America* (Boulder, CO: Westview Press, 1997).

Comblin, José, *The Holy Spirit and Liberation* (Maryknoll, NY: Orbis Books, 1989).

–'Brazil: Based Communities in the Northeast', in Guillermo Cook (ed.), *New Face of the Church in Latin America: Between Tradition and Change* (New York, NY: Orbis Books, 1994), pp. 205-25.

Costas, Orlando, *Missional Incarnation; Christ Outside the Gate: Mission Beyond Christendom* (Maryknoll, NY: Orbis Books, 1982).

Custodio, Ramón, 'The Human Rights Crisis in Honduras', in M.B. Rosenberg and P.L. Shepherd (eds.), *Honduras Confronts its Future: Contending Perspectives on Critical Issues* (Boulder, CO: Lynne Rienner, 1986), pp. 60-72.

Deiros, Pablo, *La Acción del Espíritu Santo en la Historia: Las Lluvias Tempranas* (Miami, FL: Caribe, 1998).

Driver, Juan, *La Fe en la Periferia de la Historia* (Guatemala, Guatemala: Semilla, 1997).

Dussel, Enrique, *The Church in Latin America, 1492–1992* (Tunbridge Wells: Burns and Oates, 1992).

–'Un Análisis Contextual de la Iglesia Católica en América Latina', *Pastoralia* 2.3 (1989), pp. 32-44.

Edwards, Sebastian, *Crisis and Reform in Latin America: From Despair to Hope* (Oxford, UK: Oxford University Press, 1995).

Ensor, Marisa O., *The Legacy of Hurricane Mitch: Lessons from Post-Disaster reconstruction in Honduras* (Phoenix, AZ: The University of Arizona Press, 2009).

Euraque, Darío A., *Estado, Poder, Nacionalidad y Raza en la Historia de Honduras: Ensayos* (Tegucigalpa, Honduras: Ediciones Subirana, 1996.

–*Reinterpreting the Banana Republic: Region and State in Honduras, 1870–1972* (Chapel Hill, NC: University of North Carolina Press, 1996).

Escobar, Samuel, 'Christian Reflections from the Latino South', *Journal of Latin American Theology* 1.2 (2006), pp. 6-14.

Ferrero, José María, 'Honduras: La Iglesia Ante el Gobierno del Cambio', *Puntos de Vista* 3.1 (1991), pp. 13-25.

Flora, Cornelia Butler, *Pentecostalism in Colombia: Baptism by Fire and Spirit* (Rutherford, NJ: Farleigh Dickinson University Press, 1996).

Freston, Paul, 'Pentecostalism in Latin America: Characteristics and Controversies', *Social Compass* 45.3 (1998), pp. 335-58.

Fuentes, Vilma Elisa, *The Political Effects of Disaster and Foreign Aid: National and Subnational Governance in Honduras after Hurricane Mitch* (PhD, University of Florida, 2003).

Funes, Matías, *Los Deliberantes: El Poder Militar en Honduras* (Tegucigalpa, Honduras: Editorial Guaymuras, 1995).

Galvao, Ruy de Andrade Coelho, *Los Negros Caribes de Honduras* (Tegucigalpa, Honduras: Editorial Guaymuras, 1981).

Gill, Athol, 'Christian Social Responsibility', in C. René Padilla (ed.), *The New Face of Evangelicalism* (London: Hodder and Stoughton, 1976), pp. 82-96.

Gill, Leslie, 'Like a Veil to Cover Them: Women and the Pentecostal Movement of La Paz', *American Ethnologist* 17.4 (1990), pp. 706-21.

González Carías, Silvia and Rosa Margarita Montenegro, *Sueños Truncados: La Migración de Hondureños Hacia los Estados Unidos* (Tegucigalpa, Honduras: Pastoral Social Caritas, 2003).

Guerrero Méndez, Miguel, 'La Iglesia: Fuerza del Espíritu, Su Unidad y Diversidad', in Carmelo Álvarez (ed.), *Pentecostalismo y Liberación: Una Experiencia Latinoamericana* (San José, Costa Rica: Departamento Ecuménico de Investigaciones, 1992), pp. 19-26.

Holland, Clifton, *World Christianity: Central America and the Caribbean* (Monrovia, CA: MARC, 1981).

Hollenweger, Walter, *Pentecostalism: Origins and Developments Worldwide* (Peabody, MA: Hendrickson, 1997).

Käkkäinen, Veli-Matti, 'Culture, Contextualization and Conversion: Missiological Reflections from the Catholic-Pentecostal Dialogue (1990-1997)', *Journal of Asian Mission* 2.2 (2000), pp. 263-69.

Kamsteeg, Frans. H., *Prophetic Pentecostalism in Chile: A Case Study on Religion and Development Policy* (Lanham, MD: Scarecrow Press, 1998).

Kay, William. K., *Pentecostalism* (London, UK: SCM Press, 2009).

Keen, Benjamin and Keith Haynes, *A History of Latin America* (Boston, MA: Houghton Mifflin Harcourt, 2013).

Kirk, J. Andrew, *What is Mission?* (London: Fortress Press, 2000).

Lalive d'Espinay, Christian, *El Refugio de las Masas* (Santiago de Chile: Editorial del Pacifico, 1968).

Land, Steven Jack, 'A Passion for the Kingdom: Revisioning Pentecostal Spirituality', *Journal of Pentecostal Theology* 1 (1992), pp. 19-46.

Land, Steven Jack, *Pentecostal Spirituality: A Passion for the Kingdom* (Cleveland, TN: CPT Press, 2010).

Levine, Daniel H. and David Stoll, 'Bridging the Gap between Empowerment and Power in Latin America', in S. Rudolph and J. Piscatori (eds.), *Transnational Religion and Fading State* (Boulder, CO: Westview Press, 1997), pp. 63-103.

López Trujillo, Alfonso, 'Medellín: Una Mirada Global', *La Iglesia en la Actual Transformación de América Latina a la Luz del Concilio* 1.12 (1976), pp. 10-21.

López, Darío, *Pentecostalismo y Transformación Social: Más Allá de los Estereotipos, las Críticas se Enfrentan con los Hechos* (Buenos Aires, Argentina: Ediciones Kairós, 2000).

—*Pentecostalismo y Misión Integral: Teología del Espíritu, Teología de la Vida* (Lima, Perú: Ediciones Puma, 2008).

López, Mario René, *Historia y Misión del Protestantismo Hondureño* (San José, Costa Rica: Editorial Visión Mundial Internacional, 1993).

MacCameron, Robert, 'Bananas, Labor and Politics in Honduras, 1954-1963: Foreign and Comparative Studies', *Latin American Series* 5.1 (1983), pp. 288-96.

Makay, Juan, *El Otro Cristo Español* (Ciudad Guatemala, Guatemala: Ediciones Semilla, 1989).

Mariz, Celia Loreto, 'Perspectivas Sociológicas Sobre el Pentecostalismo y el NeoPentecostalismo', *Revista de Cultura Teológica* 3.13 (1995), pp. 7-16.

Martin, Bernice, 'Latin American Pentecostalism: The Ideological Battleground', in Calvin L. Smith (ed.), *Pentecostal Power: Expressions, Impact and Faith of Latin American Pentecostalism* (Leiden, The Netherlands: Brill, 2011), pp 85-109.

Martin, David, *Tongues of Fire: The Explosion of Protestantism in Latin America* (Oxford, UK: Basil Blackwell, 1990).

Mejía, Medardo, *Historia de Honduras* (Tegucigalpa, Honduras: Editorial Universitaria, 1983).

Menéndez, Valentín, *La Misión de la Iglesia: Un Estudio Sobre el Debate Teológico y Eclesial en América Latina* (Roma, Italia: Universidad Pontifica Gregoriana, 2001).

Meza, Víctor, *Historia del Movimiento Obrero Hondureño* (Tegucigalpa, Honduras: CEDOH, 1980).

Moffitt, Robert, *Si Jesús Fuera Alcalde: Como Transformar tu comunidad* (Phoenix, AR: Harvest, 2006).

Monteiro, Yara, 'Congregación Cristiana en Brasil, de la Fundación Centenario: La Trayectoria de una Iglesia Brasileña', in Daniel Chiquete and Luis Orellana (eds.), *Voces del Pentecostalismo Latinoamericano* 4 (Concepción, Chile: RELEP, 2011), pp. 77-140.

Moreno, Pedro 'The Economics of Evangelization', in P.D. Sigmund (ed.), *Religious Freedom and Evangelization in Latin America: The challenge of Religious Freedom* (Maryknoll, NY: Orbis Books, 1999), pp. 50-68.

Natalini, Stefanía de Castro, *Significado Histórico del Gobierno del Dr. Ramón Villeda Morales* (Tegucigalpa, Honduras: Editorial Universitaria, 1985).

Núñez, Belsazar, *Identidad y Misión* (Tegucigalpa, Honduras: Editorial Benugra, 1995).

Núñez, Emilio A. and William D. Taylor, *Crisis and Hope in Latin America: An Evangelical Perspective* (Pasadena, CA: William Carey Library, 1995).

Olivera, Ademar, 'Moving Forward with the Latin American Pentecostal Movement', *International Review of Mission* (October 1998), pp 4-7.

Orellana, Luis, 'El Futuro del Pentecostalismo en América Latina', in Daniel Chiquete and Luis Orellana (eds.), *Voces del Pentecostalismo Latinoamericano* 4 (Concepción, Chile: RELEP, 2011), pp. 141-51.

Pacheco, Alexis and Guillermo Jiménez, *Hacia una Pastoral de las Personas Amenazadas por la Pobreza*, *CLADE* 3 (Quito, Ecuador: Fraternidad Teológica Latinoamericana, 1992).

Padilla, C. René, 'Los Evangélicos: Nuevos Actores en el Escenario Político Latinoamericano', in C. René Padilla (ed.), *De la Marginación al Compromiso: Los Evangélicos y la Política en América Latina* (Buenos Aires, Argentina: Fraternidad Teológica Latinoamericana, 1991), pp. 5-19.

–'An Ecclesiology for Integral Mission', in Tetsunao Yamamori and C. René Padilla (eds.), *The Local Church, Agent of Transformation: An Ecclesiology for Integral Mission* (Buenos Aires, Argentina: Ediciones Kairós, 2004), pp. 19-49.

Padilla, C. René, 'Evangelism and Social Responsibility from Wheaton '66 to Wheaton '83', in C. René Padilla and Chris Sugden (eds.), *How*

Evangelicals Endorsed Social Responsibility (Bramcote, Nottingham: Grove Books, 1985), pp. 27-33.

Pedron Colombani, Sylvie, 'Pentecostalismo y Transformación Religiosa', in Jean Pierre Bastian (ed.), *La Modernidad Religiosa: Europa Latina y America Latina* (México, DF: Fondo de Cultura Económica, 2004), pp. 133-59.

Pérez Baltodano, 'Dimensiones Culturales del Desarrollo Político e Institucional de América Latina', *Nueva Sociedad* 2.1 (2007), pp. 2-8.

Petersen, Douglas, 'Pentecostals: Who are They?' in Vinay Samuel and Chris Sugden, (eds.), *Mission as Transformation: A Theology of the Whole Gospel* (Oxford, UK: Regnum Books, 1999), pp. 76-111.

Piedra, Alberto M., 'Some Observations on Liberation Theology', *World Affairs* 148.3 (1985), pp. 151-58.

Pinedo, Enrique Niñez, *Adolescencia y Misión Integral: Nuevos Desafíos de la Educación Teológica en America Latina* (Buenos Aires, Argentina: Kairós, 2012).

Posas, Mario, *Lucha Ideológica y Organización Sindical en Honduras, 1954–1965* (Tegucigalpa, Honduras: Editorial Guaymuras, 1980).

–*El Movimiento Campesino Hondureño* (Tegucigalpa, Honduras: Editorial Guaymuras, 1981).

–*Modalidades del Proceso de Democratización en Honduras* (Tegucigalpa, Honduras: UNAH, 1988).

Read, William R., *Víctor Monterroso M. and Harmon A. Johnson, Latin American Church Growth* (Grand Rapids, MI: Eerdmans, 1969).

Robeck, Cecil M., 'Selected Bibliography on Latin American Pentecostalism', *Pneuma: The Journal of the Society for Pentecostal Studies* 13.1 (1991), pp. 193-97.

Robledo Castro, Agapito, *40 Años Después: La Verdad de la Huelga de 1954 y de la Fundación del SITRATERCO* (Tegucigalpa, Honduras: Ediciones del SEDAL, 1995).

Romero, Ramón, *Por la Democracia y Contra el Golpe: Un Análisis Independiente* (Tegucigalpa, Honduras: UNAH DVUS, 2009).

Rowlands, Jo, *Questioning Empowerment: Working with Women in Honduras* (Dublin, Ireland: Oxfam Publications, 1997).

Russell, Chandler, 'Fanning the Charismatic Fire', *Christianity Today* 12.4 (1967), pp. 36-47.

Sabanes, Dafne, *Caminos de Unidad: Itinerario del Diálogo Ecuménico en América Latina 1916–1991* (Quito, Ecuador: CLAI, 1991).

Salazar, Elizabeth, *Todas Seríamos Rainhas. Historia do Pentecostalismo Chileno da Perspectiva da Mulher* (ThM, Instituto Metodista da Ensino Superior, Brasil 1995).

Salomón, Leticia, *Las Relaciones Civiles-Militares en Honduras: Balance y Perspectives* (Tegucigalpa, Honduras: CEDOH, 1999).

Samuel, Vinay S and Chris Sugden, *The Church in Response to Human Need* (Oxford, UK: Regnum Books International, 1987).

Sanneh, Lamin O., *Encountering the West: Christianity and the Global Cultural Process* (Maryknoll, NY: Orbis Books, 1993).

Santa Ana, Julio de, *Protestantismo, Cultura y Sociedad: Problemas y Perspectivas de la Fe Evangélica en America Latina* (Buenos Aires, Argentina: Editorial La Aurora, 1970).

Saracco, Norberto, 'The Word and the Spirit in the Evangelizing Community', *Boletín Teológico Latinoamericano* 2.1 (1980), pp. 11-123.

–'Mission and Missiology from Latin America', in William D. Taylor, (ed.), *Global Missiology for the 21st Century* (Grand Rapids, MI: Baker Academic, 2000), pp. 357-66.

Schäfer, Heinrich W., *Protestantismo y Crisis Social en América Central* (San José, Costa Rica: DEI, 1992).

–'La Generación del Sentido Religioso: Observaciones Acerca de la Diversidad Pentecostal en América Latina', in Daniel Chiquete and Luis Orellana (eds.), *Voces del Pentecostalismo Latinoamericano* 3 (Concepción, Chile: RELEP, 2009), pp. 45-65.

Schäfer, Heinrich W., 'Explaining Central American Pentecostalism with Social Inequality and Conflict: On Habitus-Analysis as a Clue to Describe Religious Praxis', in C. Smith (ed.), *Pentecostal Power: Expressions, Impact and Faith of Latin American Pentecostalism* (Leiden, The Netherlands: Brill, 2011), pp. 137-56.

Schulz, Donald. E. and Deborah Sundloff Schulz, *The United States, Honduras and the Crisis in Central America* (Boulder, CO: Westview Press, 1994).

Schultze, Quentin, 'Orality and Power in Latin American Pentecostalism', in Daniel Miller (ed.), *Coming of Age: Protestantism in Contemporary Latin America* (Lanham, MD: University Press of America, 1994), pp. 65-88.

Segreda, Luis, 'Informe de Viaje', in Harold D. Hunter (ed.), *All Together in One Place* (Sheffield, UK: Sheffield Academic Press, 1993), pp. 134-48.

Segundo, Juan Luis, *Masas y Minorías* (Buenos Aires, Argentina: Editorial La Aurora, 1993).

Sepúlveda, Juan, 'Reflections on the Pentecostal Contribution to the Mission of the Church in Latin America', *Journal of Pentecostal Theology* 1.1 (1992), pp. 93-108.

–'Theological Characteristics of an Indigenous Pentecostalism', in D.A. Smith and B.F. Gutiérrez (eds.), *In the Power of the Spirit* (San José, Costa Rica: AIPRAL/CELEP, 1996), pp. 45-53.

Smilde, David A., 'Gender Relations and Social Change in Latin American Evangelicalism', in Daniel Miller (ed), *Coming of Age: Pentecostalism in Contemporary Latin America* (New York, NY: University Press of America, 1994), pp. 32-48.

Smith, Brian, *Religious Politics in Latin America: Pentecostal vs. Catholic* (Notre Dame, IN: University of Notre Dame Press, 1998).

Sobrino, Jon, *No Salvation Outside the Poor: Prophetic-Utopian Essays* (Maryknoll, NY: Orbis Books, 2008).

—*Jesús en América Latina* (Santander, España: Editorial Sal Terrae, 1997).

Solivan, Samuel, *The Spirit, Pathos and Liberation: Towards an Hispanic Pentecostal Theology* (JPTSup 14; Sheffield, UK: Sheffield Academic Press, 1998).

Soneira, Jorge, 'Los Estudios Sociológicos Sobre el Pentecostalismo en América Latina', *Sociedad y Religión* 8.1 (1991), pp. 29-47.

Spykman, Gordon, *Let My People Live: Faith and Struggle in Central America* (Grand Rapids, MI: Eerdmans, 1988).

Stoll, David, *Is Latin America Turning Protestant? The Politics of Evangelical Growth* (Berkeley, CA: University of California Press, 1990).

Tancara, Juan Jacobo, '¿Es la Voluntad de Dios? Poder, Sumisión y Rebeldía en Evangélicos/as Pentecostales', in Daniel Chiquete and Luis Orellana (eds.), *Voces del Pentecostalismo Latinoamericano 5* (Concepción, Chile: RELEP, 2011), pp. 213-21.

Tapia, Carlos, 'Adiós a las Armas: La Guerra del Fin del Mundo', *La República* (Lima, Perú, 25 de Octubre, 1994), p. 23.

Taylor, William D., 'From Iguassu to the Reflected Practitioners of the Global Family of Christ', in William D. Taylor (ed.), *Global Missiology for the 21st Century: The Iguassu Dialogue* (Grand Rapids, MI: Baker Book House, 2000), pp. 3-14.

Tojeira, José María, *Historia de la Iglesia en Honduras* (La Ceiba, Honduras: Talleres Claret, 1987).

Torres Rivas, Edelberto, *La Piel de Centroamérica* (San José, Costa Rica: FLACSO, 2007).

Vaccaro, Gabiel, 'Reseña Histórica del Movimiento Ecuménico', in Carmelo Álvarez (ed.), *Pentecostalismo y Liberación: Una Experiencia Latinoamericana* (San José, Costa Rica: Departamento Ecuménico de Investigaciones, 1992), pp. 218-235.

Valladares, Leo, 'Los Hechos Hablan por Sí Mismos: Informe Preliminar Sobre los Desaparecidos en Honduras, 1980–1993', *Comisionado Nacional de Protección de los Derechos Humanos* (Tegucigalpa, Honduras: Editorial Guaymuras, 1994), pp. 3-14.

Watanabe, José A., 'Pensamiento Pentecostal: Un Acercamiento a la Cosmovisión Pentecostal', in Daniel Chiquete and Luis Orellana (eds.), *Voces del Pentecostalismo Latinoamericano 3* (Concepción, Chile: RELEP, 2009), pp. 143-56.

Wells-Davies, Wilma, 'La Naturaleza de la Conversión Pentecostal en la Argentina: Implicaciones Missionológicas', in Daniel Chiquete and

Luis Orellana (eds.), *Voces del Pentecostalismo Latinoamericano* 3 (Concepción, Chile: RELEP, 2009), pp. 157-78.

–*Embattled but Empowered Community: Comparing Understanding of Spiritual Power in Argentine Popular and Pentecostal Cosmologies* (London, UK: Brill, 2010).

Westmeier, Karl Wilhelm, *Protestant Pentecostalism in Latin America: A Study in the Dynamics of Missions* (London, UK: Associated University Press, 1999).

White, Robert A., *Structural Factors in Rural Development: The Church and the Peasant in Honduras* (PhD, Cornell University, Ithaca, New York, 1977).

Wilson, Everett, 'Guatemalan Pentecostals: Something of their Own', in Edward L. Cleary and H.W. Stewart-Gambino (eds.), *Power, Politics, and Pentecostals in Latin America* (Boulder, CO: Westview Press, 1997), pp. 56-64.

Wolseth, Jon, *Jesus and the Gang: Youth Violence and Christianity in Urban Honduras* (Phoenix, AZ: The University of Arizona Press, 2011).

Yamamori, Tetsunao, Bryant L Myers, Kwame Bediako, and Larry Reed (eds.), *Serving with the Poor in Africa: Cases in Holistic Ministry* (Monrovia, CA: MARC, 1995).

Zaldívar, Raúl, 'Relación Estado-Iglesia y su Apertura al Protestantismo en Honduras', *Revista Vida y Pensamiento* (Marzo, 12, 1996), pp. 90-114.

INDEX OF BIBLICAL REFERENCES

INDEX OF SUBJECTS

INDEX OF AUTHORS

www.ingramcontent.com/pod-product-compliance
Lightning Source LLC
Chambersburg PA
CBHW060042100426
42742CB00014B/2663